Feminist Forerunners

for Mark

Feminist Forerunners

NEW WOMANISM AND FEMINISM IN
THE EARLY TWENTIETH CENTURY

edited by Ann Heilmann

PANDORA
LONDON, SYDNEY, CHICAGO

First published in 2003 by
Pandora Press, an imprint of Rivers Oram Publishers Ltd
144 Hemingford Road, London N1 1DE

Distributed in the United States of America by
The Independent Publishers' Group
814 North Franklin Street
Chicago, Illinois 60610

Set in Baskerville by NJ Design Associates
and printed in Great Britain by T.J. International Ltd, Padstow, Cornwall

A catalogue record for this book is available from the British Library

ISBN 0 86358 424 1 (cloth)
ISBN 0 86358 425 X (paperback)

Contents

I Desperately Seeking Sisterhood

IV The Voyage Out

List of Illustrations

Notes on the Contributors

Barbara Bair, PhD, is the Associate Editor of the Jane Addams Papers Project, Duke University, in Durham, NC. She is one of the editors, with Robert A. Hill, of *The Marcus Garvey and Universal Negro Improvement Association Papers* published by the University of California Press, and the author of several articles on women and the Garvey movement. Her latest books, for Oxford University Press, are *Though Justice Sleeps: African Americans 1880–1900* and the collaborative anthology, *To Make Our World Anew: A History of African Americans.* She was one of the curators of the Marcus Garvey Centennial Exhibition at the Schomburg Center for Research in Black Culture, New York, and has recently served as a historical advisor for a documentary film on Marcus Garvey directed by Stanley Nelson and produced for the American Experience PBS series by Half Nelson Productions in New York.

Jill Bergman is an Assistant Professor at the University of Montana, where she teaches courses in American literature and Women's Studies. She is working on a book, *Sometimes I feel like a motherless child: Pauline Hopkins's Maternal Redemptive Vision,* and is co-editing a collection of essays entitled *Our Sisters' Keepers: Theories of Poverty Relief in the Work of Nineteenth-Century American Women Writers.*

Carmen Birkle is Associate Professor of American Studies at the Johannes Gutenberg-University of Mainz, Germany. She is the author of *Women's Stories of the Looking Glass* and *Migration-Miscegeneration-Transculturation* and has published articles on American women's and ethnic literature. She is the editor of *(Trans)Formations of Cultural Identity in the English-Speaking World* (with J.

Achilles) and *Frauen auf der Spur: Kriminalautorinnen aus Deutschland, Großbritannien und den USA* (with S. Matter-Seibel and P. Plummer). She also works as an assistant editor for the journal *Amerikastudien/American Studies* and as an associate editor for the review journal *Feminist Europa*.

Dr Laurel Forster is a cultural studies lecturer at the Arts Institute at Bournemouth. Her research interests are in twentieth-century women's writing with particular reference to its social and cultural significance. She is co-editing *The Recipe Reader*, a collection of essays on the cultural context of recipe writing. She has published on May Sinclair and is currently working on psychical research and modernism, women's writing of the First World War, and women's writing in magazines.

Jane S. Gabin is Assistant Director of Undergraduate Admissions at the University of North Carolina at Chapel Hill. Her biographical essay on Elizabeth Banks introduces the recent reissue of *The Remaking of an American*. Dr. Gabin is the author of a book on the American poet Sidney Lanier and numerous articles, including entries in the *Encyclopedia of American Poetry* and the *American National Biography*. She received her PhD in English at the University of North Carolina at Chapel Hill.

Lisa Ganobcsik-Williams is a Lecturer in the Department of English and Comparative Literary Studies at the University of Warwick, UK. She is also co-ordinator of Academic Writing for the Warwick Writing Programme. Her work on Charlotte Perkins Gilman appears in *Charlotte Perkins Gilman: Optimist Reformer* (eds Jill Rodd and Val Gough), and *Approaches to Teaching 'The Yellow Wallpaper' and Herland* (eds Denise D. Knight and Cynthia J. Davis).

Ann Heilmann is a Senior Lecturer in English at the University of Wales Swansea. She is the author of *New Woman Fiction: Women Writing First-Wave Feminism* and has edited two anthologies, *The Late-Victorian Marriage Question* and (with Stephanie Forward) *Sex, Social Purity and Sarah Grand*. She has recently edited a special issues on the New Woman for *Nineteenth-Century Feminisms* and is now editing an issue on suffrage textuality for *Women's History Review*. She is completing a book on *New Woman Strategies* and working on an anthology on Victorian and Edwardian anti-feminism.

Gillian Kersley has published a biography of Sarah Grand, *Darling Madame: Sarah Grand & Devoted Friend,* and lives, teaches and practices creative writing in Bath. She has worked in a number of fields including public relations, publishing and as manager of the counselling service Bath Relate.

Eveline Kilian teaches English Literature at the University of Tübingen, Germany. Her publications include a study of the concept of the Moment in Dorothy Richardson's *Pilgrimage* (*Momente innerweltlicher Transzendenz*), as well as articles on various aspects of gender and Modernism. She co-edited collections of essays on Feminist Literary Studies (*Bildersturm im Elfenbeinturm*) and on Generation and Gender (*GeNarrationen*). She has just finished a book-length project on gender bending and the construction of gender identity in contemporary English literature.

Sabina Matter-Seibel teaches American Language and Literature at the University of Mainz in Germersheim, Germany. Her research centers on the culture and literature of the American South and on women's writing in the nineteenth century. Her publications include *Der Süden im Spätwerk Faulkners* (The South in the Late Novels of William Faulkner) and numerous articles on women writers in the nineteenth century. She is the co-editor of *Frauen in Kultur und Gesellschaft: 2. Fachtagung Frauen- und Genderforschung in Rheinland-Pfalz* (Women in Culture and Society: Second Conference on Women and Gender Studies in the Rhineland-Palatinate), and she is working on an interdisciplinary project researching women's crime fiction. She is currently finishing a book on tradition and innovation in women's writing in the United States, 1850–1900.

Andrea Peterson lectures in the Department of English and Drama at Loughborough University, where she recently completed her PhD thesis on Vera Brittain at Loughborough University. Her published work includes 'A Process of Redefinition: Vera Brittain's Autobiographical *Testaments*', in *Inquiry* vol.18; and various entries in Margaretta Jolly, *The Encyclopedia of Life Writing*; and Sarah Gamble's *The Icon Critical Dictionary of Feminism and Postfeminism*. She is currently working on a critical study of Brittain's novels.

Patricia Pulham was born in Gibraltar and spent her childhood there before emigrating to the U.K. She completed her PhD thesis on Vernon Lee at

Queen Mary College, University of London, and currently lectures on Romantic Poetry, the nineteenth-century novel, and the women's movement. She has written a number of forthcoming articles on Lee and late-Victorian aestheticism, the Arts in the Victorian period and Victorian poetry, which are to be published in 2002–3.

Sue Thomas is the author of *The Worlding of Jean Rhys*, co-author (with Ann Blake and Leela Gandhi) of *England through Colonial Eyes in Twentieth-Century Fiction*, and compiler of *Elizabeth Robins (1862–1952): A Bibliography*, and many other titles in the Victorian Fiction Research Guides Series. She has published extensively on late nineteenth- and twentieth-century women's writing and decolonizing literatures. She is Reader in English and Coordinator of the English Program in the School of Communication, Arts and Critical Enquiry at La Trobe University, Melbourne.

Leigh Wilson teaches in the English literature department at the University of Westminster, where last year she completed her PhD on May Sinclair and narratives of cure. She is continuing to look for ways to read Sinclair, as well as working on psychical research in the early twentieth century.

Christa Zorn holds a Master in English and History from the University of Hamburg and a PhD in English from the University of Florida. She is an Associate Professor of English at Indiana University Southeast and also coordinates the Women and Gender Studies Program. Her area of expertise comprises late Victorian and early Modernist literatures. She has just finished a book manuscript under the title *Vernon Lee: Aestheticism, History and the Female Intellectual at the Turn of the Century*.

Acknowledgments

This book developed out of an international conference hosted at Manchester in July 2000 and organized by the English Department of Manchester Metropolitan University in association with the English Department of the University of Wales Swansea. In the course of three days some one hundred academics from thirteen countries presented a wide variety of new critical insights into the theme of 'Feminist Forerunners: The New Woman in the National and International Periodical Press, 1880 to the 1920s'. The internationalist vision, interdisciplinary angle, intellectual curiosity, and feminist ethos of speakers and audience made for an atmosphere crackling with excitement. I am grateful to all participants for contributing to the vibrant interchange of ideas and inspiring spirit of camaraderie which marked the event. Inevitably, only a small sample of the compellingly far-ranging essays that resulted from the conference could be considered for the parameters of this collection. Special thanks go to my co-organizers, Margaret Beetham and Janet Beer, as well as to MMU's Conference Officer, Rachel Finneron. I also wish to thank Caroline Lazar, Elizabeth Fidlon and Margaret Brittain from Pandora for their editorial support and encouragement, and Mark Llewellyn for his help with indexing. Quotations from manuscript material in The Elizabeth Robins Papers are reproduced with the permission of the Royal United Kingdom Beneficent Association, the Backsettown Trustees, and the Fales Library, New York University. Permission to reproduce parts of Jane Gabin's introduction to Elizabeth Banks, *The Remaking of an American*, is by courtesy of the University Press of Florida.

Introduction

Ann Heilmann

The impact of first-wave feminism, and in particular the New Woman movement, on the formation of *fin-de-siècle* and early twentieth-century thought and cultural practice has received ever increasing attention at the turn of the millenium. At a time of far-reaching social, political, and cultural transformation, it was the variety of New Woman identities that exercised the turn-of-the-century imagination. The site of ceaseless debate and narrative exploration as well as literary innovation, the New Woman forged and occupied the interface between mass-market consumerism and proto-modernist aestheticism. Whether an emblem of sexual anarchy or fashionable modernity, heralding degeneration or renovation, she became a prime signifier of crucial paradigm shifts in culture and society. She personified the turn-of-the-century crisis of category precisely because of the polymorphous nature of the categories and meanings that could be ascribed to her. As New Woman critics and writers then and New Woman scholars now are keen to point out, '*The* New Woman did not exist.'[1]

New Woman Hybridities

Ironically, perhaps, the wider questions raised by the textual and semiotic hybridity of the New Woman, such as the cross-national links between turn-of-the-century feminisms, are undercut by the stability of prevailing critical frameworks. However fluid the New Woman is perceived to be as an agent of cultural transformation, she tends to be cast as a white middle-class woman of British or North American descent, whose heyday was the decadent 1890s. But what about the internationalist potential of New

Womanism? Did feminists across different countries and ethnicities conceptualize and popularize 'modern' womanhood in similar ways? What reso-
nance could white paradigms of feminist modernity carry for black women
with a legacy of slavery and imperialism? These were some of the thoughts
that prepared the ground for the 'Feminist Forerunners' conference on
which this book is based.

Feminist Forerunners marks a new departure in New Woman criticism
by addressing the cross-national and ethnic dimensions of the field.
Internationally wide-ranging, the fifteen 'feminist forerunners' examined in this collection are seen within the specific cultural environments
that shaped their respective sexual and textual politics. To expand existing parameters, familiar subjects of *fin-de-siècle* and modernist criticism
(Sarah Grand, Elizabeth Robins, May Sinclair, Dorothy Richardson) are
placed alongside under-researched journalists and writers (Vernon Lee,
Lou Andreas-Salomé, Sui Sin Far, Helen Reimensneyder Martin,
Elizabeth Banks). The troubling aspects of white feminist investment in
biocentric, eugenic, and racial discourses (Charlotte Perkins Gilman) are
highlighted when juxtaposed with the political liberationism of the
'Colored American' New Woman (Pauline Hopkins, Zitkala-ša). The
picture that emerges is one of great diversity, mediated by a shared
preoccupation with the nature of femininity within the parameters of
political claims for equality or epistemological explorations of difference. Mindful of Virginia Woolf's dictum that 'in or about December
1910 human character changed',[2] the focus of inquiry is the early twentieth century, while the emphasis remains on first-generation New Women
(born in the 1850s to 1870s rather than 1890s);[3] only three of the fifteen
writers presented here belong to the second generation (Vera Brittain,
María Cristina Mena, Amy Jacques Garvey).

Feminist Forerunners?

'Have you seen that funny old thing with the short grey hair?', a self-
assured flapper sneers at the sight of Radclyffe Hall's New Woman protagonist in *The Unlit Lamp* (1926): 'Honey, she's a forerunner, that's what she
is, a kind of pioneer that's got left behind. I believe she's the beginning of
things like me.'[4] Hall's passage suggests that one of the reasons why we
are so attracted to the mirror of the past is to assure ourselves of the

progress we have made in the face of patriarchal structures in our lives. It also highlights the difficult balancing act on which this book is engaged: it seeks to offer considered appraisals of pioneering women, while avoiding the pitfalls of too uncritical a celebration or too fearful a distancing act whose emotional investment reveals itself in the force of its disclaimer. Woolf's claim that 'we think back through our mothers if we are women'[5] is of obvious importance to feminist identity formation and is here explored both in its vertical (Brittain's admiration of Olive Schreiner) and horizontal (Gilman's influence on Lee) dimensions. What may be less evident is the way in which this notion affects our own subjectivities and critical assessment of the writers whom we conceptualize as 'foremothers'.

The complex processes that are involved in 'writing' (creating) the feminist forerunner—writing about her identity, writing our identities into her—are set out in the first four essays in this book. Moving from explorations of matrilinearity to the ethnic reconceptualization of New Womanism, the second part then looks at the ways in which black activists and feminists revolutionized white paradigms while at times also curiously revisiting them. The feminist challenge to established paradigms is the focus of the third group of essays, which interrogate the 'different voice' of 'feminine' writing practices and psychoanalytic and modernist forays into 'womanliness'. The final section considers the feminist forerunner's 'voyage out' into the twentieth century and pays particular attention to women's responses to World War One.

The ambiguities and contradictions resulting from the multiplicity of New Woman identities—across a range of individuals but also within each of the women studied—is central to the 'stories' this collection sets out to tell and explore. Indeed, the concept of story-telling is an appropriate metaphor for the themes examined throughout and holds particular significance for the first part of this book.

Desperately Seeking Sisterhoods

The 'Biographer's tale' affords an appropriately self-reflective starting point to this collection. In 'Fatal Attractions? Reflecting on the Affinities between *Fin-de-siècle* Nineteenth and Twentieth-Century Women Writers', chapter 1, Gillian Kersley gives a refreshingly personal account of the (auto)biographical dimensions of second-wave re/envisionings of first-wave lives, particularly when old battlegrounds map out familiar ground a hundred years on. Kersley found that her biography of the social purist and suffragist Sarah Grand (1854–1943), a writer notorious for spicing her fictions with syphilitic villains, soon assumed the shape of a 'joint' biography of Grand and her acolyte, Gladys Singers-Bigger (1888–1969).[6] In view of the wealth of biographical material collated by Singers-Bigger in her diaries on and correspondence with 'Darling Madame', this development was arguably overdetermined. On the other hand, by illustrating that one person's biography always contains the biographies of others (including that of her or his biographer), Kersley presents a challenge to the mainstream/malestream biographical focus on 'great' men in isolation. Indeed, as Susan Standford Friedman has argued, women's autobiography typically structures the quest for identity around collective experience. It tends to locate female ego formation not in the Freudian mirror stage (with its move towards a separate sense of self), but in the dynamic interaction between 'the shared and the unique'.[7] In her contribution to this collection, Kersley suggests that women's biography follows the same principle.

The shared and the unique aspects of first and second-generation New Womanhood are explored in chapter 2 by Andrea Peterson in her essay on 'Alternative Wifestyles: Vera Brittain's Feminist Journalism of the 1920s and the Influence of Olive Schreiner'. If Singers-Bigger's heroine-worship of Grand points to the ironies of defining 'Old' and 'New' Woman identities in synchronic and generational terms, Brittain's emotional investment and political interaction with Schreiner's work and ideas indicate that the gap that developed after the turn of the century between British equality and difference feminists could at times be bridged. Just as the new Old Woman of the 1920s discovered her emotional affinities with the *fin-de-siècle* New Woman, so the 'New Feminist'[8] felt invigorated by the 'Old Feminist's' radical positions. A belated Old Girl harking back to Victorian values in the age of the Flapper, Singers-Bigger was enthralled by the vitality of the ageing New Woman Grand while, for her part, Grand was able to relive the iconoclasm of her early years in the younger woman's admiration at a time when, in her beliefs and offical function as a Mayoress, she had come to represent the establishment. Brittain's response to Schreiner (1855–1920) traces the opposite journey by looking back in order to move beyond earlier paradigms.

Strongly influenced by Schreiner's *Story of an African Farm*—to the point of naming herself and her partner after its protagonists—and particularly inspired by *Woman and Labour,* Brittain (1893–1970) nonetheless disagreed with the New Woman's conclusion that marriage and a career did not mix. Like Schreiner's contemporary Mona Caird (1854–1932) she believed that women should not only demand the right to, but also carry into practice, their desire to command a share of 'both sides of the apple of life'.[9] In fact, Brittain's concept of the 'semi-detached marriage', in which both partners would retain their independence and might live apart, bears striking analogy with Caird's vision of 'combined independence and companionship' as outlined in her 1915 novel *The Stones of Sacrifice,* which portrays such an ideal marital relationship.[10] What distinguished Brittain from her forerunners, however, Peterson argues, was her conviction that women could achieve domestic and professional fulfilment without undue sacrifice. In addition to offering her readers practical advice based on her own experience, she followed Charlotte Perkins Gilman's lead in promoting the need for far-reaching structural change by advising on the expediency of labour-saving devices and communal kitchens.

Like Schreiner, Gilman (1860–1935) held an immediate and lasting appeal for her contemporaries, as Patricia Pulham shows in 'A Transatlantic Alliance: Charlotte Perkins Gilman and Vernon Lee' in chapter 3. As the translator and reviewer of *Women and Economics,* Lee (1856–1935) was instrumental in familiarizing a European audience with Gilman's ideas. Drawing on the correspondence between the two writers and her scrutiny of Lee's annotations to Gilman's works, Pulham traces the intellectual exchange and mutual appreciation between these two strong personalities. Their priorities and preoccupations were quite divergent—'feminine' interiority and biological difference for Lee, the reality of women's oppression for Gilman. Although she was initially hostile to the suffrage movement, her close reading of *Women and Economics* and lively discussions with the author effected a gradual change of attitude in Lee. While remaining opposed to suffragette militancy, Lee came publicly to express her support of the women's movement in 'The Economic Parasitism of Women' (1908).

That sex parasitism was shortly thereafter to emerge as the central tenet of Schreiner's *Woman and Labour* (1911) offers one more incidence of the foothold Gilman's writings had gained in the early twentieth-century feminist imagination. Indeed, her influence continues today and not accidentally inspired the title of this book. Gilman's metaphor of parthenogenesis, fictionalized in *Herland* in 1915, could be regarded as emblematic of the writers, journalists, and artists studied in this collection, pointing as it does to their self-creation as New Women, their professional aspirations and success in determining their lives. Yet the unambiguous racism of Gilman's later years goes a long way towards demonstrating that all forerunners do not necessarily hold a progressive or egalitarian vision. This begs the question of how we, as late-twentieth and early twenty-first century feminists, deal with what Judith Allen has called 'anathema discourses'.[11]

In chapter 4 Lisa Ganobcsik-Williams therefore examines the underbelly of Gilman's belief in social evolution. Her essay on 'Charlotte Perkins Gilman and *The Forerunner*: A New Woman's Changing Perspective on American Immigration' subjects to close scrutiny Gilman's invocation of a distinctly nativist concept of nationhood. Pledged to the 'prevalent cultural myth of "Anglo-Saxon" superiority', Gilman emphasized that 'the formation of American democracy required particular abilities that only the most highly evolved people—white Americans of specific ethnic backgrounds—had developed.'[12] As Ganobcsik-Williams argues, Gilman's fear of immigrants settling in the United States culminated in her response to the educated and politically vocal sections of the ethnic population. Ironically, Gilman thus replicated the discursive strategies and hegemonic structures of the dominant social group that she had devoted her life to fighting. This was a missed opportunity of multiracial and cross-cultural sisterhood, viable as a concept in earlier abolitionist feminism and explored but rarely by white New Women with multinational roots like Schreiner. It was, however, addressed by ethnic and black feminist writers, who had a stake in dismantling the interlocking regimes of race and gender oppression.

From New Woman to Black Womanism

In 'Multiculturalism and the New Woman in Early Twentieth-Century America' (chapter 5) Carmen Birkle presents close readings of four turn-of-the-century New Woman short-story writers, essayists and feminist activists who skilfully inserted their complex ethnicities into the expanding periodical market of the 1900s to 1930s. In stories like 'A Warrior's

Daughter' (1902), the editor of the *American Indian Magazine*, Zitkala-ša (1876–1938), interwove the Native American traditions of the trickster and warrior tale with feminist role-reversal plots. The cunning of the trickster figure also informs 'Mrs Spring Fragrance', a story by the British-born Chinese-American/Canadian Sui Sin Far (1865–1914). Reflecting on her multicultural hybridity, her autobiographical essay 'Leaves from the Mental Portfolio of an Eurasian' (1909) concluded 'I have no nationality', a statement later paralleled by Woolf's declaration in *Three Guineas* (1938) that 'as a woman I have no country'.[13]

That subversion and impersonation were more than literary metaphors is indicated by the complex mental acrobatics required of ethnic writers who had to survive in a market catering for nativist sentiments. Thus by manipulating the contemporary taste for local colour, the Mexican-American writer María Cristina Mena (1893–1965) was able to inject the voice of ethnic alterity into anti-immigration periodicals like the *Century Magazine*. In her story 'The Gold Vanity Set' (1913) she drew attention to the connection between racial prejudice and sexual exploitation, suggesting that cross-racial and cross-gender compromise was the first step towards easing the plight of the Mexican Indian woman. Similarly, the German-American Lutheran Helen Reimensnyder Martin (1868–1939), herself an active suffragist and prolific novelist, was primarily concerned with the Old Woman's awakening. When, as a result of her husband's hostility to female education, her daughter's life threatens to replicate her own, the cowed wife in 'Mrs Gladfelter's Revolt' (1923) is propelled into open resistance and rewarded with her husband's startled recognition that for once he has met his match. The short story, Birkle concludes, offered an ideal medium for interrogating the multiple processes that arose from the combined onslaught of cultural prerogatives, racial and class bias, and gender-role expectations.

Did African-American New Woman writers deploy similar discursive strategies to address the wrongs of black womanhood? As the editors of 'New Negro' journals, Pauline Hopkins (1859–1930) and Amy Jacques Garvey (1896–1973) were relieved of the burden of 'passing' in a white periodical marketplace but, as the remaining essays in this section demonstrate, they nonetheless had to contend with some resistance from within their own ethnic and political camps. Amid cross-fire from patriarchal and racial hegemonies, they succeded in articulating and disseminating to a wide female readership a compelling message of feminist survivalism. Instrumental in establishing a strong sense of female community in the emerging black magazine culture, they can be regarded as pioneers of 'womanism', the African-American feminist position Alice Walker defined in 1967 in *In Search of Our Mothers' Gardens*:

> A black feminist or feminist of color…[who wants] to know more and in greater depth than is considered 'good' for [her]…In charge. *Serious*…Appreciates and prefers women's culture…and women's strength…Committed to survival and wholeness of entire people, male *and* female…Loves herself. *Regardless*.[14]

In chapter 6 Sabina Matter-Seibel considers 'Pauline Hopkins's Portrayal of the African-American New Woman in *Contending Forces* and *The Colored American Magazine*'. She argues that *Contending Forces*, Hopkins's narrative contribution to the surge of black activism in the post-Reconstruction period of the 1890s, served the dual purpose of raising black consciousness and furthering white readers' education. The African-American New Woman novel thus reshaped the parameters of its British sister genre, which also addressed a twin audience, feminist 'insiders' and anti-feminist opponents of the New Woman (Old Women and Old Men). In her radical rewriting of the Tragic Mulatta trope, Hopkins allows her protagonist Sappho to survive rape, programmatically validating her as an unblemished True Woman who, in Walker's terms, loves herself 'regardless'. Nonetheless the text pinpoints the limited measure of freedom that even a strong New Woman can carve out for herself if she happens to be black. In fact, Sappho is able to emerge as a truly empowered 'new' woman only by reclaiming her son. The African-American New Woman thus comes into her own by redefining herself as a mother, her split self healed by her recognition of the central place she occupies in the collective struggle for liberty. Like the British suffragettes, Hopkins drew on religious symbolism to inscribe the black woman's cause with the passion and redemption of Christ.

While the prevailing images of white New Womanhood 'encouraged middle-class white women to seek autonomy, pleasure, and consumption, black women's New Womanhood focused on building community and uplifting the race in the face of extreme discrimination and abuse'. As Jill Bergman illustrates in chapter 7, Hopkins 'used the forum of the *Colored American Magazine* as a means of fostering, "A New Race of Colored Women"' among her readers. She did this by 'encouraging academic and professional achievement among African-American women and by claiming for them a strong and unified identity', celebrating black women specifically for their contribution to communal advancement and 'championing the black women's club movement'. Ultimately, however, Hopkins's self-confident propagation of black nationalist feminism jarred with the accommodationist policies and masculinist agenda of the male leadership.

The black New Woman's radicalism is further scrutinized in '"Our Women and What They Think": Amy Jacques Garvey, New Negro Womanhood, and the Woman's Page of the *Negro World*' (chapter 8). Here Barbara Bair argues that Marcus Garvey's Universal Negro Improvement Association (UNIA), 'traditionally viewed as a "New Manhood" movement arising out of New Negro activism in the wake of World War One', was equally a New Womanhood movement, which had its 'premier propagandist' in Amy Jacques Garvey, Garvey's second wife. 'In 1924 she introduced a new women's page into the UNIA's influential *Negro World* newspaper, for which she served as associate editor.' Entitled 'Our Women and What They Think', the page 'served as a platform for black female activism and international feminism, representing the New Negro New Woman consciousness of the UNIA's women. In offering a broad range of opinion it expanded the discussion of black women's roles beyond the more constricted ideas of gender and women's place held by the organization.' Drawing on a range of contributors, Bair traces Jacques Garvey's role in promoting a vision that blended black womanism and feminist internationalism.

While stressing the importance of racial maternalism and political radicalism, Garvey and Hopkins also encouraged identification with the white New Woman's quest for freedom of movement, economic independence, and beauty. Under their editorship aesthetic appeal went hand in hand with racial advancement, Art Nouveau covers and women's articles self-confidently proclaiming the message that black was beautiful. Empowering though this was, the conflict that ensued between the effort to boost the black New Woman's pride in her race and the promotion of the 'fashionable'—white—body beautiful ultimately remained unresolved as black readers were urged to purchase products that promised whiter skin, thin-ner lips and straightened hair. Ironically, the black feminist movement thus reaffirmed the white body superior even as it wrote the 'different voice' of the black New Woman into existence.

Similar contradictions between the self-assertive celebration of 'feminine' difference and the revalidation of essentialist notions of the 'eternal female' can be traced in the work of the writers examined in the next section.

In a Different Voice

Preoccupied with explorations of feminine interiority, the (proto)modernist writers considered here inferred psychical from biological difference and are therefore frequently classed as anti-feminists. As the carefully histori-cized essays by Thomas, Zorn, and Kilian illustrate, they were primarily concerned with conceiving philosophical frameworks, which in some respects prefigure modern French feminism's concept of *écriture féminine*.

In chapter 9 Sue Thomas takes issue with some of the central inter-pretive paradigms in current New Woman criticism. Instead of concep-tualizing the genre as a Foucauldian 'reverse discourse',[15] she argues that it might be useful to pay closer attention to the aesthetic questions it raised. These were issues to which many contemporary critics responded with considerably more acumen than the notion of 'a "reaction-forma-tion" against women and the feminine'[16] would suggest. Her essay on 'Elizabeth Robins, the "New Woman" Novelist, and the Writing of Literary Histories of the 1890s' offers a reappraisal of a writer (1862–1952) whose early work in literary histories of the New Woman tends to be seen as reactionary. Drawing on archival research, Thomas considers the competing critical discourses in the British reception of Robins's early writings, 'A Lucky Sixpence' (1894), *George Mandeville's Husband* (1894) and *The Open Question* (1898), examining in close detail which reviewers and which newspapers and periodicals mobilised 'discourses of morbidity, degeneration, disease, Ibsenism and the New Woman, and the contexts in which these concepts were employed'. The complex picture that emerges indicates that anti-feminist reviewers enjoyed somewhat less authority than that with which they are usually credited. In fact, by invoking the realist aesthetic and classical tragedy as models for reading Robins's work, the contemporary debate was structured around mainstream iconography rather than responses to ideological or modernist iconoclasm. This, Thomas concludes, raises doubts about the validity of the narrative of 'rupture' that underlies contemporary literary criticism of New Woman fiction.

Chapter 10 re-evaluates the (re)visionary psychoanalytical work of the Russian-born writer of French-German descent Lou Andreas-Salomé (1861–1937). In 'Lou Andreas-Salomé's Literary Response to the Woman Question in Turn-of-the-Century Germany' Christa Zorn offers a close analysis of Salomé's 1899 essay 'Der Mensch als Weib', a 'psychological study of femininity in mytho-biological metaphors' whose essentialism attracted sharp censure from contemporary German feminists. Concerned, like Vernon Lee, with the emancipation of women's inner life, Salomé created a gynocentric psychological discourse which reversed central tenets of Freudian psychoanalysis; indeed, it was man who, for Salomé, embodied lack, whereas woman was complete in herself. Salomé's reconceptualisation of femininity deconstructed the phallogocentric order as well as the conventional binary opposition between male and female. Like Hélène Cixous some seventy years later, and like a fellow forerunner of French feminism, the contemporary writer George Egerton (1859–1945), she envisaged an autonomous femininity that was 'meant to define woman to herself, not to men'.[17] In her 'non-representational language', which straddled science, philosophy and myth, as well as her resistance of closure and lack of a unifying doctrine, Zorn argues, Salomé anticipated aspects of modern feminist theory.

If chapter 10 draws attention to the modernist aesthetic in Salomé's philosophical framework, chapter 11 examines the modernist writer Dorothy Richardson (1873–1957) and her conceptualization of femininity, which aligns her with French feminist and Russian formalist theory. In '"Female Consciousness": Aesthetic Concepts and Feminist Thought in Dorothy Richardson's Writing' Eveline Kilian explores Richardson's ambivalence towards female emancipation in the novel cycle *Pilgrimage* (1915–67). Differentiating between male and female modes of consciousness and perception, Richardson juxtaposes 'a fact-oriented mind thinking in propositions and centred on "becoming" with the holistic (and Romantic) conception of a "synthetic consciousness" predominantly concerned with "being"'. This synthetic consciousness distinguished the 'womanly woman' from men. Richardson's womanly woman (a concept she used differently than *fin-de-siècle* New Woman writers)[18] aims at a state of consummate unselfishness which, paradoxically, is achieved only by a consummately self-centred consciousness. Similarly, her notion of 'impersonality', which resembles Woolf's concept of the androgynous mind in *A Room of One's Own*, posits absolute detachment as the precondition for the state of subjectivity, an ideal that only the womanly woman is able to attain. Freedom is therefore an inner quality and as such not directly contingent on external surroundings. On the other hand, as Kilian points out, Richardson was well aware of the restrictions that were placed in women's and particularly writers' lives, and elsewhere deplored the lack of equality of opportunity in the professional world that circumscribed their achievements. Though subordinated to her aesthetic vision, this nascent concern with women's social reality points to Richardson's affinities with writers like Virginia Woolf and May Sinclair, who combined an interest in feminine interiority and stream-of-consciousness techniques with the production of socio-political feminist theory and, in Sinclair's case, political activism.

The Voyage Out

The last part of this book continues the analysis of feminist forerunners' post-Darwinian and psychoanalytic revisionism, and considers the implications of the feminist 'voyage out' into the 20th century by examining two different responses to World War One.

Chapters 12 and 13 offer complementary readings of May Sinclair (1863–1946). In her essay on 'May Sinclair's Interpretation of the New Woman' Laurel Forster argues that Sinclair rewrote nineteenth-century degeneration theory by Spencer and Lamarck in order to celebrate the New Woman as quasi-Nietzschean *Übermensch*. As in Salomé's work, the inversion of mainstream biological and psychoanalytic theories served to release femininity from the grasp of male science. Unlike Salomé, however, Sinclair was actively committed to the political movement for women's rights: a member of the Women Writers' Suffrage League and the militant Women's Freedom League, she reacted with great passion to anti-feminist attacks on the suffrage movement. In *Feminism* and 'A Defence of Man' (both 1912) she refuted essentialist arguments that pathologized the women's movement. In her fiction she promoted the New Woman's biological function as 'nature's double vitality experiment', suggesting that, in response to man's insistence on separate spheres, which obstructed human progress, nature had produced a 'new' type of woman who incorporated the best qualities of both genders. Reshaping the *fin-de-siècle* feminist trope of feminism's evolutionary role, two short stories published as *Two Sides of a Question* (1901) and novels like *The Creators* (1910) and *The Combined Maze* (1913) constructed the New Woman as a paragon of superior physical and mental strength.

As Leigh Wilson illustrates in 'She in Her "Armour" and He in his Coat of Nerves': May Sinclair and the Rewriting of Chivalry', this idea is developed further in *Tasker Jevons* (1916) and *The Romantic* (1920). In these war novels the female protagonists' identification with Joan of Arc effects a reversal of gender norms. Because of her association with the pre-war suffragettes, 'Sinclair's use of Joan of Arc within the context of the trenches' resulted in a 'radical redefinition of the concepts of chivalry' and romantic desire. As in Salomé's 'Der Mensch als Weib', lack is codified as an essentially male attribute, while woman embodies military valour, public 'manhood', and human wholeness.

Feminist chivalry of a different kind was demonstrated by another member of the Women Writers' Suffrage League, Elizabeth Banks (1870–1938), the subject of the last essay in this volume. Jane S. Gabin examines the life and professional practice of this 'American on Fleet Street', an adept impersonator who undertook a number of undercover investigations into the lives of domestic servants, crossing-sweepers and flower-sellers. Known as the 'Lady of the Round Table' at the *Referee*, a conservative London weekly where she was the only woman on the staff, she successfully resorted to subterfuge in order to champion women's suffrage despite the editor's staunch prohibition of her engagement with the subject. A working-class American who spent most of her working life in London middle-class circles, Banks destabilized the categories of gender, class, and nationhood all at once. Like Elizabeth Robins a transatlantic New Woman, she turned her position as 'cultural ambassador' to good account by supplying both nations with local colour sketches about one another. If Robins, in her guise as C. E. Raimond, played the devil's advocate for the Old Man, Banks drew on her alter egos to work for the suffrage cause. By the outbreak of the First World War, Banks had established

sufficient cultural capital to host a relief-fund event attended by the literary élite of the day. However, as Gabin points out, Banks's love of mystery
and her dynamic play with outsider and insider positions ultimately resulted
in self-erasure. What remained behind were her carefully controlled autobiographical texts, *Campaigns of Curiosity* (1894), *Autobiography of a 'Newspaper
Girl'* (1902) and *The Remaking of an American* (1928).

In her effort to shield her privacy, Banks resembled the writer with
whom this book began, for Sarah Grand, too, was unwilling to lift the 'various disguises'[19] she had assumed in the course of her public career, and
responded with considerable irritation to any attempt to break the silence
she maintained on her marriage. Feminist forerunners, it may be concluded,
were keen to uncover the secret workings of their society, but were reluc-
tant to disclose too much personal information about themselves. It is one
of the aims of this collection to address this imbalance and retrace the
personalities behind the political and theoretical frameworks of early
twentieth-century feminism.

I *Desperately Seeking Sisterhood*

1. Fatal Attractions?

Reflecting on the Affinities between Fin-de-Siècle Nineteenth- and Twentieth-Century Women Writers

Gillian Kersley

Sarah Grand was born in 1854, and was famous for coining the phrase 'The New Woman', for writing 'indelicate' and 'unwomanly' novels and campaigning for a fairer deal for women, particularly within marriage. She died in obscurity in 1943 aged 88. Her most famous novel was *The Heavenly Twins*, first published in the 1890s.[1]

My role as midwife to her slow rebirth, over one hundred years later now, was as her biographer.[2] This paper is very much a Sarah-and-me approach to the similarities of conflict shared by two women writing at the ends of the 19th and 20th centuries and the biographical process involved for one woman writing about another.

There were two of us twentieth-century women who became deeply involved with Sarah Grand: Gladys Singers-Bigger who left her very personal seven volumes of diaries of Sarah-worship in the 1930s to the Bath Library, when she died in 1970, and I who vicariously took over in the 1980s. Gladys had the edge—and the drawbacks—of loving a conventional old lady who, by then, had done it all and was basking in Bath society. I had the problem of just-missing Sarah's Bath contemporaries, mainly dead, but overlapping some of Gladys' friends. As a biographer I sat dangerously between a reasoned interpretation of historical fact and the fuzzy memories of what remained of their acquaintances.

Virago Press handed me Sarah on a plate. Elaine Showalter had just discovered and introduced her in 1977 (in *A Literature of Their Own*), mentioning that in 1920 Sarah moved to Bath and her last years were 'flat, stale, and unprofitable, despite her position as mayoress (honorary hostess), and the adoration of a younger woman, Gladys Singers-Bigger'.[3]

So, there in Bath Reference Library lay 'unpublished journals and records of Sarah Grand's life'[4]—and me, nearby, sending Virago unpublishable novels. Introduce the two, they decided, and shut one up with involvement in the other!

I was introduced to Sarah, following Elaine's superb lead, by Gladys' emotional diaries. These made a separately intriguing story and were the perfect introduction for a non-biographer. Fact towered over fiction and I became deeply involved in their relationship. Neither Virago nor I realized at the time how I could come to empathize with Sarah and identify with her struggles.

For a biography to be readable, the author has to have some kind of relationship with her subject. It is well known that biography tends to be autobiography, and autobiography is even more a form of fiction than biography—the borders blur. The biographer tends to become her subject. However, the more I read of Gladys's diaries, the more I sympathized with pathetic Gladys. Sarah, in those 'flat, stale and unprofitable years', appeared unworthy of such devotion—insensitive, autocratic, rather mean. Fame does not necessarily improve one's character! I learned a lot about her elderly personality, and didn't much like her. This was not a good beginning for our relationship and few people I came across in the late 1970s had heard of Sarah, apart from vaguely as author of some book called *The Heavenly Twins*.

Still, for me it was great to have an entirely new focus of reading, and the possibility of writing something more acceptable than my string of unpublishable novels. It didn't take long to realize that Sarah's frustrations in the 1870s and '80s were echoed by mine a century later. That period for her was formative and coloured all her later work. She did not give up in the face of a lousy marriage and repeated rejection of her novels, but capitalized on her experience and won through to recognition and fame. Inspiring!

Conveniently for me, apart from the diaries, the Library owned boxes of Sarah memorabilia. There were some four hundred letters, notes and cards, most of them still in their envelopes and tied together with ribbons. There were files of magazines and pamphlets containing many of Sarah's articles and short stories. Four enormous, elegantly bound volumes containing all the press cuttings about her time as Mayoress (1922–1929), and photographs. But in the late 1970s none of her work was in print and I began a jigsaw puzzle hunt for anything referring to her.

The more I read of New Woman novels and nineteenth-century history, the more the themes of the 1880s and 1890s appeared still relevant to today. Sarah's views (and those of her peers) about education, employment, marriage and the accepted role of women could still be describing, at the least, provincial middle-class life a whole century later. There remained a belief (as I had experienced) that it was more necessary to educate a son than a daughter, and that if a woman married her interests and occupation should, ideally, be confined to home and hearth. Unless she contributed to the household materially, she was 'the dependent'. However well she might cook, advise, save, minister and administer, her activities outside the family could only be frivolous. There was no point in encouraging her to aim higher than to be a good secretary and then a good wife. Many of my contemporaries did exactly that.

Sarah fought to improve the lot of women, particularly in marriage, and her novels made her name notorious in the 1890s. At the time of the controversial Contagious Diseases Acts (introduced to cut down an appallingly high incidence of venereal disease, particularly in the Army) she was married aged 17 to an army surgeon more than twice her age. She became not only disillusioned with her marriage but most upset by her husband's behaviour. When they returned from five years in the Far East (an amazing bonus for a Victorian girl and of which she made great use in her stories) he became connected with a Lock hospital. These hospitals were used for the forcible surgical examination of women to check for venereal disease. Women deemed prostitutes or potential prostitutes were picked up at random off the streets—there was no control on the men who spread the disease. It appears that Sarah's husband also had flirtations and mistresses on the side. So she was not only disapproving of his involvement with the kind of hospital she deplored, but horrified by his morals and behaviour, and probably frightened about the possibilities of contracting syphilis herself. When she became so disillusioned with her husband, she switched from writing her frequently rejected simple short stories to novels with a strong bias against men, and particularly about immoral husbands and the horrors that such behaviour could cause. At that time it was taboo for subjects like sex and syphilis to be mentioned, let alone by a woman. But Sarah was by no means one of the striking radicals or Shrieking Sisterhood. She preached morality and purity and believed in marriage. She was a suffragist rather than a suffragette—and by no means alone in what she wrote advocating marriage.

However, before *The Heavenly Twins* was published (at first anonymously) and because that provided her with an income—something that doesn't happen these days!—she left her husband and son, after twenty years of marriage, moved to London and changed her name from Frances McFall to Madame Sarah Grand.

So, gradually I piled up the facts and got a fair view of her background and motivation, with Gladys' diaries at my elbow and urging me on. The jigsaw puzzle hunt for details in itself became obsessive and led to as many interesting encounters (with Elaine Showalter and Martha Vicinus in particular) as the frustrating dead-ends with heirs and copyright. I learned to appreciate Sarah and her own earlier frustrations and achievements more and to understand her irritation and behaviour, so much later, with Gladys. But Gladys remained my guide because of the wealth of biographical material in her diaries. She could not be ignored and her miserably unful-filled life seemed a great counterpoint to Sarah's. No biography can deal with an individual in isolation and although Sarah met and knew many famous fellows in the literary world (Meredith, Hardy) and influenced many more, Gladys wrote herself into feminist history by association. For me, she remained important and demanding inclusion.

When it comes down to the actual construction of a biography, I real-ized, it is impossible to avoid one's own sympathies or prejudices, simply by how one presents the facts. How can one tackle seriously historical matter without to some extent personalizing it to make it readable? Was that a darkest night? Did she experience that rebuff as pain-full? Did she walk here, feel that, on this day? I find the author cannot avoid injecting her own concerns or beliefs into the material. Although presenting the facts as reasonably as possible, she is using her own reasoning. However unprej-udiced she may try to be, she can only be guided by her own interpreta-tion. I was brought up in a medical family and educated in the sciences and believed in an analytical/empirical approach to my subject, but I realized pretty early on that this subject was governed by emotions with which I identified. It followed that my own emotional response could not be excluded. The more I read of other biographies, the more I realized that political or personal agendas crept in, or dominated, particularly with feminist issues. Also, and more importantly in my view, the mere graphs and logic of a life did not make for an easy read. Sarah's story was poignant from start to finish. How her beliefs were formed and how she herself matured, dealt with and then promulgated these beliefs was all emotional, autobiographically based on her own experience, rather than analytical. Swept up in all that, I followed her line.

I set out quite instinctively and with no clear idea of what I was composing. A biography, I felt, was an expanded C.V. so that those interested in that part of history could pick Sarah up and slot her into their preoccupations with New Woman fiction. It would be an exercise in tidying up all her material and researching her background. What led me further than that at the time was Gladys and the relationship between a strong conservative feminist and a weak wimpish conservative. This showed an interesting balance, and so what followed became more of a joint biography. No man lives in isolation, anyway, and Gladys gives a more human view of Sarah in her unproductive middle age than I could make of her period of fame.

Now that, seventeen years after my book was published and Sarah and her peers and what they achieved are being more closely examined, it becomes even more apparent that some fundamental things have still not changed. We are still governed by patriarchal structures and attitudes. The law, in particular, favours power and money, which tend to be in the hands of dominant males. There remain similarities of conflict with a still male-oriented home and workplace. But Sarah's efforts to enlighten the reading public about what she saw as social injustice stand proud alongside the many later campaigns for equality. I am delighted that finally she is becoming recognized as one of the feminist forerunners.

2. Alternative Wifestyles

Vera Brittain's Feminist Journalism of the 1920s and the Influence of Olive Schreiner

Andrea Peterson

The New Woman of the 1890s can clearly be seen as an influential fore-runner of the 1920s feminist. In this paper I aim to assess the extent to which Vera Brittain's early journalism was influenced by the New Woman as represented both in the popular press and in the works of Olive Schreiner; and also the ways in which Brittain's feminist articles sought to redefine the image of the modern career woman. I will begin by contextualizing Brittain's journalistic career, before examining the extent to which Schreiner's works are intertextually echoed in many of the articles written by Brittain during the 1920s.

Although best known for her autobiography *Testament of Youth*, Vera Brittain (1893–1970) worked as a freelance journalist for five decades and contributed to various British, American, Canadian, German and Scandinavian newspapers, periodicals and magazines.[1] The Vera Brittain Archive holds copies of 'over a thousand articles, book reviews and open letters',[2] and between the wars Brittain was one of the 'most influential journalists' in London.[3] As is evidenced by her writing in other genres, Brittain aimed to promote three political causes: feminism, socialism and pacifism. She had always wanted to be a writer, in particular, a novelist. When she began working as a journalist, Brittain believed she was serving her literary apprenticeship. She maintained that the discipline of writing and placing freelance articles would provide both an income and valuable training, and later described journalism as 'a useful literary handmaid'.[4]

As a journalist, Brittain was at her most prolific during the late 1920s and early 1930s. It was during the 1920s that she focused most unswervingly on her own particular brand of feminism which was not only based on her personal and somewhat atypical experience, but was also clearly influenced by the ideas espoused by Olive Schreiner (1855–1920) in *Woman and Labour* and *The Story of an African Farm*. Although Brittain never abandoned her feminist beliefs, during the 1930s she wrote increasingly on international relations and pacifism. This was partly due to the long-awaited publication of *Testament of Youth*, and partly in response to the threat of a second world war. Consequently, for the purposes of this paper, I have limited my research to Vera Brittain's feminist journalism published between 1922—the year that she moved to London with Winifred Holtby—and 1930—the year her journalistic output first began to decline.

This period was important for Brittain both personally and professionally. She married in 1925, then spent a year in America with her husband before experimenting with what she called 'semi-detached marriage'. This arrangement, whereby she and her husband lived apart for six months a year in order to pursue their separate careers, is detailed in various articles, including 'Semi-Detachment: A Modern Solution of the Marriage Problem', which was published in the *Evening News* in 1928.[5] Her two children, John and Shirley—now Shirley Williams, the Baroness Williams of Crosby—were born in 1927 and 1930. In addition to some 287 articles, this period saw the publication of Brittain's first two novels, *The Dark Tide* (1923), and *Not Without Honour* (1924); her feminist study of *Women's Work in Modern England* (1928); and *Halcyon, or the Future of Monogamy* (1929), which is her satirical 'history' of marriage in the 19th, 20th and 21st centuries. From 1926 onwards, she was also working intermittently on *Testament of Youth*.

Brittain later remarked that she did not achieve journalistic success until the late 1920s because it took her 'at least seven years to learn' how to write articles 'containing Human Interest'.[6] By 'Human Interest' she means those 'love-affairs, sex crises and maternal self-indulgences', which were 'irreverently familiar in journalistic terminology under the comprehensive abbreviation of "H.I."'.[7] Brittain later reminisced of her early career:

> During those first anxious years of struggle to enter the most remorselessly competitive of professions, one of my greatest disadvantages lay in the complete failure of my appearance to convey any impression of

intelligence…[M]y still immature and naïve exterior struck those for whom I wanted to work as humorous in the extreme…[Hence, the] persistent 'H.I.' of popular journalism…infuriatingly…presented itself to a pen whose owner desired to write earnestly of political, international, and literary problems!…In the early nineteen-twenties I had still to discover that direct propaganda, however accomplished, is ineffective compared with the success in 'putting over' subversive doctrines…through the medium of light dissertations upon…innocent-looking domestic topics.[8]

I would suggest that therein lies the key to Brittain's success as a feminist journalist. Although she wrote for such profoundly feminist periodicals as *Time and Tide*, she came to understand that this was, to some extent, 'preaching to the converted' and that it was necessary to spread the word to a much wider (and unwitting) audience via the male-dominated world of daily newspapers. The titles of articles such as 'The Age for Marriage', 'Marriages That Last', 'Keeping His Love', and 'A Man Must Be Considered', belie their strident feminist content.[9] It is notable that Brittain's original title for this latter article was shortened on publication from the infinitely more scathing, 'A Man Must Be Considered. But As What?'[10]

Before examining some of Brittain's articles in more detail, I will focus on some popular textual representations of the New Woman. I will then outline the way in which the New and Old Feminisms of the 1920s developed out of the New Womanism of the *fin de siècle*. Finally, I will assess the extent to which Brittain's journalism can be seen to correspond with and make recourse to many of the ideas put forward by Olive Schreiner decades earlier.

The wide range of material included in this book emphasizes how difficult it is to proffer a succinct definition of the term New Woman. However, it is generally agreed that the term was originally applied to the heroines portrayed in a certain type of late-Victorian literature which fictionalized the dangers of women's financial dependence on men; oppressive marriages; the glorification of self-sacrifice; and wasted feminine talent. Later, the term New Woman also came to represent an 'individualistic, self-defined woman who educated [herself] for economic independence and [a] public life'.[11] The New Woman supported women's suffrage, advocated women's rights, and rejected the restrictive sexual ideology of the 19th century. Lyndall, the heroine of Olive Schreiner's *The Story of an African Farm*, is often seen as the archetypal New Woman; moreover, both the character of Lyndall and Schreiner's novel had great personal significance for Vera Brittain. Before examining Schreiner's characterisation of Lyndall in more detail, I will focus on one of the most problematic aspects of New Womanhood; that is, the rejection of the sexual ideology of the 19th century.

Various preparatory sketches for a new kind of femininity competed to replace the deeply entrenched iconography of the 'Angel in the House'. In 'the periodical press of the 1890s', the New Woman 'was carica-tured...as a "mannish" figure' who preferred 'education and a career to marriage, children and domesticity'.[12] It was widely believed that her education indulged some sort of transsexual fantasy and turned her into a 'desexualized half-man'.[13] Confusedly, she was alleged to vacillate between heterosexual licentiousness and rampant homosexuality. If she somehow succeeded in fulfilling her reproductive role by becoming a mother, she was supposed to experience uncontrollable infanticidal urges. In short, as Sally Ledger concludes in her detailed study, 'one of the defining features of the dominant discourse on the New Woman...was the supposition that...[she] posed a threat to the institution of marriage'.[14] Indeed, more often than not, she was identified 'as a single woman' and 'defined by her marital status'.[15] Although initially limited to a few male journalists writ-ing for a handful of periodicals, these extreme and alarmist views were swiftly perpetuated and popularized by major newspapers such as the *Daily Telegraph*, irrespective of the fact that most New Woman writers actu-ally sought to reform marriage rather than eradicate it and frequently promoted sexual abstinence.[16] Indeed, what many New Woman writers 'wanted to achieve was to convince their readers of the expediency of a far-reaching overhaul of marital relations, not to promote the more radi-cal idea that the concept should be abandoned altogether'.[17]

In recent years, the term New Woman has broadened both its para-meters of definition and its chronology. Ledger cites various feminist histo-rians, such as Judith Walkowitz and Lucy Bland, who have used the term New Woman to describe both 'late nineteenth- and early twentieth-century

feminists', thereby inaugurating 'a genealogy of first- and second-generation New Women', with the second generation living and writing in the
1920s and 1930s.[18] Nevertheless, the original New Woman of the 1880s
and 1890s is a figure quite distinct from the New Feminist of the 1920s.
The protracted battle for women's suffrage had long since divided feminists into two rival factions: the National Union of Women's Suffrage
Societies—which, under the leadership of Eleanor Rathbone, later became
the National Union of Societies for Equal Citizenship—and the Women's
Social and Political Union. This division had led to 'criticisms that the
women's movement was concentrating on one issue of largely middle-
class interest, at the expense of the...needs of working-class women'.[19]
During the 1920s, the women who supported these two major feminist
organisations became known as New and Old Feminists.

In 1925 the National Union of Societies for Equal Citizenship unveiled
what it called the New Feminism. Despite its new name, NUSEC's New
Feminism actually 'marked a general shift' away from 'emphasis on equal
opportunities towards emphasis on the distinctive needs of women'.[20] In
particular, the New Feminism focused on the needs of working-class mothers. In contrast, the Six Point Group continued to champion equal rights
and equal opportunities for women—issues that were somewhat anachro-
nistically deemed 'Old', especially given that the Equal Opportunities
Commission has found that even in the 21st century women are still not
treated equally and continue to be discriminated against in the workplace.
The six goals that gave the Six Point Group its name were: to introduce
widows' pensions; to introduce laws ensuring mothers' equal rights of
guardianship over their children; to reform the laws dealing with child
assault; to reform the laws determining the rights of unmarried mothers;
to obtain equal pay for women teachers; and to secure equal opportunities
for women working in the Civil Service.[21] Vera Brittain worked for the Six
Point Group for many years; hence, she is often assumed to be an Old
Feminist. Nevertheless, I believe that Brittain's journalism challenges this
assumption by expressing sympathy for the New Feminist goals of the
1920s without eschewing the emphasis on equality demanded by Old
Feminism. Indeed, I would agree with Alan Bishop's assertion that Brittain
often 'avoided identifying herself [too] closely with [any] factions involved
in disputes that threatened the common cause'; hence, '[h]er feminism

represented a creative reconciliation of "old" and "new" feminist priorities'.[22] In order to illustrate this, I will now examine a range of articles written by Brittain during the 1920s, focusing on her 'creative reconciliation'
of her New Feminist ideals with Olive Schreiner's New Womanist treatise.

Vera Brittain was still at school when she first read Olive Schreiner's *Woman
and Labour*. She later declared it the 'Bible of the Women's Movement',
and it evidently shored up her dreams of continuing her education and
becoming a professional writer.[23] The fact that, even by 1913, such ambitions were still widely equated with the single, mannish New Woman is
evidenced by an anecdote retold in *Testament of Youth*. Brittain writes:

> so unpopular…was the blue-stocking tradition…that my decision to
> go to an English town to study the literature of my own language
> caused me to be labelled 'ridiculous', 'eccentric', and 'a strong-minded
> woman'.
>
> For a few weeks my mother had quite a bad time at…teas and
> Mothers' Union meetings….
>
> 'How *can* you send your daughter to college, Mrs. Brittain!' moaned
> one lugubrious lady. 'Don't you want her ever to get *married?*'[24]

Nevertheless, the following year Vera Brittain went up to Somerville
College, Oxford. It was whilst studying for her Oxford Senior that Brittain
first read *The Story of an African Farm*. She received a copy of Schreiner's
novel as a gift from Roland Leighton, a young man she had recently been
introduced to by her brother, Edward Brittain, and to whom she later
became engaged.

Roland included a letter with the novel that asked, 'When you have read
it let me know what you think of it and whether you agree with me that
Lyndall is rather like you'.[25] Vera immediately identified with Lyndall, the
young heroine 'with a tiny body…dark brown hair & large intellectual
brown eyes'.[26] She replied, 'I think I *am* a little like Lyndall, and would
probably be more so in her circumstances, uncovered by the thin veneer
of polite social intercourse'.[27] However, it was Lyndall's relationship with
Waldo that most fascinated Vera and Roland. She not only identified with
Lyndall, but he chose to adopt the role of Waldo. Whilst serving in France

during the First World War, Roland wrote to Vera: 'Like Waldo I love to sit in the sun, and like him I have no Lyndall to sit with'.[28] Henceforth, references to *The Story of an African Farm* and its main protagonists pepper their correspondence until December 1915, when 'death intervened with its final full-stop—though ironically it was "Waldo" [Roland] who died', and '"Lyndall" [Vera] who was left alone.'[29]

By introducing Vera to *The Story of an African Farm*, Roland had effectively connected her with two influential New Woman writers: Olive Schreiner, and his own mother, Marie Connor Leighton. Marie Leighton was a well-known writer of popular romantic fiction, and her earnings provided her family's main source of income. Well aware of this economic fact, Roland respected both his mother's occupation and her feminist beliefs. Marie Leighton was open about *The Story of an African Farm* having had 'an immense influence on her life', and was pleased to learn that 'it was going to be the same' for a new generation of feminists.[30]

But how did *The Story of an African Farm* and *Woman and Labour* influence Vera Brittain? Alan Bishop has suggested that in her later life, Brittain tended to represent the influence of these two works as 'romantically monolithic'; however, several critics have pointed subsequently to the inconsistencies between Schreiner's feminist treatise and her novel and, in the light of these criticisms, Bishop has traced the antithetical effect of the two texts on Brittain's feminism and pacifism, as expressed in her wartime diary.[31] I will now endeavour to extend Bishop's inquiry by examining the effects of *The Story of an African Farm* and *Woman and Labour* on the development of Brittain's feminism during the 1920s.

Bishop argues that *The Story of an African Farm* exerted a 'mainly negative' effect on Brittain during the First World War, as 'it helped to justify an obsessive concern with her own suffering' and 'drew her away from her pacifist inclinations'.[32] Unlike Bishop, I am primarily concerned with the influence Schreiner's works exerted on Brittain's feminism during the 1920s. After the First World War, Brittain's references to *The Story of an African Farm* gradually decrease, and its influence becomes increasingly difficult to discern. Whereas Brittain was explicit about her belief in *Woman and Labour* as the 'Bible of the Woman's Movement', *The Story of an African Farm* was a much more personal text; indeed, she confided to her diary that '*The Story of an African Farm* plays the part of a Bible *with me*'.[33] I would argue that, because of her personal and romantic investment in the narrative, *The Story of an African Farm* most probably influenced Brittain's postwar attitudes towards marriage and motherhood, although she does not always agree with Schreiner's more negative views.

In her journalism of the 1920s, Vera Brittain consistently portrays marriage, motherhood and, indeed, sexual intercourse, as fulfilling and enriching for women. In contrast, Lyndall might seem to have a low opinion of woman's matrimonial lot; as she exclaims, 'I am not in so great a hurry to put my neck beneath any man's foot; and I do not so greatly admire the crying of babies'.[34] In common with many other New Woman writers, however, Schreiner promoted the reform of marriage rather than its abolition and she was perturbed when readers of *The Story of an African Farm* concluded that she must be 'opposed to life-long and deathless marriage between man and woman'.[35] Arguably, her exploration of the different types of relationships men and women might enter into can make her attitude to marriage appear rather ambivalent. Later in the novel, for example, Lyndall defends '[m]arriage for love', declaring it 'the beautifullest external symbol of the union of souls'; yet she castigates 'marriage without [love as]…the uncleanest traffic that defiles the world', and is scornful of the woman who marries simply for status, selling herself 'for a ring and a new name'.[36] Confusingly, Lyndall refuses to marry the man she loves, the unnamed father of her child, but, instead, agrees to marry the effeminate Gregory Rose—apparently to save her reputation. It has been suggested that this is evidence of Schreiner's 'low opinion of sexual attraction',[37] although later, in *Woman and Labour*, she was to declare 'sexual love' to be 'essentially Good and Beautiful'.[38]

While Schreiner's treatment of heterosexual relationships is indeed ambivalent, her depiction of motherhood remains consistently negative. Lyndall's baby is hardly mentioned. We do not learn its sex and Lyndall seems to regard it as a kind of parasite, saying, 'It crept close to me; it wanted to drink, it wanted to be warm…I did not love it…I did not care for it'.[39] In contrast, Brittain constantly promotes the positive aspects of marriage and motherhood and this would seem to be a crucial difference between the New Feminist and the New Woman: the New Feminist, having examined the range of alternatives to conventional marriage explored by her forerunners, had determined to promote the benefits of companionate marriage and motherhood—especially in combination with some form of fulfilling and economically empowering work outside the home. In this respect, the influence of *Woman and Labour* is more readily discernible than that of *The Story of an African Farm*.

In *Woman and Labour*, Schreiner proclaims the necessity of 'a movement towards common occupations, common interests, common ideals, and towards an emotional sympathy between the sexes'.[40] After an historical survey, tracing woman's gradual alienation and ultimate exclusion from the workforce, Schreiner argues that women might now find new occupations:

> every individual unit humanity contains, irrespective of race, sex, or type, should find exactly that field of labour which may most contribute to its development, happiness, and health, and in which its particular faculties and gifts shall be most effectively and beneficially exerted for its fellows.[41]

According to Schreiner, woman's reclamation of her right to work is of paramount importance. A working woman is not only man's equal economically and intellectually, but she is also his equal sexually; hence, an empowered woman can enjoy an active sex life with her husband, whereas her forerunners had been encouraged to abstain from sexual intercourse because their 'sexual relationships [were] based, not on the spontaneous affection of the woman for the man, but on the necessitous acceptance by woman of material good in exchange for the exercise of her sexual functions'.[42]

The positive influence of *Woman and Labour* is immediately obvious in Brittain's journalism as there are several articles containing direct references to Schreiner's text. Like Schreiner, Brittain advocates the merits of professional and economic equality for women. For example, in an article entitled 'Happiness and Sex. Do Women Enjoy Life Less Than Men?', Brittain reminds her readers:

> From poverty, loneliness, ennui and frustration, the 'labour and the training that fits us for labour' demanded by Olive Schreiner in 1911 can so effectually rescue us that no woman need be penniless or bored or solitary except as the result of her own lethargy.[43]

Hoping that the Sex Disqualification (Removal) Act of 1919 had opened up many more professions to women, Brittain endeavoured, throughout the 1920s, to undermine those 'ancient conventions and prejudices' which she believed obstructed women's progress even more effectively than legislation.[44] In an article called 'The Professional Woman: Careers Affected by Marriage', she decried 'the convention that a woman's work' is seen as nothing more than 'a kind of superior hobby'.[45] In addition, Brittain fervently embraced Schreiner's notion of female parasitism, as detailed in the first three chapters of *Woman and Labour*. Schreiner had argued that 'if not given work, or if not made fit for it,' the female parasite would 'gradually pull her race down with her into a state of vacuity and degeneration,' as 'weak and parasitic mothers' would bear only 'weak and enervated children'.[46] *The Nation and The Athenaeum* published a lengthy article entitled 'Married Teachers and Social Hypocrisy' in which Brittain explains:

> The Industrial Revolution, combined with Victorian middle-class envy and admiration of 'conspicuous consumption', produced that peculiar phenomenon, the female parasite, whose threat to society was first pointed out by Olive Schreiner in 'Woman and Labour'…Once this human parasite had been produced, the social code which not only tolerated but flattered her taught her that she had justified her existence when she had acquired the right to wear a wedding ring, and had produced one or two children…To the women who have carried into a more energetic age this out-of-date system of values, the living proof that marriage and a profession can be happily combined threatens their comfortable justification of their own parasitism…[T]hey want to see marriage wreck a keen worker's future. Their…jealous resentment…can be so easily camouflaged as devotion to the welfare of the future generation.[47]

Later, under a provocative headline claiming that the 'Superfluous Women are Really The Tennis Mad who Neglect their Homes', Brittain published a more accessible attack on the 'middle-class parasitic female'.[48] Quoting Lady Rhondda's essay 'Leisured Women,' Brittain claims that those 'middle-class parasitic female[s] "who do not see their children…for more than two or three hours in the twenty-four"' nevertheless make those "'children, and the home they do *not* bear the brunt of looking after, into an excuse for doing nothing else'".[49]

Although she defends the career-oriented single woman in this article, I would agree with Linda Anderson that Brittain cannot wholly detach herself from 'an ideology that promoted marriage as a form of success for a woman'.[50] The fact was that in 'her determination not to abandon her career', she 'was undoubtedly swimming against the popular ideological tide'.[51] Even with legal reform on their side, most middle-class women still felt that they had to choose to become either a 'desexualised half-man' with a compensatory career, or a ladylike hostess with a breadwinning husband and perfect children. Vera Brittain was adamant that no woman should have to make this 'intolerable choice'.[52]

In an unpublished article entitled 'The Crisis in Morals. Prudery versus Knowledge', Brittain quotes from Schreiner's 'Introduction' to *Woman and Labour* in support of her argument for the 'liberation of both the married and the unmarried' from 'prudery and censorship'. However, since the majority of women still wanted their 'sexual relationships with men…sanctioned by legal marriage',[53] Brittain emphasizes the need for a more enlightened approach towards sex within marriage, arguing that 'a large percentage of matrimonial failures are due to physiological or psychological maladjustments which could easily have been corrected'.[54] She also suggests that both men and women should be trained 'in sex technique' and the use of 'contraceptives'.[55] Similar ideas had already been expressed by some of Brittain's feminist forerunners. At the turn of the century New Women had reinterpreted '[w]omen's right to education…to include the right to vital sexual information', and '[t]hree demands' had been 'at the forefront' of their 'feminist vision of social and marital reconstruction: sex education for all, an end to the sexual double standard, and the civic duty of (male) chastity'.[56] That Brittain failed to place her article indicates that the earlier feminist campaign had failed: sex was still a taboo subject and 'prudery' still triumphed over 'knowledge'.

Heavily influenced by several contemporary sexologists, including Havelock Ellis, Walter Gallichan and Magnus Hirschfeld, Brittain condemned 'the convention that the sex life of spinsters remains permanently in abeyance'.[57] Indeed, Brittain was very concerned that the single New Woman of the 1880s and 1890s was now in danger of becoming an

'Old Maid'. It should be noted, however, that she never used this term in a derogatory way, and usually applied it only to working spinsters. For example, in 'The Modern "Old Maid"', Brittain implores '[t]hose authorities who imagine that, by closing the doors of professions to married women, they are encouraging motherhood and protecting the home', to 'study the useful and enjoyable life of the present-day spinster before…mak[ing] up their minds that no woman who had a chance of marriage would choose to be an old maid'.[58] In the lengthy article 'Is It Foolish To Be An *Old Maid* From Choice?', Brittain concludes that 'it is not so much foolish, as cowardly, to become an old maid from choice', as women who choose not to marry do not have so many difficulties to overcome as their married counterparts.[59]

Brittain frequently emphasizes that '[e]ach normal person, whether man or woman, is endowed by Nature with a mind and a body, and is intended…to fulfil the requirements of both'.[60] Consequently, many of her articles are prescriptions for 'having it all'. They offer practical advice gleaned from her own experience. She suggests that the 'acceptance by all professions of a certain number of part-time members' would enable 'the majority of married women' to continue working during 'the early years of motherhood'.[61] One of her more radical demands was that 'English husbands learn…to take their full share of domestic responsibility' by sharing household chores and childcare with their wives.[62] This echoes Schreiner's notion that rather than a sexual revolution, what was needed was an 'interevolution between sexes', in order that there might be a 'real and permanent human advance'.[63] In recognition of this, Brittain herself would later write that '[f]or Olive Schreiner the freedom and equality of women was less a political movement than the product of a totally new relationship between the sexes'.[64] Actually, by the mid 1920s Brittain had begun to echo Schreiner's argument that men must change their ideas and practices as well as women. Schreiner's works generally gesture toward 'long-term relationships', that allow 'both partners…individual freedom and the exclusive right to their own bodies';[65] however, her novel '*From Man to Man* breaks off at the precise point at which New Woman meets New Man'.[66] In contrast, Brittain's journalism starts at the point at which their honeymoon ends, the point at which New Feminist wife begins to negotiate an alternative 'wifestyle' with her New Feminist husband.

Brittain advocates that all households take full advantage of the latest 'labour-saving devices'[67] and, like the American New Woman writer Charlotte Perkins Gilman, calls for 'communal kitchens...laundries, crêches and nursery schools'.[68] Furthermore, she imagines how women's lives could be made easier by the creation of 'labour-saving houses, properly trained domestic workers, more community kitchens, laundries and well-run restaurants, [and] more open-air nursery schools'.[69] Nevertheless, these 'labour-saving' measures are intended solely to facilitate women's return to the workforce and not to create more leisure-time. Indeed, Brittain seems to have embraced Schreiner's notion of female parasitism to such an extent that leisure has been eradicated from her utopian vision of family life. Ultimately, she envisages that

> the ideal households of the future will be those in which, by labour-saving devices, all necessary work has been reduced to a minimum, and that which is left is shared between the wives and husbands who delight in making homes for one another.[70]

In one of her later articles, published in 1955, Vera Brittain actually describes Olive Schreiner as 'a forerunner...coming to be recognized as one of the most remarkable pioneers produced by the nineteenth century'.[71] By developing the ideas put forward by Schreiner in *Woman and Labour*—and, to a lesser extent, in *The Story of an African Farm*—Brittain aimed to offer the married woman a practical alternative: a 'wifestyle' that stormed the marriage bar, allowing the married woman to combine a career with motherhood. As Brittain herself notes in an article headed 'The Incomplete Woman', the popular press had perpetuated an image of the New Woman 'as a "masculine woman", a "virulent female", an "abnormal type", or a "sexually embittered spinster"'.[72] Through her journalism, Vera Brittain used the press as a means to alter this, but, rather egotistically, she chose to model the New Feminist in her own overtly feminine and fashionable image.

3. A Transatlantic Alliance

Charlotte Perkins Gilman and Vernon Lee

Patricia Pulham

The lives of Charlotte Perkins Gilman and Vernon Lee were almost exactly contemporaneous. Lee, born in 1856, was four years older than Gilman and both women died in 1935. In contrast to Gilman, who has featured prominently in our literary consciousness since the 1960s at least, Lee, once famous enough to be mentioned in Robert Browning's poem 'Inapprehensiveness' (in his 1889 collection, *Asolando: Fancies and Facts*) has been consigned to relative obscurity.[1] Until fairly recently the name 'Vernon Lee' has meant little to all but a handful of scholars who, unearthing her work in a wide range of fields, including history, philosophy, aesthetics, politics, sociology, travel writing and fiction, have no doubt been astonished that a woman of her intellectual stature has been virtually ignored for the best part of sixty-five years.

First appearing on the literary scene at the age of twenty-four with a critical work, *Studies of the Eighteenth Century in Italy* (1880), Vernon Lee was promptly acclaimed for her erudition and introduced to literary and artistic circles that included such prominent figures as Dante Gabriel Rossetti, Walter Pater, and Henry James.[2] Given her early success and the profusion and quality of her subsequent production, one would expect Lee's name to have become part of our collective memory, to be remembered with the same respect that is given to her literary admirers, Browning and James. Yet this is not so, nor, it would appear, has it been so in the recent past. In his dissertation written in the 1950s (published in 1987), Burdett Gardner observes that, despite being appreciated by critics such as Desmond MacCarthy and Mario Praz, in 'the standard histories and reference works one seeks her name largely in vain', concluding that, 'Indeed, it would almost seem that a conspiracy of silence has prevailed against her'.[3] Fortunately, this unhappy neglect of Lee is slowly being redressed by the recent attention of scholars such Carlo Caballero, Jane Hotchkiss, Christa Zorn (formerly Zorn-Belde), Catherine Maxwell, Gillian Beer, Kathy Alexis Psomiades, and Angela Leighton, whose work is helping to restore her to her rightful place in history.[4] This essay will, I hope, play a small part in this process. I aim to demonstrate the respect in which Lee was held by Charlotte Perkins Gilman and to highlight Lee's influential role in the dissemination of Gilman's *Women and Economics* (1898). In addition, I wish to show that this was not a one-way process and that Gilman's work had a considerable effect on Lee, making her reconsider her own stance in relation to the Woman Question.

In Gilman's autobiography there is only a cursory mention of Lee in a diary entry for 1904 which records that whilst in Italy with her daughter, Kate, Gilman stopped overnight in Florence to call on her friend, Mrs Hackett, 'in whose house *Women and Economics* had been begun; and to call on "Vernon Lee" in her villa near by, who had written an introduction to the Italian edition.'[5] However, Gilman's existing letters to Lee, held by Somerville College, Oxford, and spanning the period 1900 to 1904 suggest a warm admiration and gratitude for the part she plays in the introduction of her work to a European audience. Their correspondence begins less than auspiciously perhaps, for it seems that Gilman's first letter (dated 28 November 1900) is a reply to one from Lee regarding the translation of *Women and Economics* into Italian, in which she questions the lack of bibliographical detail in Gilman's work and challenges some of her points on economic independence. Gilman replies:

> The lack of bibliography in *Women and Economics*—as well as the scarcity of definite quotation or reference, is due to a few personal conditions. My education consisted mainly in solitary study along lines of special interest, mainly sociological, and in such books and other literature as I was able to get to from time to time. For six to eight years I read in this way, with increasing interest but no systematic record. Then followed many years of broken health and partial recovery; full of wide experience, but no regular study. When at last I was able to write somewhat—since 1890—I was not able to study, and

in the fall of 97, when this book was written, was travelling from place
to place…a good deal, and making desultory visits. It was finished
in a boarding house in New York with as much labor as I was able
to give—but that activity did not include a wide and thorough
research into my early sources of information.[6]

Lee was not the only person to request clarification regarding this matter,
yet, significantly, Gilman's autobiography logs a quite different response
when the scholarship of *Women and Economics* is questioned by Dr. E. A.
Ross, a sociologist she had known at Stanford, for here she writes:

> He asked why I had not put in a bibliography. I told him I had meant
> to, but when it came to making a list of books I had read bearing on
> the subject, there were only two. One was Geddes's and Thompson's
> *Evolution of Sex*, the other only an article of Lester F. Ward's, in that
> 1888 *Forum*.[7]

Interestingly, in a letter to Lee written in 1904, Gilman recommends
that Lee should read Ward's *Pure Sociology* which contains a chapter that
develops the gynaecentric theory broached in the 1888 article, and this
book, together with *The Evolution of Sex*, is cited in Lee's essay 'The
Economic Parasitism of Women' in the collection *Gospels of Anarchy*
published in 1908.[8] What seems particularly important about this passage,
however, is the difference between Gilman's replies to Lee and to Ross
which implies that Gilman took pains to excuse herself to Lee in a manner
she didn't deem necessary when formulating her answer for Ross. This, I
would argue, suggests a respect for Lee and her work, as well as an anxious
need to elicit Lee's sympathy, understandable perhaps as this early letter
precedes the writing of Lee's preface to the Italian edition of *Women and
Economics*.

In contrast, Gilman's response to Lee's comments relating to the content
of the book is far more confident and forthright. In her annotated edition
of *Women and Economics* in the British Institute in Florence, Lee takes issue
with Gilman concerning the analogy made between the biological and social
organism in the section entitled 'Union of Male and Female Qualities.'
Gilman's recourse to the world of 'insects and crustaceans' to find evidence

of male inferiority sits uneasily with Lee, who writes in the margins, 'Mammals are different in size, strength energy, the females [markedly] inferior as the expenditure during gestation would lead one to expect', and she considers Gilman's biology generally somewhat 'leaky'.[9] It is apparent from Gilman's letter of 28 November 1900 that Lee has raised the subject and questioned the validity of her opinion. Gilman writes:

> Now for your own position that woman's natural sex-distinction makes her 'a weaker intellectually and muscularly more worthless creature' than man. I refer you at once to the whole field of savage life, ancient and modern, where women fulfill their sex functions freely and do much muscular work besides. I do not know how they compare intellectually with men in their stage of development; they probably differ by industrial education. Again in peasant life generally, women do much muscular work, and compare intellectually— admitting educational differences—very favourably with men. In commercial life in France, women take part in commercial activities and compare favourably with men in this field—the education being fairly equal…But now, begging the whole question, admitting for the sake of argument that woman is muscularly and intellectually inferior to man and cannot 'compete' with him; *that does not shake the claim for her economic independence in the least.* Inferior men, and inferior classes of men, can maintain their economic independence. They do not ask to be 'supported'…because they cannot 'compete' with cleverer and stronger people.[10]

Evidently, Gilman's answer had a substantial effect on Lee, for by the time the Italian version of *Women and Economics* is published, she tells the reader:

> In writing this preface for a translation of Mrs Stetson's *Women and Economics*, and in recommending the original to my Anglo-Saxon readers, I am accomplishing the duty of a convert. I believe that *Women and Economics* ought to open the eyes, and, I think, also the hearts, of other readers, because it has opened my own, to the real importance of what is known as the Woman Question.[11]

Lee claims that her conversion to Gilman's point of view resulted from the book's objective outlook, 'because in it the rights and wrongs of *Femina, das Weib*, were not merely opposed to the rights and wrongs of *Vir, der Mann*, but subordinated to those of what is, after all, a bigger item of creation: *Homo, der Mensch*'.[12] In her 1994 dissertation on Lee, Christa Zorn argues that although Lee calls herself a 'convert' to the Woman Question, 'she does not speak from the same space as Stetson [Gilman] whose book focuses on sociological and political questions'.[13] For Zorn, Lee's approach is literary: she comments on Stetson's book 'as literary critic, not as feminist'.[14] Yet as Zorn herself observes, Lee, in her preface, 'rewrites' Stetson's book 'for a European audience through influential contemporary male discourses (Darwin, Durkheim, Marx, Michelet)'—discourses which are themselves sociological and political—and in this manner 'simultaneously express[es] her female viewpoint and point[s] out the foibles of [the] male discourses she cites':[15]

> By pitting against one another various discourses in late nineteenth-century Western capitalism (such as Darwinian evolutionism, socialism, anthropological racism, and Nietzschean *Übermensch* philosophy) she deconstructs these discourse[s] through their own implications…Always in favour of 'showing' instead of 'telling', Lee uses this principle to steer the reader's attention to the 'universal' argument in order to convince a potentially critical audience.[16]

It seems that while Lee and Gilman may not 'speak from the same space', there are interesting points of convergence and I would argue that the fundamental link between the two women lies in their humanist convictions. In a speech delivered at the London Pavilion on 19 May 1913 and published in *The Suffragette* (6 June 1913), Gilman states:

> I am called a feminist: I am not a feminist; I am a humanist.[17] The reason why I have had to stop and study the position of women, why I have had to stop and wait for twenty years and work for the freedom of womankind is because woman in her present position is the stumbling-block of the world. The world cannot go further nor faster nor higher until it has brought up the rearguard![18]

These are sentiments which are clearly visible in *Women and Economics*, and it is this point of view which would have struck a chord with Lee. This is not to say that Lee did not have reservations concerning the suffrage movement. Letters from Ethel Smyth to Lee indicate that Lee disagreed with the militant action advocated by certain members of the women's movement. In a letter dated 15 November 1912 (?), Smyth writes:[19]

> I want you to do something for me—write an article for our paper 'The Suffragette'—Mrs Pankhurst wants it to be very good on the side of things not connected necessarily with W[omen's] Suffrage...Of course if you feel moved to write something 'feminist'—do—only not something à la Bernard Shaw which can be equally used by the enemy...I know you're not a militant but I believe you will allow that reforms move on as many legs as a centipede...Of course if you think us all wrong; fit only for the pit, it's another matter but I don't believe you do.[20]

Her next letter dated 15 December 1912 (?) suggests that Lee has refused her request. Smyth replies, 'I quite understand that you or anyone sh[ould] disapprove of militancy...I still half hope you may send me a little article against militancy if you like!!'.[21] Following Lee's second refusal in answer to this letter, Smyth writes on 24 January 1913 (?):

> My dear Vernon, I wonder if you would do this: state your...objections to our doing what (remember) I have seen you trying to do on [*sic*] another field force the pace!...What I want you to do, if you will, (in that you, a distinguished woman, possibly voice many others, [and] would do so in a way they cannot attempt) is, what Mr. Venus was requested to do,—bring your powerful mind to bear on the subject of your own convictions—or your own instincts if you like to put it so—in this matter, [and] let me put the result into 'The Suffragette'.[22]

Lee's reluctance to accede to Smyth's request is, I suggest, based on the fact that Lee's own understanding of the importance of female emancipation centres on the accession of woman to citizenship. Militancy, by the very nature of its violent character, is in conflict with the concept of 'good citizenship' and one can speculate that Lee's unwillingness to appear in *The Suffragette* is likely to have been due to its support for militant action. This concern with citizenship is one which, as Lisa Ganobcsik-Williams demonstrates in the next chapter, is shared by Gilman, and evidently colours Lee's championship of female suffrage. It is unsurprising, then, that in her introduction to Gilman's book, Lee should advocate the removal of those 'legal and professional disabilities' which prevent women from forging a place for themselves in society.[23] Yet, despite her reservations, Lee *did* write an article on suffrage, although it is uncertain whether it was ever published in *The Suffragette* or elsewhere. The Vernon Lee archive at Colby College, Waterville, Maine, contains the galleyproof of an essay by Lee which bears the handwritten title 'Why I Want Women to Have a Vote', an article in which the enfranchisement of women is specifically linked to the importance of citizenship. Lee argues:

I find that I want women to have the vote not because they deserve it (how many men would have it at that rate?); not because I think them wonderfully useful members of the community (few members, even male, *are* wonderfully useful); but because women might be made less undeserving of a vote—and men less undeserving through their influence—exactly by being given it. For the vote, even if used badly or not at all, is the recognition that the times are gone by when it was opportune that women, like Milton's Eve, should live for God through Man— a mode of life definable in un-Miltonian prose as parasitic and irresponsible. Democracy requires that the number of people habitually recognising duties larger and more complex than those of family life, the number of efficient citizens, should increase steadily, and that the proportion of human cattle, human furniture, and machines, and even of human *objets d'art* should steadily diminish…Now women's capacity, great or small, for civic efficiency is not at present asked for…All there might be of it is wasted, allowed to become, at best, so much dilettante's excellence…Nor does our wastefulness of such civic capacities end here. Women are not a class apart…For every woman there is a man; and the man will be none the better citizen for the presence of a woman who is no citizen at all.[24]

Unfortunately, because the article lacks publication information it is impossible to date. However, its content suggests that it was written after Lee's 'conversion'. Despite its neutral tone, equally sceptical of the merits of men and women, it is clear that Lee's thoughts on the matter of the female vote have been heavily influenced by Gilman's theories even though they may not correspond exactly and are constrained by Lee's reluctance to align herself with either gender. That the article was written at all is testament to Lee's change of heart, for it is hard to believe that the woman who considered women to be 'weaker intellectually' than men would have advocated the extension of women's rights into the realms of civic responsibility.

When one visits the Vernon Lee Library at the British Institute in Florence, one observes that Gilman features among a select group of authors who have more than one work in this collection. Apart from *Women and Economics* (1898), one finds *The Home: Its Work and Its Influence* (1903), *Human Work* (1904), and *The Man-Made World* (1911), all of which are liberally inscribed with marginalia. Marked passages in Lee's copy of *The Home* resonate interestingly with aspects of her own life, and in particular those writings which relate to the social sexualisation of girls in Chapter 13, 'The Girl at Home'. Gilman writes:

> Since we first began to force upon our girl baby's astonished and resisting brain the fact that she was a girl; since we curbed her liberty by clothing and ornament calculated only to emphasise the fact of sex, and by restrictions of decorum based upon the same precocious distinction, we have never relaxed the pressure. As if we feared that there might be some mistake, that she was not really a girl but would grow up a boy if we looked the other way, we diligently strove to enforce and increase her femininity by every possible means.[25]

Lee marks the sentence, 'As if we feared that there might be some mistake, that she was not really a girl but would grow up a boy if we looked the other way...' and adds the comment, 'As some small girls undoubtedly hope'.[26] In these few short words, one senses Lee's return to her childhood, and wonders less at her adoption of the sexually ambiguous pseudonym 'Vernon Lee.' Although, as Christa Zorn argues, 'Lee seems to have "lived" feminism more than she expounded it..."trained for art and literature as most girls of her generation were trained for marriage or domesticity'", it appears, nevertheless, that the young Violet Paget experienced those pressures which Gilman identified as those of her sex.[27] It would seem that Gilman's works touched Lee not only intellectually and politically, but also personally.

It is impossible to tell from the copies of the texts themselves whether they were sent to Lee at Gilman's request. However, it is certainly likely as in a letter dated 15 December 1902, Gilman asks Lee, 'Did you get a copy of *Concerning Children* I ordered sent you last spring or summer?'[*sic*] and adds 'At present I am deep in a new one on "work" a sort of social philosophy; and hope to publish in the Spring. Be sure you shall have a copy of that'.[28]

Concerning Children does not appear in the Lee Library collection but clearly Gilman kept her promise regarding the book on 'work' which, judging from the intended date of publication, is most probably *The Home: Its Work and Its Influence*, and in a letter dated 1904 Gilman writes:

> I mean to send you…an early copy of *Human Work*, the greatest thing I have done yet—; which comes out this Spring…I am deeply inter-ested in having you read this last. *Concerning Children* was but a hand-ful of essays; *The Home* is but a criticism; but this Work book is a presentation of my philosophy of human life; explaining and connect-ing all I have written before.[29]

Gilman's regard for Lee's opinion is evident not only here, but also in her earlier letter of 15 December 1902, where she thanks Lee for her review of *Women and Economics* in the *North American* in July 1902, and in which she acknowledges that,

> It is by far the most satisfactory of any review or discussion I have seen. On analysis and comparison it brings out the main points at issue, and treats them admirably…But it pleases me most in itself; that it will reach and persuade many who have not read the book— and will not. I thank you very warmly.[30]

It is clear that, in Gilman's view, Vernon Lee's approval was worth having, and that Lee's published appreciation of her work ensured its dissemination to a larger audience than it might otherwise have reached. This, I claim, is confirmation that, despite the lack of attention given to her work for much of the last century, Lee's opinion once mattered and held considerable intellectual sway. It was certainly prophetic, for in her essay 'The Economic Parasitism of Women', speaking of anthropological arguments locating the differing evolution of male and female brains in the developing processes of civilization, Lee writes:

> I have a very strong feeling that the desirability of any particular thing in the future has nothing to do with its existence or non-existence in the past; and that the question of the position of women, say, in the year 2000 A.D., will depend not upon the position of women in the year—well, the year 20,000 before the Deluge—but upon the condition of the world at large, the intellectual, moral, particularly economical state of men and women, in our own times.[31]

In one of her letters to Lee (28 November 1900), Gilman is equally prescient. Lee, questioning whether the name 'Stetson' or 'Gilman' should appear on the translated copy of *Women and Economics*, receives the reply:

> As to the name on the translation, Stetson I think—that book being written by Mrs Stetson. Those that follow will be Gilman, though the new one just out or nearly out—*Concerning Children* has the 'Stetson' bracketed under to bridge the chasm. A temporary nuisance, this changing women's names—we shall outgrow it.[32]

Both these women display a sociological awareness and an intellectual lucidity that was bound to foster mutual appreciation and lively debate. From the short extracts included here, it is evident that this continued for a number of years and manifested itself not only in their correspondence but also in the silent dialogue that exists in the annotated editions of Gilman's works in the Vernon Lee Library at the British Institute in Florence.[33]

4. Charlotte Perkins Gilman and The Forerunner

A New Woman's Changing Perspective on American Immigration

Lisa Ganobcsik-Williams

Charlotte Perkins Gilman (1860–1935) is known today as a pioneer of American feminist theory. In this article, however, I explore a different component of the wider reform vision that Gilman formulated and prescribed for late nineteenth and early twentieth-century American society. Although her social vision took women's rights as a central tenet and driving force, Gilman often stressed her belief in 'humanism', by which she meant the progress of the human race as a whole. 'I am not primarily "a feminist,"' she wrote, 'but a humanist. My interest in the position of women, in the child, in the home, is altogether with a view to their influence on human life, happiness, and progress'.[1] Social service to promote a 'common good' was a basic element of Gilman's humanist or civic republican philosophy, and she believed that the United States, as a new nation with a participatory form of government, provided the world's best opportunity to create a rational citizenry committed to improving the quality of life for all people.

Gilman's democratic socialist reform theories, though groundbreaking on many fronts, were not always well-received by the general public, whose fundamental habits of thinking and acting she was attempting to influence and alter. After establishing an international reputation as a social critic with books such as *Women and Economics* (1898), *Concerning Children* (1900), and *The Home* (1903), Gilman noted a decline in the willingness of commercial editors to publish her manuscripts. 'If one writes to express important truths, needed yet unpopular, the market is necessarily limited,' her autobiography explains. 'As all my principal topics were in direct contravention of established views, beliefs, and emotions, it is a wonder that so many editors took so much of my work for so long'.[2] In response to this lack of reception, Gilman decided, at age forty-nine, to start her own magazine, which would allow her to 'publish and edit myself and preach'.[3] From 1909 through 1916, Gilman singlehandedly wrote, edited, and published a twenty-eight page monthly, *The Forerunner*, which included poetry, stories, one serialized novel and one sociological book each year, book reviews, essays, and sermons. While she continued to publish elsewhere and to deliver public lectures, with *The Forerunner* Gilman created and maintained a unique, public writing space for developing and disseminating her humanist social philosophy—a writing space that was uncensored and uncritiqued by editors and which had an audience of yearly subscribers. Gilman stopped publishing the magazine in 1916, having, after seven years, 'relieved the pressure of what I had to say'.[4]

Although *The Forerunner* was a space for broadcasting her developing theories on women's rights, including the right to participate in government policymaking, Gilman also used this platform to address other issues and social oppressions. One subject she repeatedly took up was immigration. Like other public figures, Gilman was concerned with how the American government would handle problems resulting from turn-of-the-century immigration—a surge unprecedented in scale and ethnic diversity. Beginning in the 1890s, this third historical wave of immigration 'ascended to its zenith in 1907 and then fluctuated at a level above 650,000 per year until the outbreak of the World War'.[5] During this period, immigration from traditional sources such as Germany, Great Britain, Scandinavia, France, Switzerland, Holland, Belgium, and Luxembourg was eclipsed by an outpouring from 'two distinct [and distinctly different] geographic regions', the Mediterranean and the Slavic.[6] By 1907, the presence of 'new immigrants' who differed from Americans of white, Protestant origin in social customs, religious beliefs, and appearance had become unmistakable.[7]

As a social critic, Gilman contributed to public debate about how best to assimilate such immigrants into American culture. In this article, I examine Gilman's views on immigration and ethnicity as expressed in *The Forerunner*. While *The Forerunner* writings rightly helped to establish Gilman's reputation as an early feminist, the same forum in which she articulated her liberatory ideas on gender oppression served as a site for her less palatable theories (for today's feminists) on immigration and on ethnicity. Exploring Gilman's work in this way sheds light on the complexities and limits of her feminist/humanist vision.

Gilman's views on the issue of immigration narrowed markedly over time, and by the 1920s she had developed a strong bias against foreigners settling in the United States.[8] This intolerance was nativism, the belief 'that some influence originating abroad threatened the very life of the nation from within'.[9] Gilman's social reform vision was grounded in the newly-authoritative language of science, and she theorized the principle of 'social evolution' to explain that, as a result of social factors, different groups of people had evolved to different stages of readiness to participate wisely in a democratic system of public policymaking. Secure in claiming her own Anglo-American heritage as traceable to the white Puritan founders of the United States,[10] she formulated a 'scientific' philosophy of social control that endorsed nativist schemes for managing immigrants and immigration procedures. In this article, I explore Gilman's changing theories and recommendations for how the nation could cope socially and legislatively with the pressures of immigration. By looking through a chronological framework at Gilman's narrowing position on immigrants, it becomes clear that she utilized scientific discourse in different ways to justify and lend authority to her shifting attitudes.

Although Gilman's nativist views were considered extreme by many of her liberal friends and fellow social reform activists,[11] the development of her response to the dramatic increase in American immigration throughout her lifetime followed a general, national pattern of reaction. Her writings on immigration in *The Forerunner*, however, reveal that Gilman also experienced a more specific reaction based on her belief in her concept of humanism: she increasingly perceived unregulated immigration to be a threat to her vision of a homogenous American public comprised of enlightened, rational women and men. As Dale M. Bauer argues, the aging 'Gilman feared that immigration would result in democratic rule by dysgenic—or degenerate—mobs that would put an end to the social progress she had spent her life imagining'.[12] That Gilman used *The Forerunner* to propound a social vision which would limit the input of immigrant voices is ironic; she established her magazine in order to counteract the exclusion of her own voice from the public sphere, yet she readily sought to repeat the same exclusion when it came to immigrant perspectives. Although *The Forerunner* gave Gilman an opportunity to develop her social philosophy free from pressures of commercial restraint, on the issue of immigration, this same advantage became something of a drawback, because there is no debate within *The Forerunner* to challenge Gilman's increasingly harsh viewpoint. Even when other views did surface inadvertently in the pages of *The Forerunner*, Gilman effectively ignored the implications they held for her own arguments by invoking her humanistic philosophy to justify her role as a social commentator in recommending measures that she believed would best serve society as a whole.

Gilman's Early Optimism

Changes began occurring in American immigration patterns during the 1880s. As historian David Leviatin explains, the archetypal 'Protestants of northern and western European background, arriving in the United States as families and settling on farms in the rural countryside,' gave way to an influx of single young males, mainly Catholics and Jews fleeing poverty and persecution in Eastern and Southern Europe and settling in large American cities.[13] In the early and mid-1890s there was a reaction against such foreigners in American society, evidenced by a flowering of hereditary patriotic societies, the establishment of an Immigrant Restriction League in Boston, and the support of a number of corporations and labour unions for a literacy test to limit immigrant intake. John Higham argues that this response was prompted by the widespread economic depression of 1893–1896, during which employment was scarce, and that following a return to prosperity at the beginning of 1897 and into the early years of the 20th century, Americans' 'ethnic fears did not cut deeply' despite the changing patterns of immigration. Economic confidence prevailed, as well as a social confidence that 'the ordinary processes of a free society' and the 'general institutions and atmosphere of American society' would act as sufficient structures for fashioning immigrants into citizens.[14]

Susan Lanser detects anxiety about immigrants in Gilman's work as early as the 1892 story 'The Yellow Wallpaper'. As Lanser points out, Gilman wrote 'The Yellow Wallpaper' while residing in California, the state most open to immigration from the islands and nations of the Pacific, and one in which 'mass anxiety about the "Yellow Peril"' had succeeded in pushing through the Chinese Exclusion Act of 1882, a federal ban on Chinese immigration to the United States. Lanser argues that the tale's protagonist sees climbing out of the wallpaper of her room 'foreign and alien images that threaten to "knock [her] down, and trample upon [her]"…images that as a white, middle-class woman of limited conscious-ness she may neither want nor know how to read'.[15] Thus, Lanser claims, 'The Yellow Wallpaper' reveals Gilman's own uneasiness about the power of uncontrolled foreign influences on the culture of the United States.

While I don't discount Lanser's interpretation, especially in light of anti-immigrant attitudes of the early 1890s, I want to stress that two of Gilman's first pieces to address the issue of immigration directly, 'The Making of Americans' and 'Malthusianism and Race Suicide,' were published follow-ing the nation's return to economic confidence and offer an optimistic view of immigrant potential.[16] Larry Ceplair notes that in these 1904 articles from the *Women's Journal*, Gilman celebrated 'the mingling of peoples that goes to make up our own people,' and criticized those who feared the increase in immigration.[17] Gilman's sentiments are strikingly in tune with other social commentators of the day who endorsed the 'commingling' and 'intermin-gling' of various peoples within the American nation.[18]

In addition to the 'relaxed, assimilationist mood of the new century',[19] Gilman's optimism in these articles was perhaps influenced by her involve-ment in the urban social settlement movement during the mid-1890s. Gilman lived and worked at the Hull House settlement in Chicago in 1895 and 1896, and her interaction there with a community of scholars and reformers who were deeply committed to improving the lives of immigrants undoubtedly boosted her confidence in the potential of immigrants to become produc-tive members of society.[20] However, continued yearly increases in the number and ethnic diversity of immigrants entering the nation, coupled with the growth of Progressivist philosophies of managerialism in educational and social reform, also influenced Gilman, as a reform activist, to adopt stricter views on the need for the American government to establish frameworks for more systematically managing immigrants.[21]

Gilman's Plan for Managing Immigration

Gilman's reaction to the current of immigration that peaked and contin-ued steadily in the years following the publication of her optimistic articles was to put faith in the concept of management. Her earliest scheme for managing immigration appears in *Moving the Mountain*, serialized in *The Forerunner* in 1911. In this utopian novel, vast social improvements have occurred in the United States, resulting from social evolution and women's realisation that they can be involved in governing the country. The new 'human' vision implemented by women treats the immigration process as a controlled experiment in acculturation.

The keystone of this process is an assimilationist scheme based on a social evolutionary theory, 'the reintegration of peoples,' whose premise is that displaced people naturally integrate into their host society, and that it is impossible to stop this 'sociological process…but quite possible to assist and to guide [it] to great advantage'. Nellie, Gilman's mouthpiece in the story, explains that immigrants' education, or more precisely, their 'Compulsory Socialization,' now begins before they leave their home countries, since the United States government requires them to be 'antiseptically clean, they and all their belongings, before entering the ship'. Once aboard, this social-ization to 'American' standards of cleanliness and order continues, as immigrants are assigned rooms instead of being relegated below decks to 'steerage'. Upon reaching ports of entry, aspiring immigrants are escorted by a 'reception committee' through the ornamental gates of 'an experi-ment station in applied sociology'. Long Island has been converted into such a station, and replaces Ellis Island, through which the majority of those arriving from Europe entered the United States. This new station provides prospective citizens with basic training in America's industrial, agricultural, and domestic technologies.

When another character in the story labels these policies a 'forcing system', Nellie argues that immigrants 'ha[ve] to submit to our handling,' so that 'no immigrant is turned loose on the community till he or she is up to a certain standard'. She stresses that these policies are more humane than early twen-tieth-century methods of immigration control: '[P]oor, brutal…Ellis Island' has been superseded by a showpiece '"Reception Room" of our country'.[22] Through the socialization program, she insists, 'we give them the chance' to 'be something better'. *Moving the Mountain* reveals that Gilman's initial suggestions for a federal policy on immigration recognized immigrant poten-tial, and sought to offer 'real scientific care, real loving study and assistance' in teaching American ways of life.[23] At the same time, however, these suggestions were strategies for forcibly assimilating immigrants, and for the containment and deportation of those who did not, even after intensive training, meet 'American' standards of citizenship.

The Issue of Americanization

During the First World War, 'Americanization' became 'a great popular crusade,' promoting immigrant 'assimilation, education, and advancement'.[24] In *The Forerunner* in 1914, three years after *Moving the Mountain* appeared and at the beginning of the war in Europe, Gilman published 'Immigration, Importation, and Our Fathers,' an article in which she defends citizenship standards by historicizing the formation of a definitive American national character. The United States, argues Gilman, was founded by a group of like-minded people who shared fundamental ideas about government, and it is this vision that true Americans continue to uphold.

The problem today, Gilman argues, is that there is a rapidly growing number of immigrants who, through ignorance or lack of interest, know nothing about this vision of citizenship. Following this logic, Gilman makes a distinction between immigration and importation. An immigrant is 'intelligent enough to know about another country and to recognize its advantages'. Most of her era's newcomers, however, are not immigrants, but poor and ignorant 'imported labor' enticed by employers and steamship companies.

Gilman's tone in 'Immigration, Importation, and Our Fathers' is increasingly suspicious toward some categories of immigrants. No longer envisioning her country's open immigration policies as a moral duty to rescue the oppressed, as she did in *Moving the Mountain*, but as an act of charity and hospitality, Gilman suggests that the United States is in danger of being exploited by nations sending unskilled labourers.

Still attempting to strike a balance between open and restricted policies, however, Gilman's article proposes a more refined version of her previous immigration scheme. Her solution, a National Training School of Citizenship, through which all immigrants must pass, takes the form of a welcome, that is 'warm, hearty—and compulsory'.[25] In this scheme, immigrants are apprenticed to a national school, from which they are slowly graduated, and the products of their labour pay for maintaining the overall programme. Immigrants will have no input into the programme; instead, it is to be managed by social scientific experts.

In 'Immigration, Importation, and Our Fathers,' Gilman admits that her training scheme may involve an element of labour exploitation. However, she insists, it is far less exploitative than what current immigrants encounter daily in their new homeland: 'What becomes of the immigrants now? Are they not exploited, outrageously, by everyone, from the steamship agent to the employer, landlord, and shopkeeper?'[26] In some ways, of course, Gilman was right. Immigrants, especially those who did not speak English, were susceptible to gross economic impositions. However, by attempting to coerce the immigrant population into developing a homogenous American national character, Gilman's schemes were designed to take advantage of immigrants in a different way, by taking away their right to speak in public forums until they had been divested of their former culture and traditions and could frame their thoughts from an 'American' perspective.

Fears of Immigrant Retaliation

John Higham argues that during the First World War, the Americanization movement changed. By 1915, its tone continued to be liberal and its emphasis remained on social welfare, but 'the impulse behind the new interest in Americanization was fear of [immigrants'] divided loyalties' to their old and new nations.[27] In 1915, in an article in *The Forerunner*, 'Let Sleeping Forefathers Lie,' Gilman's tone has changed to one of urgency, anxiety, annoyance, and fear. Although the United States was founded as a 'social, economic, and political experiment,' she explains, the founding fathers were not scientific: 'They were, of course, totally igno-rant of the great steps in natural science which have so lifted the world's thought; they were very primitive economists, and no[t] sociologists at all'. America's unscientific founding fathers, therefore, did not realise their unrestricted immigration policy would open the nation to a take-over by rapidly-multiplying foreigners. Calling for measures to restrict yearly immigration, Gilman presents an assimilation scheme which is similar to her previous proposals, but adds the proviso that potential immigrants must apply and be accepted before leaving their home countries. Thus, the scheme has become a quota system: 'We should receive every year, at various ports, as many of these applicants for citizenship as we can so educate and place—no more'. Gilman tries to make this stricter process sound less harsh by invoking a paternalistic metaphor: immigrants are orphaned children in need of a 'national adoption center' to perform the vital work of 'renationalization'.[28]

In *The Forerunner* of 1915, Gilman also tried a more positive rhetorical approach to dealing with the threat of immigrant power. In *Herland*, that year's serialized novel, Gilman applies a constructive outlook on immigration to depict a scheme for assimilating immigrants into a technologically and culturally evolved society. To illustrate this model, Gilman compares Americans unfavorably with a more highly-developed fictional people, the Herlanders, and implies that US immigration policies should be revised in order to assimilate foreigners more effectively. Through a utopian frame, *Herland* portrays the experiences of three Americans, Van, Jeff, and Terry, as they undergo compulsory training in the history, geography, technology, customs, citizenship duties, and political processes of a newly created and culturally superior nation. As a result of this preparation, Jeff and Van are able to settle in Herland as informed, immigrant citizens, while Terry, who chooses not to adapt to the country's social and political standards, is eventually deported as an alien.[29]

Herland illustrates how Gilman would expect immigrants to assimilate by being brought up to the social evolutionary level of the more highly-evolved nation. In the novel's sequel, *With Her in Ourland*, serialized in the *The Forerunner* in 1916, Van returns to the United States with his Herland wife Ellador. Making an extended tour of the country, Van and Ellador refer to Herland's political, social, and economic system as a model for diagnosing and prescribing solutions to problems brought on by unrestricted immigration.

The main problem Van and Ellador identify is that the collective intellect and public-spiritedness of the American people has begun to fragment. Because of its unique history, American society requires qualities that old-world monarchies and feudal systems did not: namely, 'the conscious intelligent co-ordinate action of all the people'. In a democracy, insists Ellador, everyone must participate: 'It's no miracle…just people co-operating to govern themselves'. '[T]raining in democratic thought, feeling and action, from infancy', is Ellador's prescription for all Americans. The progressed American mind will be like the Herland mind, whose quality has been developed by Herland's cultural system. Van describes this standard of brainpower as awesome in 'its breadth and depth', 'calm control', and 'rationality'.

The basic problem posed by unrestricted immigration to the United

States is that immigrants understand democracy even less than Americans do, Ellador tells Van. Immigrants have potential to be re-made as American citizens, but millions are not, because no organized governmental efforts are put forth to teach them. Americans have not been conscious of their responsibilities to society, and have not taken immigration seriously enough; as a result, the United States has become 'clogged and confused, weakened and mismanaged, for lack of political compatibility'.

Gilman could envision rationalists like herself working for government bureaus to plan and implement educational programs in citizenship for both Americans and immigrants. As much as she would have liked to, however, Gilman could not envision enforcing her educational schemes on Americans: 'Our people are not pawns on a chessboard; they can't be managed to prove theories,' Van admonishes Ellador. Immigrants, however, could be managed, and rudimentary mechanisms for bodily control, such as cleanliness checks and medical exams, were already in place at clearance centers like Ellis Island. In *With Her in Ourland*, therefore, Gilman once again takes ports of entry as a starting point for immigrant indoctrination, and recommends a scheme to Americanize immigrant minds through training as they arrive.[30]

Science and Immigrant Restrictionism

With Her in Ourland is an important text in the development of Gilman's nativist stance, because it marks a turning point in her application of science to ethnicity. Until this point, Gilman's argument was that people of all nations are in the process of evolving. In *With Her in Ourland*, however, she adds to this basic evolutionary structure the qualification that some ethnic groups are more fitted than others to become American citizens. Whereas in the 1904 article 'Malthusianism and Race Suicide' Gilman found 'amusing' the distinction made by many Americans between themselves and immigrants: 'as if none were Americans save those whose foreign stock came over in a certain century, charter members, as it were—all later additions inferior!',[31] in *With Her in Ourland* she argues that people descended from the same mix of ethnic groups that produced America's founding fathers have the best chance to develop democracy to its highest point.

Gilman's emphasis in *With Her in Ourland* is that the 'original' Americans arrived with the intention of building a nation, and possessed understanding of how to do it. Thus, Gilman claimed that early English and

Northern European settlers were American natives in terms of originating the concept of democracy. This view is in some ways less discriminatory than those which claimed Anglo-Saxons to be American natives because they were the first to have owned the land, for in Gilman's theory, there is room for people of other ethnic groups to acquire the democratic state of mind. However, in *With Her in Ourland*, Gilman begins to retreat from the openness of her position by adopting a scientific idea of temporary 'race' stratification: although individuals of every nationality are ready to become citizens, ethnic groups as a whole are at different stages of development, and not all have reached the democratic stage. Certain ethnicities are genetically progressive and others are not; therefore immigration of some groups should be restricted.

Based on these convictions, Ellador criticizes the founding fathers' lack of foresight: 'Here you were, a little band of really promising people, of different nations, yet of the same general stock, and *like-minded*—that was the main thing…it never occurred to you that the poor and oppressed were not necessarily good stuff for a democracy'. Gilman was convinced that for democracy to succeed, all citizens needed to possess a similar standard of education and shared cultural understandings. Therefore, Ellador explains, Americans' endeavour to develop a democracy comprised of rational, culturally homogenous citizens will be hindered by the task of assimilating increasing numbers of nationalities 'with all their differing cultures, ideas, tastes, and prejudices'. This reasoning, as demonstrated in *With Her in Ourland*, eventually led Gilman to adopt a stance against unrestricted immigration.

By admitting that those she considered to be the first Americans were a mix of mainly northern Europeans who came together at a certain place and time to establish a new nation, Gilman was able to rationalize the category of 'native,' and to make a distinction between 'legitimate' and 'illegitimate' immigrants. Echoing her descriptions of true immigrants and imported labourers in 'Immigration, Importation, and Our Fathers,' *With Her in Ourland*'s definition of legitimate immigrants adds to the qualities of skill and eagerness for democracy an important scientific qualification: the biological inheritance to participate in democracy. By the time Gilman wrote *With Her in Ourland*, she had come to view most twentieth-century immigrants as illegitimate, and to criticize liberals who pushed for the re-establishment of open-door federal immigration policies.[32]

The Cacophony of Immigrant Voices

In my introduction, I noted that Gilman's social-evolutionary views on immigration altered markedly over time. My conclusion returns to this claim to suggest reasons for Gilman's long struggle with the problems posed by American immigration.

Gilman felt secure in talking about gender because she believed oppressed women had little or no voice for themselves, and, at this stage, required intellectuals such as herself to represent their best interests by speaking for them publicly in logical, reasoned language. Unlike the 'American' women for whom she imagined she was speaking, however, the immigrant communities that Gilman encountered were extremely vocal. In fact, the loud clamour of their voices was difficult to ignore. The influence of immigrants on American society worried Gilman because their intrusion into her everyday life as a New York city resident led her to believe that they were extremely capable of speaking out publicly and of initiating political processes that would run counter to those in which she envisioned 'American' women participating.[33] In 'Among Our Foreign Residents,' one of her final articles on immigration in *The Forerunner*, Gilman admits she sees evidence that immigrant groups were developing a public voice, and criticizes those who, in her view, dissociated themselves from American cultural values by congregating in clubs and societies that encouraged them to pledge loyalty to the countries and cultures they had left behind.[34]

Seven years after she printed 'Among Our Foreign Residents' in *The Forerunner*, and following her involvement in nativist 'Americanization' societies, Gilman published 'Is America Too Hospitable?', an article which took the anti-immigrant sentiments she developed over *The Forerunner* years to a further conclusion: fear of the power of immigrant intellectuals.[35] This article extends what was becoming apparent by the time 'Among Our Foreign Residents' appeared in *The Forerunner* in 1916: that Gilman was increasingly afraid of immigrant voices. In this article, Gilman attacks immigrant intellectuals who were trying to speak for their own constituencies—and by implication, were attempting to usurp the position of reformers like herself. Gilman feared what immigrant voices had to say—they 'come here to criticize and improve us'—and that the commotion of their speech would drown out the authority of established social commentators.[36]

In 'Among Our Foreign Residents' and more markedly in 'Is America Too Hospitable?', Gilman condemned immigrant discourse communities as hostile to 'native' American ideals of liberty. Thus, in her treatment of immigration and ethnicity, Gilman's liberal or humanist vision breaks down, because at the same time that she was hoping to further democracy through assimilation schemes, she was trying to find ways to literally limit democratic participation. She attempted to limit the actual idea of democracy, and to claim it as the possession of a public comprised primarily, (at least initially), of white 'American' women and men—a public in which feminist reformers could persuade other citizens by making reasoned arguments.

Ultimately, then, immigrant voices threatened Gilman's conception of her own identity and status as a social reformer. As I have argued, her vision of democracy was an experiment which rational people such as herself could logically and successfully manage. The daily influx of immigrants seemed to make the outcome of this social experiment more uncertain by constantly changing the controlled conditions which the social scientist had to address. Moreover, immigrant groups could not be neatly categorized because their collective identity was fractured across a multitude of ethnic communities. In response to these changing conditions, Gilman regularly had to reformulate the way she thought about the question of managing immigrant populations.

Judith Allen has argued that feminist scholars have shied away from studying Gilman's later work because of 'the aging Gilman's gradual embrace of a range of theoretical and political stances uncongenial, anathema[tic], and even ludicrous, to contemporary readers'.[37] Allen pays particular attention to writings which reveal Gilman's engagement with 'anathema discourses': terminology and concepts such as nativism, which today are widely seen as detestable, and which run Gilman the risk of being ostracized or condemned by feminist scholars.

My focus has been to trace the continuity between Gilman's liberal social-democratic vision and the 'anathema discourses' she espoused. This article has concentrated on the theories of ethnicity and immigration that Gilman developed in *The Forerunner* at the height of her career as a reformer and civic commentator.[38] These writings reveal Gilman's recognition that feminism, for which she was best known, could not be treated in isolation, and show how she attempted to theorize issues of immigration and ethnicity as a feminist concern.

II From New Woman to
Black Womanism

5. Multiculturalism and the New Woman in Early Twentieth-Century America

Carmen Birkle

By now, it is widely known that as a response to the Cult of True Womanhood of nineteenth-century Victorian America the so-called New Women[1] at the turn to the twentieth century were highly instrumental in furthering the feminist issues of the women's movement such as women's suffrage and women's economic independence. While most critics and scholars interested in the *fin de siècle* have for a long time assumed that the women's movement was almost exclusively a white middle-class affair, recent interest in multiculturalism has altered our perception of this period.

At the turn to the 20th century in the United States, the Native American Zitkala-ša (1876–1938), the Chinese American Sui Sin Far (1865–1914), the Mexican American María Cristina Mena (1893–1965), and the German American Helen Reimensnyder Martin (1868–1939) became successfully published authors who created strong New Women in their short stories.[2] These characters, often out of despair, manipulate their husbands by subtly and gradually integrating liberating ideas into their everyday lives, without, however, ever breaking out of their cultural contexts. Instead, they use precisely their respective ethnicities to bring about cultural changes. These New Women prove that Zitkala-ša, Sui Sin Far, María Cristina Mena, and Helen Reimensnyder Martin instrumentalized in their short stories the slogan 'the personal is the political' to express their feminist ideas. I will argue that while many of their male characters stubbornly hold on to traditions and reject interaction with other cultures, many of their female protagonists turn into cultural mediators who are open for outside influences which they often appropriate and transform within the framework of their own cultures.

All four authors profited from major social, cultural, and economic changes in American society at the turn of the century. They seized the opportunities offered to them by a rising interest in the genre of the short story, supported by a new mass market for magazine publications. New printing technologies, increased and better transportation through the construction of the railroad as well as the development of yellow journalism helped the foundation of new magazines, often addressed to a mass audience such as *McClure's*, *Munsey's*, or the *Ladies Home Journal*, which easily competed with the established and more elitist magazines such as *Atlantic Monthly*, *Harper's*, *Century*, and *Scribner's* by dropping prices as low as ten cents per issue. At the same time, many so-called minority magazines were established. This 'ethnic press' was, of course, very heterogeneous and— perhaps with the exception of the African-American press—has found little recognition, mostly because the majority of ethnic newspapers and magazines suffered from a lack of financial support and were consequently of very short duration.

All four writers under consideration here had very different relationships to magazines and their editors and to journalism as such and were influenced by this trade in their writing. After having published three autobiographical (fictional) stories of her educational development in the *Atlantic Monthly* in 1900 and having published in *Everbody's Magazine*, the political activist Zitkala-ša became a member of the Society of American Indians (founded in 1911) and was the editor of this society's *American Indian Magazine* (founded in 1913) from 1918–19. Sui Sin Far became a journalist out of financial necessity and contributed essays and short stories to *Century*, *Good Housekeeping*, the *Independent*, the *Dominion Illustrated*, a small Canadian magazine, the *Montreal Star*, and other mostly regional magazines such as the *New England Magazine* and the Western journals *Land of Sunshine*, *Overland Monthly*, the *Westerner*, the *Los Angeles Express*, and even went to Jamaica as a reporter. María Cristina Mena's major journalistic endeavours were her publications for *Century*, and her correspondence with the magazine's editors reveals the strong editorial 'censorship' they imposed on her. Helen Reimensnyder Martin, to the contrary, published her highly critical pieces in such well-known magazines as *McClure's*, *Cosmopolitan*, *Century*, and *Hampton's Magazines* in order to promote her ideas of women's rights, often embedded in the exotic context of New Mennonite communities. In short, all four women writers were actively involved in the magazine industry of the time; their stories bear the marks of the respective editorial policies, but also shaped these policies and acquainted, or even confronted, an American mass readership with critical multicultural issues.

In Zitkala-ša's 'A Warrior's Daughter' (1902), Sui Sin Far's 'Mrs Spring Fragrance' (1910), María Cristina Mena's 'The Gold Vanity Set' (1913), and Helen Reimensnyder Martin's 'Mrs Gladfelter's Revolt' (1923), the construction of ethnicities based on values highly estimated by the respective ethnicities such as physical strength, language, religion, and education, and rooted in specific geographies as cultural contact zones, such as Indian Territory, San Francisco Chinatown, Mexico, and Pennsylvania Germany, serves as a means for the negotiation of issues of gender and culture within which women undermine established patterns of cultural organization, move freely in hitherto ignored cultural contact zones, and motivate transculturation.

Zitkala-ša (1876–1938)

Zitkala-ša, born as Gertrude Simmons on the Yankton Reservation in South Dakota as the daughter of a Native American mother and a white father, and later married to Raymond T. Bonnin, assumed authority over her life by rejecting her father's last name and christening herself 'Red Bird,' thus claiming not only her Native American heritage but also her mother's. She received her education at the White's Manual Institute in Wabash, Indiana, the Earlham College in Richmond, Indiana, and the Boston Conservatory of Music, and taught at the Carlisle Indian School in Pennsylvania. In 1901, she published the collection of Lakota stories, *Old Indian Legends*, with the trickster figure Iktomi as the protagonist in most of the stories through which she rejected 'the idea of an individual author producing an original written text' and 'highlights her role as one of many story-tellers.'[3] Throughout her life, Zitkala-ša advocated the rights of women, working with the General Federation of Women's Clubs, and of Native Americans, collaborating with the Bureau of Indian Affairs, founding the National Council of American Indians, and, as a member of the Society of American Indians, editing their journal, the *American Indian Magazine*. These organizations, her collaboration with John Collier and his American Indian Defense Organization as well as her constant public lectures in Sioux dress finally helped to achieve the enactment of the Indian Citizenship Bill in 1924. Because of internal disagreements, the Bonnins left the SAI, which subsequently dissolved in 1920. Gender and the intermingling of races were her thematic focuses in her autobiographical short stories ('Impressions of an Indian Childhood', 'The School Days of an Indian Girl', and 'An Indian Teacher among Indians'), essays, legends, the Indian opera *Sun Dance* (1913), composed in collaboration with William F. Hanson, and her study *Oklahoma's Poor Rich Indians: An Orgy of Craft and Exploitation of the Five Civilized Tribes—Legalized Robbery* (1924).

Through the influence of the SAI, Zitkala-ša began to lecture widely on 'Indian citizenship, employment of Indians in the Bureau of Indian Affairs, equitable settlement of tribal land claims, and stabilization of laws relating to Indians'.[4] She advocated 'citizenship not to oppose tribal organization, necessarily, but to protect tribal rights and treaties. She argued that civil rights would provide the legal mechanism to protest invasive government policy and to advocate for individual and tribal self-determination'.[5] Elected secretary of the organization, she and her husband moved to Washington, D.C., where she initiated her public work for the society by writing the poem 'The Indian Awakening' for the inaugural issue of the *American Indian Magazine* (*AIM*) in 1916. While this poem emphasizes close ties to the spirit of the dead, to Native American traditions, as well as to nature, at the same time it reflects hybridity through the combination of Indian and Christian religions. This hybridity becomes the guiding (or driving?) force in the twenty-two years of Zitkala-ša's[6] public life.

The *American Indian Magazine*, with Arthur C. Parker as editor, was founded in Washington, D.C., in April 1913, as the *Quarterly Journal of the Society of American Indians*, but changed its name to *American Indian Magazine* in 1916 with the subtitle *A Journal of Race Ideals*. Its objectives were 'the advance of the Indian', Indian citizenship, 'presenting the history of the American Indian peoples,…presenting information concerning their status, and…dispelling myths concerning them'.[7] The magazine became the major voice critical of the Bureau of Indian Affairs[8] and printed further poems by Zitkala-ša in which she claimed America for the Indians.[9] In 1917, she published 'The Red Man's America' in which she rewrote the words of 'America, the Beautiful': 'My country! 'tis to thee, / Sweet land of Liberty, / My pleas I bring. / Land where *our* fathers died, / Whose offspring are denied / The Franchise given wide, / Hark, while I sing!' She asked for the enactment of the Gandy Bill outlawing the use of peyote and ended with a plea to God: 'Grant our home-land be bright, / Grant us just human right, / Protect us by Thy might, / Great God, our king!'[10]

During her editorship, she wrote numerous editorial comments for the journal in which she voiced her political ideals and claims and did not 'limit herself to the prior subjects of women contributors, such as health and education',[11] but claimed 'America! Home of the Red Man!'[12] in defence against the statement of a white traveller whom she met on her way to the SAI's annual conference in 1918 in Pierre, South Dakota: 'You are an Indian! Well, I knew when I first saw you that you must be a foreigner'.[13] She rebelled and became herself a Native American New Woman.

For a discussion of the New Woman figure in her work, I will look at Zitkala-ša's short story 'A Warrior's Daughter', originally published in *Everybody's Magazine* in 1902, and republished in 1921 in *American Indian Stories*. I read this story on two levels: on the one hand, it empowers Native American ethnicity, giving its members a renewed sense of pride in a community and tradition which have endured and survived forced migration, ghettoization in reservations on Indian Territory, violent battles with the U.S. army as well as attempts at cultural annihilation through enforced 'Americanization' as defined by mainstream America in the 19th century. In this respect, the story reads as a resistance piece to Zitkala-ša's three autobiographical essays-stories about her 'Americanizing' Eastern school education. On the other hand, the story is also a continuation of these earlier essays through the creation of a strong female character whose awakening implies resistance to Eastern acculturation and whose growing awareness of gender roles results in her determination to fight for her own (marital) happiness.

'A Warrior's Daughter' focuses on the legends of Indian warriors but subverts traditional gender roles by turning the 'loyal' daughter into a warrior and trickster. Tusee, an eight-year-old child/woman with a 'buoyant spirit', has a lover in whose presence she turns into a woman with an awakening sexuality reflected in her craftwork, 'the petals of a wild rose growing on the soft buckskin'.[14] Her lover's only chance to win her as a wife is to follow her father's command of bringing him 'an enemy's scalp-lock, plucked fresh with [his] own hand'.[15] During this attempt, he himself becomes the prisoner of the enemy. In contrast to traditional gender roles, 'she [Tusee] plans to cheat the hated enemy of their captive'.[16] Equipped with a knife, she secretly steals into the camp, deviates the guard's attention by flirting with him, and animal-like 'gives a wild spring forward, like a panther for its prey' and kills the captivator with the words, 'I am a Lakota woman!'[17] Tricksterlike, she then disguises as an old woman 'with a bundle like a grandchild slung on her back', metamorphoses back into 'its [the figure's] youthful stature', and frees her lover, who, in his weakness, becomes like a 'hysterical Victorian woman' and faints.[18] Tusee, to the contrary, draws strength from his weakness: 'The sight of his weakness makes her strong. A mighty power thrills her body. Stooping beneath his outstretched arms grasping at the air for support, Tusee lifts him upon her broad shoulders. With half-running, triumphant steps she carries him away into the open night'.[19] Although, as Laurie Lisa claims, 'this woman as warrior image might have seemed to be antithetical to a white audience that historically viewed Indian women as slaves or menial drudges, there was precedent in Plains Indian culture that expected gender roles could be reversed'.[20] Because her readership was predominantly Anglo-Saxon, Zitkala-ša clearly reversed the gender expectations of these readers while catering to those of her Native American readers and appealed to women to conceive of a possible redistribution of gender roles and to fight for their ideals.

For this gender reversal in the story, she uses the Indian figure of the trickster who can assume various masks and personae at any time. 'Her disguise as a bent woman with a bundle on her back echoes a Lakota trickster tale in which Iktomi throws grass into his blanket and carries it as if it is a great burden in order to trick and catch some ducks'.[21] Tusee as a trickster figure plays with male gender expectations when she performs the flirtatious young woman and the caring old grandmother. In these roles, the stereotypical images of women as whores and mothers become performances which then question culturally constructed ideas of femininity. Tusee also becomes an emblem of matrilinearity since she is daughter, wife-to-be, and grandmother at the same time and thus embodies the idea of female bonding within an ethnic context. Simultaneously, I would argue, that Zitkala-ša herself as the author of this tale assumed the mask of a trickster figure by using the Native American context of a warrior story in order to emphasize the strength of Native American women to become (potential) saviours of the Native American people threatened by literal extinction and assimilation through their encounters with Anglo-Saxon America.

Sui Sin Far (1865–1914)

The Chinese American/Canadian Sui Sin Far, born in England as Edith Maud Eaton to a Chinese mother and a British father, lived in England, Canada, Jamaica, and the United States, never married, earned her living as stenographer, journalist, and fiction writer, and was probably the first person with a Chinese background to thematize the complex experiences of Chinese Americans in the United States in short fiction. In her autobiographical essays, 'Leaves from the Mental Portfolio of an Eurasian' (*The Independent* [1909]) and 'Sui Sin Far, the Half Chinese Writer, Tells of Her Careeer' (*Boston Globe*, 5 May 1912), and her short stories, such as 'Mrs Spring Fragrance' (1910), she interwove cultural hybridity with a strong feminist stance demanding the right for women, particularly Chinese-American women, to control their own lives both in legal and economic terms.

Sui Sin Far grew up as a British girl, going to a British school, when she was made aware of the fact that she was different from her playmates, an event that very much shaped the rest of her life and her work, 'the day on which I first learned that I was something different and apart from other children'.[22] She began her career as a published writer under the name Edith Eaton in the fall and winter of 1888–89 with six short stories and two essays in a new magazine, the *Dominion Illustrated*, 'devoted to the promotion of Canada'.[23] Sui Sin Far started to work as stenographer, typist, and journalist at a lawyer's office and the *Montreal Star* and also opened up her own office (1894–95). While she had always been confronted with racism before, to which she reacted with surprise and incomprehension, 'Papa is English, mamma is Chinese. Why couldn't we have been either one thing or the other? Why is my mother's race despised?',[24] she was now asked to write about Chinese people:

> I meet many Chinese persons, and when they get into trouble am often called upon to fight their battles in the papers. This I enjoy. My heart leaps for joy when I read one day an article signed by a New

York Chinese in which he declares 'The Chinese in America owe an everlasting debt of gratitude to Sui Sin Far for the bold stand she has taken in their defense.'[25]

Yet, she also experienced reverse discrimination, 'full-blooded Chinese people having a prejudice against the half white. Fundamentally, I muse, all people are the same. My mother's race is as prejudiced as my father's'.[26] In 1897, she went to Kingston, Jamaica, as a reporter and suffered from racism against both Blacks and Chinese people, and had to return to Montreal because of malarial fever. In the same year, she published her essay 'The Chinese Woman in America' in the *Land of Sunshine*. It is an essay in which Sui Sin Far seeks to explain and describe the Chinese woman to American eyes and shows her as someone who does not mingle with Americans and who yearns for a return to China. Thus, Chinese women do not seem to want Americanization. 'By depicting Chinese women as icons of the Orient with "sensibilities as acute as a child's," Sui Sin Far employs a popular turn-of-the-century orientalism'.[27] She thus characterized Chinese women as non-threatening to white America and made them more acceptable as exotic objects. When Sui Sin Far subsequently suffered from inflammatory rheumatism, she moved West first to San Francisco, then to Seattle, and finally to Los Angeles. Out West, she wrote many of her Chinese stories and essays on Chinatowns and had publications in many regional magazines. In June 1912, the Chicago publisher A. C. McClurg published 2,500 copies of her short-story collection *Mrs Spring Fragrance*. From 1911 until 1913 she wrote several stories for the *New England Magazine* and the *Independent* and finally returned to Montreal to live with her family where she died in 1914.

Most of her life and work was concerned with a life in-between cultures, a life of biological and cultural hybridity and unbelonging. Understanding both sides of her ancestry helped her to deal with her hybridity, which was not simply constituted by one culture added to another, but by a transculturated difference from both individual components: 'I do not confide in my father and mother. They would not understand. How could they? He is English, she is Chinese. I am different to both of them—a stranger, tho their own child'.[28] It was not before the publication of her autobiographical essay 'Leaves' that she had a term for this particular in-betweenness.

In 'Leaves', for the first time, 'she explicitly identifies herself as a Eurasian and speaks with an insider's voice.'[29] She concludes:

> After all I have no nationality and am not anxious to claim any. Individuality is more than nationality. 'You are you and I am I,' says Confucius. I give my right hand to the Occidentals and my left to the Orientals, hoping that between them they will not utterly destroy the insignificant 'connecting link.' And that's all.[30]

Sui Sin Far's short stories reflect the history of Chinese people in the United States from their origins in China via the transition period of migration to the United States to the final settlements in the United States and the related problems of acculturation in this diaspora. The majority of her stories—which are almost all published in her collection *Mrs Spring Fragrance*—focus on the Chinese in the New World and their various facets of reactions to a new life.

Contrary to some critics' belief that Mrs Spring Fragrance in 'Mrs Spring Fragrance', originally published in the *Hampton's* in 1910, is a very superficial character easily manipulated by the official United States government rhetoric, I argue that she is a trickster figure moving and mediating between cultures and manipulating people. Mrs Spring Fragrance is introduced as one of those wives who follow their merchant husbands to Seattle. She easily adapts and speaks the language fluently after five years: 'There are no more American words for her learning.'[31] 'Though conservatively Chinese in many respects, he was at the same time what is called by the Westerners, "Americanized." Mrs Spring Fragrance was even more "Americanized"'.[32] The Spring Fragrances' neighbors, the Chin Yuens, live according to Chinese customs and betrothe their daughter Laura to the son of the Chinese Government schoolteacher in San Francisco at the age of fifteen, but she now loves Kai Tzu, an American-born Chinese. When Laura tells Mrs Spring Fragrance about her trouble, the latter assumes and subverts the traditional role of the matchmaker and invents a scheme with which to manipulate all participants in this wedding game: 'For a long time Mrs Spring Fragrance talked. For a long time Laura listened. When the girl arose to go, there was a bright light in her eyes'.[33] Her function as a catalyst illuminates Mrs Spring Fragrance's specialty: her ability to use and abuse language in convincing ways. During her trip to San Francisco, which she has undertaken for the sole purpose of helping Laura, she writes a letter to her husband in which she exhibits the feminine quality of submissiveness but engages in political questions and manipulations, ironically revealing the simplicity of her husband's mind:

> It [the lecture on 'America, the Protector of China!'] was most exhilarating, and the effect of so much expression of benevolence leads me to beg of you to forget to remember that the barber charges you one dollar for a shave while he humbly submits to the American man a bill of fifteen cents. And murmur no more because your honored elder brother, on a visit to this country, is detained under the rooftree of this great Government instead of under your own humble roof. Console him with the reflection that he is protected under the wing of the Eagle, the Emblem of Liberty.[34]

During her prolonged stay in San Francisco, she succeeds in joining Laura's husband-to-be with another woman without them recognizing the manipulation. She thus subverts the role of the matchmaker 'who traditionally worked for the parents of the bride and groom to arrange marriages in which romantic love played no part. In this instance, however, the matchmaker becomes a catalyst to the Western romantic convention by helping young, second-generation Chinese American lovers outwit their more traditional immigrant parents'.[35]

Like Zitkala-ša's warrior daughter, Mrs Spring Fragrance performs femininity physically and most effectively linguistically in order to achieve a happy marriage for Laura. Mrs Spring Fragrance as a trickster figure mediates between but is also critical of the American and Chinese cultures and the sexes, revealing both ethnicity and gender as socially and culturally constructed categories. According to Annette White-Parks, the story is 'concerned with the redistribution of power between races, sexes, classes, and generations, redistributions acted out on the threshold of change from old orders—Victorian England and Imperialist China—as an immigrant people found ways of adapting to new conditions'.[36] As in Zitkala-ša's story, female bonding is the basis for success.

María Cristina Mena (1893–1965)

María Cristina Mena was born in Mexico City as the daughter of a Spanish mother and Yucatecan father of European descent. Her father was a very powerful, successful, and prominent businessman dealing with American companies during the last two decades of the Porfiriato. She was educated at an élite convent school in Mexico City, Hijas de María, and later in an English boarding school. Therefore, her birth and childhood background instilled in her the knowledge of a certain privilege and also of the transience and ultimate superfluousness of national and racial boundaries. According to Gloria Velásquez Treviño, her 'life and cultural background attest to her cultural ambivalence'.[37] She grew up a national and racial hybrid, speaking Spanish, English, French, and Italian,[38] reading classic literature[39] in these languages, and tried her hand at poetry at the age of ten. Because of her family's high social standing and wealth, they were able to send her off to live with friends of the family in New York City when she was fourteen (1907), at a time when the Mexican Revolution was in its preparatory stages with constant upheavals. This was her first significant and decisive border crossing since it led to her eventually becoming an American citizen, thus in a way reenacting the Pocahontas and La Malinche myths. Not much is known about her life over the next six years other than that she continued to write poetry and finally had her first two short stories ('The Gold Vanity Set' and 'John of God') published in two major American magazines in the same year. Being published in leading American magazines as a Mexican immigrant woman must have come as a surprise to Mena and her friends and family and meant a tremendous success at that time. Over the next three years, she published eight stories[40] and one biographical essay ('Julian Carrillo: The Herald of a Musical Monroe Doctrine,' *Century Magazine*, 1915). She married the Australian playwright and journalist Henry Kellett Chambers. During the years of her marriage to Chambers until his death of a paralytic stroke in 1935, she published only one more short story ('A Son of the Tropics', *Household Magazine*, 1931). After her husband's death, she began to write children's books under her married name, often with topics similar to those of her short stories (*The Water-Carrier's Secrets*, 1942; *The Two Eagles*, 1943; *The Bullfighter's Son*, 1944; *The Three Kings*, 1946; *Boy Heroes of Chapultepec: A Story of the Mexican War*, 1953) and also transcribed them into Braille.

According to Elizabeth Ammons, María Cristina Mena 'is thought to be the first woman of Mexican heritage to publish fiction in the United States in English'.[41] This exemplary position is affirmed by Raymund Paredes who explains that 'in the nineteenth century, Mexican-American authors generally wrote for their own people. It was only after the first decade of the twentieth century that a few Mexican-Americans began to publish stories and poetry in large-circulation American magazines'[42] in English.[43] Her writing career began when *Century Magazine* asked her to write short stories presenting 'an appealing version of life in Mexico'.[44] After the publication of her first story, 'John of God, the Water-Carrier',[45] in the magazine, she received a contract for a series of short stories on Mexican life. Because the *Century*'s editorial policy was anti-immigration at that time and catered to nativists' ideas of a pure Anglo-Saxon American culture,[46] this contract asked Mena to depict Mexican life in Mexico, and although she had more than enough material to write about Mexicans in the United States, she adhered to the magazine's requirements in order to be published. Nevertheless, she struggled 'with her editors to present her own vision of Mexico, fighting against a white male editorial board which supported *Century* as a bastion of the Anglo-American literary elite'.[47] While the image of Mexicans was exoticized in the United States and the image of Mexican Americans was criminalized, Mena tried to focus on actual people of Mexico and their lives, but at the same time idealized them, which brought her fiction—in the minds of critics—close to sentimentalism. According to Mena, Americans saw the primitivism and the idealism in her stories while Mexicans saw the soul of the 'Indito' of the Mexican population.[48] Although it seems logical to attest to Mena's fiction elements of authenticity, her life in New York City and thus her displacement from 'home' as an exile at the age of fourteen should not be underestimated as influences on her fiction and her view of Mexican culture, in particular since she never had been a member of the lower Mexican classes but always an observer. She clearly was sympathetic to the plight of the Mexican 'Indito' in her stories, but her perspective was that of elitist benevolence and 'upper-class bias'.[49] With her stories, Mena wrote against prejudices deeply rooted in American society. In a letter to Robert Sterling Yard at *Century Magazine*, she wrote in March 1913:

I expect to write more stories of Inditos than of any other class in Mexico. They form the majority; the issue of their rights and wrongs, their aspirations and possibilities, is at the root of the present situation in my unhappy country, and will become more and more prominent when the immense work of national regeneration shall have fairly begun; and I believe that American readers, with their intense interest in Mexico, are ripe for a true picture of a people so near to them, so intrinsically picturesque, so misrepresented in current fiction, and so well worthy of being known and loved, in all their ignorance.[50]

In my discussion of 'The Gold Vanity Set' (1913, first published in *The American Magazine*), I will show how Mena, while supposedly idealizing Mexican society, subtly infiltrated into her fiction her criticism of patriarchal structures enforced by the Catholic Church and created female characters who break gender taboos and instrumentalize their own religious and ethnic background to undermine male authority.

'The Gold Vanity Set' is the story of the beautiful Mexican Indian woman Petra, her husband Manuelo, and the American woman Miss Young who is visiting, as a tour guide—a popularized version of an ethnographer or a participant observer—a small Mexican village. Petra and Manuelo are *peons*, members 'of the landless laboring class, or persons in compulsory servitude'.[51] Miss Young is introduced as a representative of 'American fashion'[52] whose job as a tour guide turns her into a version of the New Woman which contrasts with Mexican Indian society's gender role expectations. In contrast to the unmarried Miss Young's independence, Petra, at the age of fourteen, is treated like a servant and patiently bears her husband's moods and frequent beatings: 'Manuelo might lose his temper and strike her, but a few minutes later he would be dancing with her. Her last memory going to sleep was sometimes a blow, "Because he is my husband," as she explained it to herself, and sometimes a kiss, "Because he loves me"'.[53] Only his drunkenness arouses resistance in her. Petra's first rebellion against being photographed by Miss Young can be read as resistance to cultural appropriation as well as to exoticization and objectification. While here rebellion and ethnicity are aligned, a little later rebellion and gender come into play. When Miss Young forgets her gold vanity set, Petra steals the set. Interestingly, the mirror like the camera is another means of creating an image of the self and is also a means for the study of the self. Petra is saddened by her image because so far she has always 'seen' herself like the women in Manuelo's songs, up until then her only (textual) means to create an image of herself in her mind. When she finds the powder and the rouge in the other two caskets, she quickly learns how she can alter and supposedly improve her image with these tools. She subsequently attributes to the vanity set her husband's changed behaviour toward her as a religious sign from the Virgin of Guadalupe.[54] 'Thus did Petra discover the secret of the vanity set. But her concept of it was not simple, like Miss Young's. Its practical idea became a mere nucleus in her mind for a fantasy dimly symbolic and religious'.[55] She, therefore, offers the set as a sacrifice to the Virgin.

Although she remains an obedient and submissive wife and receives his caresses 'with the trembling joy of a spaniel too seldom petted',[56] Petra has actively incorporated the artefact of the gold vanity set into her own culture. She takes Miss Young and Don Ramón to the Chapel of the Virgin of Guadalupe where 'the gold vanity set shone at her [the saint's] breast, most splendid of her ornaments. The gold vanity set, imposing respect, asking for prayers, testifying the gratitude of an Indian girl for the kindness of her beloved'.[57] Understanding the relevance of the set, but not the cultural and religious implications, Miss Young leaves with the words: ''Well, if it saves that nice girl from ever getting another beating, the saint is perfectly welcome to my vanity set'.[58] She has manipulated gender roles by simultaneously enhancing and producing one aspect of femininity (female beauty) and subverting another (submissiveness). A feminine object used for manipulation empowers and liberates women from patriarchal abuse. Thus, both Miss Young and Petra become New Women to the degree that they can grasp the possibilities inherent in their respective cultures. The New Woman as a concept, therefore, loses its absolute quality and is revealed as dependent on culture as well as class. In this story, Mena counterbalances the limitation of the concept of the New Woman to Anglo-Saxon middle-class American women.

Helen Reimensnyder Martin (1868–1939)

The Lutheran Helen Reimensnyder Martin, born in Lancaster, Pennsylvania, to the Rev. Cornelius Reimensnyder, an immigrant German Lutheran clergyman, and to Henrietta Thurman Reimensnyder, grew up surrounded by (New) Mennonite and Amish groups. She studied English at Swarthmore and Radcliffe Colleges and taught for a while at a private school in New York City. She became most well known because of her thirty-six novels, of which *Tillie: A Mennonite Maid* (1904) and *Barnabetta* (1914) were even turned into movies, *Tillie* in 1922 (and into a play in 1924) and *Barnabetta* after a dramatization in 1916 as *Erstwhile Susan*. After her marriage to Frederic C. Martin in 1899, she moved to Harrisburg, Pennsylvania, with her husband, but travelled widely in order 'to avoid the stagnation of what Mrs Martin called "a provincial town."'[59] Throughout her life and in her fiction, Helen Reimensnyder Martin was a spokeswoman for the rights of women and worked actively for suffrage. Based on her personal background of Lutheran Pennsylvania German family life, she had first-hand experience of many injustices directed toward women. In the short story 'Mrs Gladfelter's Revolt' (first published in *The Nation* on 10 October 1923, republished in *Yoked with a Lamb*), Helen Reimensnyder Martin puts all of these interests in a nutshell.

'Mrs Gladfelter's Revolt' appears to be a regional-ethnic variation of Mary Wilkins Freeman's 'The Revolt of "Mother"' (1891) in which the New England 'Mother' Sarah Penn[60] triumphs over her husband Adoniram. Both short stories, although published thirty-two years apart, are clearly situated in a specific rural region and ethnic context, a hetero-topia by choice, which determines the distribution of gender roles. While the earlier 'Revolt of "Mother"' is about a new house to improve the daughter's chances for marriage, 'Mrs Gladfelter's Revolt' goes beyond the private sphere into the political arena of women's rights for suffrage and education. To a certain degree, Helen Reimensnyder Martin picks up Mary Wilkins Freeman's rebelling female character and suggests that further steps have to be taken away from the enclosed realm of family life on a farm in order to enhance women's emancipation.

In 'Mrs Gladfelter's Revolt', Martin presents a Pennsylvania German mother's successive steps of revolt against a tyrannical husband and a patri-archal society based on specific ideas of gender roles, education, political rights, money, and the organization of the private sphere. The narrator takes most of her vocabulary from the field of power. To describe Jacob Gladfelter, the husband, she uses terms such as 'rule', 'dominance', and 'obstinacy', which supports the four sons' 'self-assertion' and assumption of male

superiority, but makes the wife and daughter 'submissive and cowed', culmi-
nating in the wife as the husband's 'abject slave': 'From that night when,
meeting her for the first time at a barn dance, he had boldly snatched her
from her partner, carried her bodily to his own sleigh and driven away with
her under the very eyes of her dumbfounded and indignant escort, she had
been his abject slave'.[61]

This close connection between women's situation in society and abjection is theorized by Julia Kristeva in her study on *Pouvoirs de l'horreur: Essai
sur l'abjection* (1980). She relates the idea of abjection to the rejection of
women as the other. While 'slavery' suggests appropriation and property,
'abjection' implies horror, the unfamiliar closely related, as Susanne Becker
suggests, to 'the female body',[62] representing the 'fear of the other, fear of
evil-the-feminine'[63] which is potentially threatening. Abjection ultimately
'underlines the power of horror for liberation or change'.[64] Thus, by casting his wife right from the beginning into the role of the 'abject slave', Jacob
Gladfelter unknowingly prepares the ground for her revolt.

Mrs Gladfelter has internalized the system's ideas of the husband's
right to determine their children's education and her own right to vote:
'It had never occurred to Meely, Jacob's wife, to question her man's right
to rule his own household. She would have thought him less than a man
and would not have respected him if he had not governed her and their
children with a firm hand'.[65] Both agree that 'a woman must always,
according to the Pennsylvania Dutch standard of what was "womanly,"
acquiesce in the dominance of a man, either her father or her "mister"'.[66]

However, when he announces that their daughter Weezy is not supposed
to continue her education, Mrs Gladfelter 'jolted into a real protest'.[67] She
awakens to the arbitrariness and 'the bald unreasonableness and injustice'
of gender roles, as defined and constructed by the Pennsylvania German
community, and develops 'into a new being—she was almost a stranger
to herself'.[68] She ignores all her household duties when she takes her
daughter to school without telling her husband, and when she replies to
the question about what her husband thinks of all her unusual activities
that '"It makes me nothing what he says!"', even her relatives suggest she
see a doctor.[69] This implication of illness in conjunction with the rejection of prescribed femininity is a standard assumption of nineteenth-
century American society.[70] Meely now is true to her name, Gladfelter,

although her own sons mock her as a 'new woman' with which they only connote the smoking of cigarettes and a particular hair-style. Jacob insists on silence and his usual repetition of short commands or questions, but for the first time in his life his authority fails in view of Meely's 'unconquerable buoyancy':[71] 'Meely's answer was to meet his cold eyes with such unflinching determination in her own that in his utter astonishment at its unfamiliarity, he relaxed, his jaw dropped, and he stared at her in confusion'.[72] He finally achnowledges that she seems 'like a stranger' to him.[73] While he is deeply rooted in traditions, Meely wants change, change as preferred to artificially constructed and unquestioned stability. Like Mary Wilkins Freeman's Adoniram Penn who 'was like a fortress whose walls had no active resistance, and went down the instant the right besieging tools were used',[74] Jacob, 'with a strange pang of fear in his heart, saw, in the straight, fearless gaze of the little woman whom, up to this hour, he had always regarded with a queer mingling of affection and contempt, that for once in his life he had encountered his match in obstinacy. Deep down in his soul he knew that he was beaten'.[75]

This vocabulary of battles lost and won emphasizes the woman's participation in a sphere traditionally restricted to men. Meely Gladfelter wins the fight for her daughter's education and her own right to vote, in spite of the socially perpetuated idea that women's education is unnatural.[76] She remains within the social framework of her marriage, a context that is also set for her daughter, but actively shapes the conditions. She turns from the submissive wife into the strong New Woman and is, for a while, a stranger to herself. However, she grasps this strangeness and shapes it to her own liking.

In conclusion, all four women writers present women who experience the patriarchal structures of their respective societies as oppressive and, after many years of quiet endurance, follow their urges for resistance. The women dismantle the existing constructions of femininity and masculinity by performing gender and by manipulating those who are stuck in these gender fixations. Despite their rootedness in specific ethnicities, which are displaced as 'other' in U.S. American society, these female characters exhibit common interests provoked by a patriarchal society and are not limited by national or ethnic boundaries. Although the institution of marriage still is a guiding and desirable principle for the four female protagonists, they teach their partners a lesson. The warrior's daughter, Mrs Spring Fragrance, Petra, and Meely Gladfelter resist oppression through tricksterlike cunning and female bonding across the generations and shape and redefine male-dominated realms such as physical fights (Zitkala-ša)—in mainstream America athletics could be seen as equivalent—language (Sui Sin Far), religion (María Cristina Mena), and education (Helen Reimensnyder Martin) according to their own interests. The icon of the New Woman, although literally used only by Helen Reimensnyder Martin, finds its admirable personifications in the works of these highly intuitive women of ethnic America. The concept of the New Woman gains in cultural expressiveness as well as complexity and loses its mono-cultural and class bias through these writers' ethnic diversities.

All four women writers were most probably the first of their respective ethnic groups to publish short stories in English in American magazines. Within the multiplicity of newly emerging magazines and the rise of magazine production, these ethnic New Women found their place to critically discuss ethnicity and gender issues of the time. The short story was an adequate genre for the representation of subversive ideas on multiculturalism and feminism, thus constituting an ideal medium for strong and critical feminist countervoices to patriarchal and nativist America at the beginning of the twentieth century.

6. Pauline Hopkins's Portrayal of the African-American New Woman in Contending Forces *and the* Colored American Magazine

Sabina Matter-Seibel

The 1890s were a period of intense political and intellectual activity for African American women. Blacks were struggling to enter the new century as fully participating citizens and women were at the forefront of the fight. In 1892 alone, three well-known black women published books which analyzed the tangled relationships between race, gender and patriarchy. Frances E. W. Harper (1825–1911) published her novel *Iola Leroy*, Anna Julia Cooper (1859–1964) wrote *A Voice from the South* and Ida B. Wells (1862–1931) produced *Southern Horrors: Lynch Law in all its Phases*. In 1893, when it became clear that African Americans were not to be represented at the World's Columbian Exposition in Chicago, except in a highly selective manner as exotic exhibits, Wells was in the Haitian pavilion protesting the exclusion and circulating the pamphlet she had edited, *The Reason Why the Colored American is not in the World's Columbian Exposition*.

It was the 'woman's era', as Harper called it as she addressed the World's Congress of Representative Women on 'Woman's Political Future': 'The world cannot move without woman's sharing in the movement, and to help give a right impetus to that movement is woman's highest privilege'.[1] As an answer to the call for constructive work, the Club Movement among coloured women grew rapidly. In 1896, various club organizations formed the National Association of Colored Women (NACW). For the first time, African-American women could confront their oppression through a national organization.

In this 'nadir' of black history, as the post-Reconstruction period is called by historian Rayford W. Logan,[2] an appeal was made to mobilize all forces. In 1892, the wave of lynching had reached its peak. Jim Crow Laws determined life in the South; job and housing discrimination were increasing in the North. In 1896, in Plessy versus Ferguson the Supreme Court cemented the institutionalization of 'separate, but equal'. The White City of the Exhibition, supposedly a symbol of American progress, became the icon of white supremacy for African-Americans.

When in 1899 Pauline Hopkins (1859–1930) wrote her first novel, *Contending Forces; A Romance Illustrative of Negro Life North and South*, it was her attempt to voice in fiction the political debates of the day using the arguments she had honed on the lecture circuit. Hopkins meant her novel to be a 'weapon for social change'[3] and it was recognized as such. The Colored American Publishing Co-operative gave free copies to libraries and various organizations and raved, 'The book will certainly create a sensation among a certain class of "whites" at the South, as well as awaken a general interest among our race, not only in this country, but throughout the world.'[4] *Contending Forces* was actively to further African-American political interests, to raise the consciousness of white readers and to serve as 'race literature'[5] for black readers.

In turning to both a black and a white audience, Hopkins tried to revive abolitionist sentiments, especially the identification of white and black women along lines of gender. In 1899, she still believed in the New England spirit of democracy and fairness:

> I have presented both sides of the dark picture…truthfully and without vituperation, pleading for that justice of heart and mind for my people which the Anglo-Saxon in America never withholds from suffering humanity.[6]

In spite of this appeal to white readers, Hopkins's political message is clear. Racism is a 'cankering sore which is eating into the heart of the Republican principles and stamping the lie upon the Constitution'.[7] She makes it clear that the African-American community cannot wait any longer and will not back down: 'Expediency and right go hand in hand. There is no room for compromise'.[8]

The novel speaks specifically to black women and presents them with a new type of African-American woman. Immediately after completing the book in 1899, Hopkins presented her work at the meeting of the Woman's Era Club in Boston. Subsequently, it was recommended by women's clubs in all cities. Spurred by the novel's invocation 'to agitate', Alberta Moore Smith, president of the Colored Women's Business Club in Chicago, called it 'undoubtedly the book of the century'.[9]

Women in *Contending Forces* have a strong voice in political matters. Even though the meeting of the American Colored League features only male speakers, the women talk about current issues at a sewing circle that serves as a political meeting in disguise.[10] But giving black women a public voice, even if in a domestic setting, is only one aspect of empowerment. At the center of the novel is Hopkins's revision of the stereotype of black female wantonness. She fights the image in the popular media which described the behaviour of blacks as governed by their allegedly uncontrollable passions. The intersecting discourses of race purity and female virtue are questioned. For Hopkins lynching and rape are the chief means of oppression by white society. She is a radical in the vein of Ida B. Wells when she situates rape separate from the issue of violated white womanhood and as a tactic to repress any attempt at political, social and economic advancement of blacks.

In *Contending Forces*, Hopkins takes up the antebellum type of the tragic mulatta and rewrites it. Grace Montfort follows the fate typical of the Victorian fallen woman and commits suicide after having been raped. Sappho Clark, a beautiful, near-white mulatta survives rape by a white uncle, months in a New Orleans brothel and the birth of an illegitimate son. She moves North and starts a new life. Hopkins rewrites the older oppressive script and rewards the heroine with the conventional happy end of marriage to a worthy man. By relying on the old ideal of the True Woman, Hopkins establishes a difference between female virtue, an inner quality that cannot be defiled, and female propriety, which is dictated by society.[11] Sappho's purity is emphasized in the flower imagery used (she is a 'queen rose and lily in one'), and in the religious imagery that turns her into a heavenly creature: 'She is like the angels in the picture of the cruxification'.[12]

Once established as a True Woman, she can emerge as a potential African-American New Woman. Elaine Showalter defines the New Woman as university-educated, sexually independent, working for a living, enjoying her mobility, gaining a voice in public and as refusing to define herself through her role as wife and mother.[13] In short, she has more ways of life to choose from than her Victorian foremother. Sappho does show some of these traits: she is unmarried, she has moved from New Orleans to Boston, she lives alone in a boarding house and she is gainfully employed (as a stenographer, just like Hopkins herself).

But do these parallels and the fact that she does not share the fate of the Victorian fallen woman make her an African-American New Woman? Sappho's choices, if they can be called that, are all negative: she chooses not to bring up her son, she chooses not to reveal her past, she chooses not to marry as atonement for her sins. Some New Woman characteristics she adopts under pressure: her geographical mobility is actuated by her desperate conviction that Boston offers better opportunities to blacks. In describing her heroine's impressions of Boston, Hopkins's repetition of the word 'free' serves as an ironic incantation: 'Here in the free air of New England's freest city, Sappho drank great droughts of freedom's subtle elixir'.[14] Her employment is dire necessity and she has to work at home because the other employees do not want to work with a black woman.

Living apart from family means not freedom, but danger for Sappho. In fact, Sappho is a metaphorically homeless heroine, as Kristina Brooks has pointed out.[15] Sappho's movement from her parents' house via a series of public houses (whore house, convent, boarding house) reflects the search of the African American for an equal right to privacy and protection as a citizen of the U.S. In public spaces Sappho is vulnerable. John Langely, the villain of the novel, is able to enter her room precisely because she is not in her own home.

Sappho is also literally a 'new' woman as she suppresses her past. In Boston, she assumes the identity of a marriageable woman, when in reality she is a rape victim and a mother, both factors which serve to discredit her in society's eyes. Maintaining this dual identity, though, has aliented Sappho from herself: 'we grow to loathe ourselves'.[16] She sees herself as subject and object at the same time. Even the rational arguments of Mrs Willis, who lectures on women's issues and reminds the women at the sewing circle that they were immoral only under compulsion,[17] do not heal this inner split. Sappho is free only in a very limited manner, as long as nobody knows her buried self. When that is revealed, she is circumscribed by public censure. In fact, when her story is told in public at the meeting of the American Colored League, she faints away, symbolically losing control over her destiny.

Sappho's healing begins when she travels, both emotionally and geographically, back into the past, recovering her child and her heritage. In a way, Sappho has to be tamed first, has to give up her lover and become a mother to her son before she can develop into a New Woman. As Jill Bergman argues in the next chapter, there are redeeming qualities in motherhood for black women at the turn of the century. While Anglo-Saxon women were turning away from motherhood as defining women's role, African-American women, whose memory of the destruction of family bonds in slavery was still fresh, felt empowered by the claim they could make to their children. Nevertheless, when pondering the conditions of black life in the United States, Hopkins realized that both biological motherhood and mothering of the race was still a task beset by legal difficulties and psychological hang-ups. Sappho feels a 'dumb rage und spirit of revenge' that has to be expunged for a black New Woman to emerge.[18] Hopkins's thinking is womanist as she insists on a rehabilitation of the black woman, from a reclaiming of her body to uplifting the race.

For Hopkins, *Contending Forces* opened a way to earn a living through her writing, to secure her own position as an African-American New Woman, when the Colored Co-operative Publishing Company, which also published *The Colored American Magazine*, invited her to contribute to the magazine. Black women had used magazines to agitate against slavery and to work for racial uplift since mid-century.[19] Journalism was meant to educate, missionize, inspire and stir people to action. At the beginning of the 20th century African-American magazines like *The Colored American Magazine*, *Horizon* and *Voice of the Negro* proliferated. While their main goal remained the instruction of their readers, they served as organs for middle-class protest against discrimination. The editors were searching for a black literary aesthetic which would meet the needs of the day.[20] They were celebrating black progress, but also protesting lynch law, disenfranchisement, Jim Crow laws and discrimination in the North in no uncertain terms. Most of these magazines were located in Boston, not only because blacks there had been freedmen longer and had a better education than blacks in the South, but because the editors, just like Hopkins in *Contending Forces*, hoped for 'lingering abolitionist and equalitarian traditions'.[21]

The Colored American Magazine was founded in 1900 by four young men. In the first issue Hopkins's short story 'The Mystery Within Us' was published. When the next issue appeared, she had already advanced to editor of 'The Women's Department'. From November 1903 until her dismissal in 1904 she acted as literary editor. Her output during these four years is prodigious: in addition to articles on politics, business, education and religion, she publishes ten short stories and three novels in its pages. As the first black woman editor of a magazine she has the power to influence the magazine's policies. By offering a wide variety, 'Literature, Science, Music, Art, Religion, Facts, Fiction and Traditions of the Negro Race',[22] she creates a marketplace of ideas, hoping that it will make a difference in the lives of African Americans.

Hopkins makes 'a new race of colored women'[23] her cause. In 'The Women's Department', she advises women to become actively involved in social work, in politics and in business: 'One of the most remarkable movements of the twentieth century has been the ramification of women in all directions where she [*sic*] has seen the slightest chance for business or intellectual progression.'[24] She is convinced that women will provide much needed guidance in the fight for equal rights: 'our women are proving the salvation of the race in America'.[25] It is the same sentiment that Hopkins voices in *Contending Forces*: 'if our race ever amounts to anything in this world, it will be because such women as you are raised up to save us'.[26] In several articles she reports on the racism of white Women's Clubs. Solidarity between white and black women as in the abolitionist movement, which Hopkins had tried to reawaken in *Contending Forces*, is quickly becoming utopian. In her article 'Club Life among Colored Women' she reveals the bad treatment of black women by white members and interprets this behaviour as pandering to Southern white males. She severely criticizes Northern women by comparing them to the biblical Sarah who takes revenge on the hapless Hagar.[27]

In addition to her regular column, she published biographical sketches of African Americans. For Hopkins, biography is a means of shaping race history through public lives. As in *Contending Forces*, she educates her readers to middle-class norms and values, while advancing a political challenge to the status quo and a commitment to the preservation of African-American history.

Two series appeared monthly from November 1900 to October 1902, 'Famous Men of the Negro Race' and 'Famous Women of the Negro Race'. Among the men are such historical icons as Frederick Douglass, Booker T. Washington and Toussaint L'Overture.[28] In the latter, Hopkins provides a revisionist history of the Haitian revolution, but the point of view is masculine. Toussaint emerges as a benevolent patriarch. In all male portraits, emphasis is placed on the participation in history by means of public roles and on the individuality of the men.

In contrast, the women in the women's series are rather seen as an embodiment of the community endeavour and not as individual heroines. The collective portrait of 'Phenomenal Vocalists'[29] starts the series. The other group portrayals are of educators, literary workers, women of the college elite and club women. Hopkins's emphasis is on racial uplift and cultural work. She cultivates race consciousness by her insistence on collective identity. The political agenda of learned and independent womanhood is brought together with the Victorian ethos of serving humanity. Here she moves away from the domestic sphere of her novels and towards 'organized intelligence'.[30]

Interspersed among the group portrayals are biographical sketches of Sojourner Truth and Harriet Tubman. By embedding these unusual women in collective portraits, Hopkins transforms Truth and Tubman from indecorous, opinionated and excessively public women into exemplary community figures. In 'Sojourner Truth: A Northern Slave',[31] Hopkins deconstructs received history by depicting domestic drama: Truth is shown as a sexual victim, as a mother of five, as the rescuer of her son similar to Eliza in Stowe's *Uncle Tom's Cabin*. Hopkins falls back on the familiar patterns of domestic fiction. She privileges the intimate elements of this public life before liberating Truth from domestic chores when she starts travelling as a lecturer in the North. In 'Harriet Tubman ("Moses")', Tubman emerges as a feminized Christ 'in her heroic and successful endeavors to reach and save all whom she might of her oppressed and suffering race, and pilot them to the promised land of Liberty'.[32] She is thereby contained in conventional religious imagery and given a justification for her unwomanly behaviour through her role as 'Moses' for her people.

As Doreski has pointed out, Hopkins both relies on the New England tradition, employing Puritan 'exemplary biography', and diverges from it to create a revisionary race history.[33] Hopkins's appropriation of biographical strategies from Mather and Emerson is an accessible way of rendering homage to the African-American past. The biographies of black men and women are acts of recovery and commemoration. Nevertheless, women like Mary Church Terrell, Ida B. Wells and Fannie Barrier Williams, who were regarded as aggressive and improperly behaved in the white press, are significantly missing from her 'Famous Women of the Negro Race'. These African-American New Women were still too new to deserve a place among the cultural icons.

Towards the end of the century it became increasingly difficult to place the black woman in the New Negro debate. In 1895, the *Cleveland Gazette* commented on the New York Civil Rights Law which had just been passed by giving credit to 'a class of colored people, the "new Negro," who have arisen since the war, with education, refinement and money'.[34] In its emphasis on education and refinement this concept provides a place for the African-American New Woman working for racial uplift. The photograph of 'The Young Colored American' published in the fall 1900 issue of the *Colored American* shows the optimism of the time: an African-American baby sitting on an unfurling American flag, a new American for a new century, a baby to be brought up a New Negro by a black woman.[35]

But the baby was quickly growing into a man. In *A New Negro for a New Century* (1900),[36] Booker T. Washington and other contributors stress economic accomplishments and self-betterment. Here the New Negro is conspicuously male, portrayed as a materially successful man, often an ambitious entrepreneur. A hard-working and level-headed citizen without political ambitions, he deserves to be admitted into mainstream society. American middle-class standards had been favoured by Hopkins, too, but not to the exclusion of equal political rights. In fact, Hopkins had drawn a negative portrait of the new Negro in *Contending Forces*. John Langley, the villain of the novel, is a typical new Negro politician: manipulative, power hungry, greedy, ready to sell his people's interests for privileges and money.

The contending forces of the title which are dooming the black race are defined as 'lack of brotherly affiliation, lack of energy for the right and the power of the almighty dollar'.[37]

After 1895, Washington expanded his influence in the North by securing controlling interests in black newspapers and magazines. This strategy worked well to silence dissent in the black group and to spread the gospel of accomodationism.[38] By 1900, he controlled *Alexander's Magazine*, *Colored Citizen*, *Colored American* of Washington and the *New York Age*.[39] When the Colored Publishing Co-operative failed in the spring of 1904, Fred R. Moore, secretary of the National Negro Business League and a close friend of Washington, bought the paper. Readers were kept ignorant of Washington's involvement. In the summer of 1904, Moore moved the operation to New York where Thomas T. Fortune took over its editorial duties in order to escape the influence of radical black Bostonians.[40]

This signaled the end of Hopkins's editorship. In the 'Publishers' Announcements' of November 1904 Hopkins is dismissed with lukewarm praise: 'On account of ill health Miss Pauline Hopkins has found it necessary to sever her relations with this Magazine and has returned to her home in Boston. Miss Hopkins was a faithful and conscientious worker, and did much toward the building up the Magazine'.[41] Her outspoken radical ideas on race and gender were not in agreement with the accomodationist politics of Washington.[42] What was especially riling to Washington's supporters was Hopkins's insistence on writing about the past, particularly about the African-American women's history of rape, forced concubinage and miscegenation. In her editorials she emphasized the central position of black women in racist arguments. In contrast, Washington's future-oriented thinking would not allow any room, textually and psychologically, for the past. As if the new century would cancel all history, working through the experiences under slavery was impossible. For the African-American woman this denial of a 'usable past' brought on alienation and self-hatred as Hopkins had shown in *Contending Forces*. In her understanding, the black woman could not, as Fannie Barrier Williams maintained, rise like a phoenix from the ashes: 'This woman, as if by magic, has suceeded in lifting herself completely from the stain and meanness of slavery as if a century had elapsed since the day of her emancipation'.[43]

After Hopkins left, the *Colored American* became a mouthpiece for the ideologies of Washington. The approach of the magazine grew more conciliatory and the importance of the vote was deemphasized. Most articles beseeched white readers for support. In the November 1904 issue Moore outlined his intentions: 'The Magazine seeks to publish articles showing the advancement of our people along material lines, believing that the people generally are more interested in having information of the doings of the members of the race, rather (than) the writings of dreamers or theorists'.[44] Being concerned with the material advancement of blacks, Moore made no effort to attract black writers of fiction. Between 1905 to 1908, most articles published by the magazine were on business, agriculture and industrial education.[45] There was rarely literature by black women or articles about them.

Hopkins meanwhile had found another magazine more to her liking. A month after she had left the *Colored American*, her first article appeared in the *Voice of the Negro*, effectively refuting the claim that health reasons had prevented her from staying with the *Colored American*. The *Voice of the Negro*, established in 1904 in Atlanta under the editorship of J. Max Barber, was the first magazine to be edited by blacks in the South. Barber's editorial policies were similar to Hopkins's: the paper was to publish radical essays against lawlessness and bigotry and speak for full political participation.[46] Nevertheless, Hopkins did not have the opportunity to focus on the new black woman as she had done while at the *Colored American*. The *Voice* and Barber were writing for 'The New Negro Man'.[47] The northward migration of Southern blacks, black urbanization and a growing class of black industrial workers foregrounded male values. The meaning of the term 'New Negro' acquired meanings specific to males, the working class and radical politics.[48] Race discourse became increasingly fragmented, and issues of class superseded issues of gender.

Hopkins shifted the focus in her own writing away from gender. While she had first asserted the presence of Afro-Americans within an Anglo-American context, she now reinterpreted their African heritage. With her fourth novel, *Of One Blood*, which describes a return to a mythical African kingdom, Hopkins had already joined a tradition of black writers who argued for the recognition of ancient African contributions to world civilization.[49] Between February and July 1905 the *Voice of the Negro* ran a series of articles by Hopkins on 'The Dark Races of the Twentieth Century'. In 1905 she published a *Primer of Facts Pertaining to the Early Greatness of the African Race*.[50] In both cases, she uses the male persona of a scientific expert and the imperial, scholarly language of cultural relativism. Hopkins had undergone a development from domesticity to nationalism.

Hopkins had had doubts about the fate of the new black woman as early as 1900. At the end of *Contending Forces*, Sappho is still homeless in American society. Together with her husband she leaves on a ship to England with vague plans of establishing a school 'across the water'.[51] Though it is the conventional happy end in marriage, Hopkins does not present a vision of a fullfilled married life. The social context has not changed enough to accommodate Hopkins's womanist revision of the African-American woman. Racist attitudes, the eliding of her history and the focus on black material advancement as a male privilege has the black New Woman sailing off—first to Europe like Sappho, and later to Africa.

7. 'A New Race of Colored Women'

Pauline Hopkins at the Colored American Magazine

Jill Bergman

> The Negro woman having risen from no greater depths, though enslaved, than the Anglo-Saxon woman, feels her womanhood stir within her and boldly advances to scale the heights of intellectual advancement, feeling that the door has been opened for her to take an active, intelligent and resolute part in the march of human progress. It seems almost as if the inspiration of the times had created a new race of colored women, a new tide set in, new forces called into play, a new era in the world's history and through all this the moral and social regeneration of a race.
>
> *'Famous Women of the Negro Race'*[1]

The era of the New Woman has been described in terms of a generational transition. In *Disorderly Conduct*, Carroll Smith-Rosenberg calls the New Women 'daughters' who 'repudiat[ed] the Cult of True Womanhood in ways [their] mother[s]—the new bourgeois matron[s]—never could'.[2] These daughters abandoned their mothers' ethos of self-sacrifice; instead they sought education, autonomy outside the patriarchal family, professional visibility, and political power. Old ideals of domesticity were dropped in favour of more progressive notions. African-American women watched this movement with great interest. As Pauline Hopkins indicates in the epigraph, taken from her 'Famous Women of the Negro Race' series, advances made by white women—what she refers to as 'the inspiration of the times'—gave black women hope that they could participate in this progress. They believed that white women's progress opened a door for black women's similar advances. In the quotation, Hopkins offers for her readers' contemplation the possibility that the advent of the New Woman had facilitated a 'new race of colored women' as well. In her work as editor and contributor for the *Colored American Magazine* from 1900 to 1904, Hopkins monitored and facilitated this progress by focusing much attention on African-American women. In her fiction featuring female protagonists, her series 'Famous Women of the Negro Race,' and other written and photographic portraits of successful 'race women'—black women interested in the improvement of the race— she informs her readers of black women's work and progress and appropriates the ideals of New Womanhood, claiming for the African-American daughters some of the same advancement enjoyed by their white sisters.

However, the generational model does not accurately describe the rise of the black New Woman. Most African-American contemporaries of the white 'bourgeois matrons' had been slaves and excluded from ideals of True Womanhood. In the Reconstruction and post-Reconstruction eras, while the white 'daughters' were abandoning domestic ideals as confining, black women embraced these newly accessible ideals as a means of claiming womanhood and citizenship for themselves.[3] Several scholars have noted that black women writers of the late 19th and early 20th centuries appropriated the antebellum domestic novel forms and ideals as a means of repudiating prevalent stereotypes.[4] Like other turn-of-the-century African-American women, Hopkins is not ready to abandon the domestic ideals of the bourgeois matron, in part because she has just got a chance to join the bourgeoisie.[5]

Another significant reason Hopkins does not abandon the domesticity of the 'mothers' for the New Womanhood of the 'daughters' is because of New Womanhood's emphasis on individual rights. The shift from the ideals of domesticity as lived by the bourgeois matron to the ideals of New Womanhood amounted to a shift from self-sacrifice to self-development. According to an 1898 essay in the periodical *Club Woman*, 'The new woman decides that the woman ought not to be sacrificed to the mother.'[6] In other words, rather than conceiving of herself solely as mother, woman should think of herself as an individual. She should begin to put her needs and interests on par with—or even above—those of her family. Hopkins's portrayal of New Womanhood indicates some ambivalence about this ethos. While she favours much of the progress experienced by women under the ideals of New Womanhood, in the post-Reconstruction era of severe racial oppression African Americans typically saw the needs of the race as more pressing than the needs of women. As the motto of the National Association of Colored Women, 'Lifting as We Climb', illustrates, women's progress needed to serve the progress of the race.[7] Hopkins believed this, and, to return to the epigraph, she saw the 'new race of colored women' as a vehicle for 'the moral and social regeneration of a race.' Elements of the bourgeois matrons' domesticity—in particular the ideal of the glorified, redeeming mother—suited this vision of uplift. Far from abandoning the bourgeois matrons' ideals, then, Hopkins merges them with the ideals of New Womanhood to create a new race of black women who take a distinctly maternal approach to racial uplift.

The *Colored American Magazine*, published from 1900 to 1909, was, according to Abby Johnson and Ronald Johnson, 'the first significant Afro-American journal to emerge in the twentieth century'.[8] In its first issue, it declared that it met the 'immediate need of a Race Journal' and described its diverse contents as being 'devoted to Literature, Science, Music, Art, Religion, Facts, Fiction and Traditions of the Negro Race.'[9] Although some confusion exists over Hopkins' precise role at the magazine—her name did not appear on the masthead as editor until March 1904—Hazel Carby believes that Hopkins's role has been 'vastly underestimated.'[10] A 1947 article by William Stanley Braithwaite, who contributed frequently to the publication, puts her in an active role from the magazine's inception.[11] The philosophical consistency between her numerous contributions and the magazine's overall message would seem to indicate that she wielded a great deal of influence. And I will argue that Hopkins had much to do with making this important race journal one that specifically addressed the interests and highlighted the accomplishments of black women, in spite of its more general readership. Indeed, during her tenure as editor Hopkins virtually made the *Colored American Magazine* an organ of African-American New Womanhood and maternal racial uplift.

In many ways Hopkins appears to subscribe to the tenets of New Womanhood in the pages of the *Colored American* and attempts to share in the advances it had afforded white women. A brief biographical sketch of Hopkins in the January 1901 issue—probably heavily influenced by Hopkins, if not in fact written by her—attributes to Hopkins many classic

1. *Colored American Magazine*, vol.5, no.6, October 1902.
Covers like this one featured portraits of stylishly dressed 'race women'
surrounded by floral borders.

New Woman traits. Most significant is the staunch, almost excessive, insistence upon her middle-class status. The New Woman, according to Smith-Rosenberg, was typically a 'member of the affluent new bourgeoisie' with 'economic resources' and 'social standing' that allowed her a measure of freedom.[12] The biography carefully accentuates Hopkins's impressive family history and her connections to the anti-slavery movement as a means of placing her firmly within the black middle class:

> By her mother Miss Hopkins is a direct descendant of the famous Paul brothers, all black men, educated abroad for the Baptist ministry, the best known of whom was Thomas Paul, who founded St. Paul Baptist Church...the first colored church in this section of the United States. Susan Paul, a niece of these brothers, was a famous colored woman, long and intimately associated with William Lloyd Garrison in the anti-slavery movement. Miss Hopkins is also a grandniece of the late James Whitfield, the California poet, who was associated with Frederick Douglass in politics and literature. His poems are in all the libraries of the Pacific coast, and Mr Douglass had them in his library.[13]

I quote this paragraph at length not only to demonstrate how painstakingly the writer establishes Hopkins's rather slight link to Frederick Douglass, but also to indicate the perceived value of her family information. The whole biography occupies little over a page in length, and yet it devotes a fifth of that space to establishing Hopkins's class status through her familial connection to prestigious activists, religious leaders, and literary people. The article focuses on her own education as well; although she did not pursue a post-secondary degree, the profile boasts that she was 'educated in the Boston public schools, and...graduated from the famous Girls' High School of that city.' And like the New Woman, Hopkins followed a career rather than marriage. After a brief foray into literary work, she pursued stenography before writing her first novel and joining the staff at the *Colored American*.

Not only is the editor portrayed as something of a New Woman, but the magazine itself promotes black New Womanhood. Its covers appear to be designed to attract a female readership with its floral borders, scrolling artwork, and portraits of women whose stories are told in the issue (*see* figure 1). And the magazine's content delivers what the covers promise. Although not limited to women's issues, a high proportion of the articles report the activities of women. With her twelve-part series 'Famous Women of the Negro Race,' Hopkins celebrates the professional and social accomplishments of black women. The series title misleads somewhat because apart from three famous women profiled (Harriet Tubman, Sojourner Truth, and Frances Harper), Hopkins focuses her attention on lesser-known, distinctly middle-class women of the race—women who could reasonably serve as models for her female readers. A monthly column entitled 'Here and There' sets out to 'publish monthly such short articles…as will enable our subscribers to keep in close touch with the various *social* movements among the colored race.'[14] For example, this column reports the appointment of 'fourteen negros, [*sic*] three of whom are women, to do census work in Augusta, Ga', touts the accomplishments of soprano Rosalie Tyler and teacher Bessie C. Winfield, and introduces the officers of a women's club in New York. In January 1901, an article entitled 'Boston's Smart Set' provided photographic portraits of 'eight popular Bostonians'—all women.[15] The 'Women's Department,' a column edited by Hopkins, appeared in only one issue early on, offering information similar to that in 'Here and There.' It seems to have been absorbed into that column, perhaps due to redundancy. Indeed, as I've shown, much of the magazine can be read under the heading of the 'women's department'.

But while Hopkins uses the *Colored American* to promote the tenets of New Womanhood among her readers, using 'the inspiration of the times' to advance the new race of colored women, she also shows a certain ambivalence, if not disdain, for some aspects of New Womanhood. I make this point with a small but telling use of an image by Hopkins. The popular image of the athletic woman on a bicycle is a familiar icon of New Womanhood, representing the freedom and independence associated with the movement. The Charles Dana Gibson illustration (figure 2) is just one of many familiar examples. Hopkins uses the image of the bicycle-riding woman, too, but for a different effect. In her first novel, *Contending Forces* (published in 1900 by the same company that published *The Colored American*), she juxtaposes two female characters. The novel's heroine, Sappho, exhibits traits of New Womanhood as an educated, professional, middle-class woman.[16] A comic character in one of the subplots, Mrs Ophelia Davis, is a fifty-year-old woman whose dialect and former servant status clearly mark her as beneath the middle class.[17] Hopkins further demarcates the contrast between these characters with their names: Ophelia is a man-centered woman who pursues a relationship with the local minister, a man half her age; Sappho, although pursued by male characters and eventually married to the novel's exemplary male character, appears woman-centered in her independence, her female friendships, and her commitment to community progress. While Sappho and other exemplary characters focus their attentions on the alleviation of the injustices facing their race, Ophelia Davis provides comic relief by riding a bicycle with the minister. By linking Ophelia, a well-meaning but silly character, with the bicycle fad, Hopkins draws attention to frivolous aspects of New Womanhood and provides a sharp contrast to the important race work to be done, thus registering Hopkins's judgment of the pursuit of personal pleasure and indicating her ambivalence about some aspects of New Womanhood.

2. Charles Dana Gibson, 'Scribner's for June', 1896

Hopkins offers a more glaring indictment of New Womanhood in her comments on women's voting rights. She explains, 'There is quite a ripple among women just now in favor of woman suffrage. We believe it to be a good thing if limited in some degree...[W]e ought to hesitate before we affiliate too happily in any project that will give [white women] greater power than they now possess to crush the weak and helpless.'[18] The racism of white women showed Hopkins that gender solidarity must come second to race solidarity, a belief that was confirmed in May 1902, when the General Federation of Women's Clubs voted to exclude 'colored' clubs. This event clearly outraged Hopkins—she wrote about it in both the July and August issues following the vote and reflected upon it again in October of that year. 'We look in vain', she wrote, 'for a trace of the graciousness attributed to the female character or the meek gentleness of Christ in the position assumed by the Anglo-Saxon woman toward her dark-skinned sister.'[19] The federation's vote probably confirmed her belief that the appropriation of New Womanhood for the advancement of black women must serve as a means to the more pressing goal, the progress of the race. This is where I see an important distinction in the manifestation of New Womanhood as it appears in the pages of the *Colored American*, the difference between the mothers and the daughters. The legacy of the bourgeois matron with her idealized domesticity that the white daughters rejected provided African-American women with a powerful model in the form of the redeeming mother. The New Womanhood that Hopkins celebrates and promotes blends the redeeming mother with the progressive daughter.

The redeeming mother was a key figure in nineteenth-century American domesticity informing the ideal of the bourgeois matron. As Jane Tompkins explains in her insightful discussion of the cultural work of *Uncle Tom's Cabin*, antebellum domestic fiction portrayed a worldview in which mother love was a source of significant power. She argues that 'the popular domestic novel of the nineteenth century represents a monumental effort to reorganize culture from the woman's point of view' by applying feminine values to the situations encountered in daily life. *Uncle Tom's Cabin*, she asserts, was 'a brilliant redaction of the culture's favorite story about itself—the story of salvation through motherly love'.[20] She goes on to explain the centrality of separate spheres to this doctrine: 'by resting her case, absolutely, on the saving power of Christian love and on the sanctity of motherhood and the family, Stowe relocates the center of power in American life, placing it not in the government, nor in the courts of law, nor in the factories, nor in the marketplace, but in the kitchen'.[21] Fannie Barrier Williams described this power in a 1902 article on the club movement and racial uplift: 'It took the colored people a long time to realize that ...to be a citizen of the United States was serious business, and that a seat in Congress was an insecure prominence unless supported by good women, noble mothers, family integrity and pure homes.'[22] And Hopkins herself uses the rhetoric of salvation when she asserts that 'our women are proving the salvation of the race in America.'[23] Two aspects of the redeeming mother are important for understanding Hopkins's project of revising New Womanhood: the notion that mothers have the power to save, and the faith in private, maternal power over the public power of government.

At the turn of the century, a time of severe and legalized racial discrimination, one can easily understand why the philosophy of a redeeming mother would be attractive to African-American women. Given the numerous abuses of motherhood under slavery, motherlessness came to represent to the slave community, and later to the post-Reconstruction community, the alienation and disenfranchisement forced upon African Americans. The music of the African-American community gave testimony to the use of this symbol, such as the spiritual that lamented, 'sometimes I feel like a motherless child, a long ways from home.'[24] Logically, Hopkins imagined a maternal style of racial uplift that would address this metaphorical motherlessness. Her portraits of exemplary race women show them to measure up to the model of white New Womanhood—particularly in terms of education and class standing—but also portrays them in a position of mothering their race.

Several New Women introduced in the *Colored American* exemplify this maternal quality. The magazine's fourth issue runs a profile of Mrs Rosa Bowser apparently written by Hopkins. Bowser has made a name for herself as a 'race woman' through her numerous activities: founder of the Richmond, Virginia Women's League, president of the Richmond Mothers' Club, and president of the women's department of the Reformatory Movement, to name a few. Quoted in the context of her work for the establishment of a reformatory, she appeals to her listeners in the name of motherhood:

Let us be interested in ourselves; these children are on the downward road;…as fast as the bad rise, we rise with them; and so long as they are degraded, we are degraded. If the parents can not, or will not, bring up their children so that they can become good citizens, then it is clearly the duty of some one else to look after them.[25]

This active New Woman conceptualizes the needs of troubled youth in

terms of a lack of parenting, and she relates the better parenting or mothering of those children directly to the race's progress. She understands her
work, therefore, not in terms of individual freedom and advancement, but
in terms of community, of improving the race by helping the children.
Indeed, the individual freedom to raise one's children comes under threat
here for the greater good of the race. She calls upon her fellow race
women to provide the mothering that children, and the race, lack.

In the women's club movement we find what Hopkins believed to be
the most effective vehicle of maternal racial uplift in the hands of the black
New Woman. According to Patricia Marks's study of representations of
the New Woman, 'the exceptional proliferation of women's clubs during
the last decades of the century testified to the growing independence' of
turn-of-the-century women,[26] and clubs proliferated among black and
white women alike. The black women's club movement had its beginning
in the early 1800s in various US cities with enough black, middle-class
women to sustain a membership. These groups joined together for a variety of purposes, sometimes to socialize, sometimes to meet community
needs.[27] With the end of the Civil War, and then with the failure of
Reconstruction, the purpose of such groups became uplifting the 'folk' of
the race and building a life under freedom, as well as raising the standard
of womanhood so as to refute claims by whites that black women fell
outside that classification. Women's clubs were grassroots, private sphere
groups with a national agenda and served a variety of purposes for these
women seeking a secure place among the nation's middle classes. Hopkins
describes the goals of women's clubs as 'further[ing] the interests of the
race generally and...our women particularly' by 'awaken[ing] in [them]
an active interest in the events of the day, and giving to them through such
an organization an opportunity of hearing and participating in the discussion of current topics.'[28] It was a meeting place of race women, many of
whom were successfully pursuing professional or artistic careers. Thus the
club provided positive examples of black New Womanhood to its members.
Its maternal agenda came in its attempt to improve and 'civilize' the lower
classes of blacks, showing them to be capable of the same level of civilization found in bourgeois culture.[29] This effort had an evangelical character to it which Hopkins describes this way: 'We believe it to be the club
women's task to "little by little turn the desire of the world from things of

RIP TO PARADISE. Sixth Letter. MR. JOHN O. FREUN

THE
COLORED AMERICAN
MAGAZINE

CENTS A MONTH   JUNE, 1904 $1.00 A YEAR.

A MONTHLY ILLUSTRATED MAGAZINE
DEVOTED TO THE INTERESTS OF
THE COLORED RACE.

JEROME B. PETERSON
Consul at Puerto Cabello, Venezuela
See Editor's Notebook

PUBLISHED BY
THE COLORED CO-OPERATIVE PUBLISHING CO.
181 PEARL STREET, NEW YORK

3. *Colored American Magazine*, vol.7, number 6, June 1904.
On these *Colored American* covers (here and figure 4), the race women
have been replaced with successful business men.
In the graphics for June 1904, drawings of two men—one a labourer
and one a scholar—have replaced the earlier cover's illustration of
Phyllis Wheatley and Frederick Douglass.

4. *Colored American Magazine*, vol. 8, number 2, February 1905.
On this cover, a floral border has the addition of thorns, qualifying the soft
floral cover of the earlier look.

the flesh to things of the spirit. She must make [the] world want to do things that raise it higher and higher.'"[30] With the spiritual language here, she recalls the moral, redemptive mission of the bourgeois matron and reaffirms that the goal of women's progress is the race's uplift.

As an editor with a vision for maternal racial uplift, Hopkins created in the *Colored American* a black women's club in print form. She chose new/race women to hold up as examples. She educated her readers on issues of importance to the race through the articles she herself wrote for the magazine.[31] And she used the magazine to form readers into a community in much the same way that women's clubs sought to do. With the 'Here and There' column, she offered news of race-related events, political and social, taking place around the country, and invited readers 'to contribute items of general views and interest.'[32] The column thus functioned, in principle, like women's club meetings in which members discussed current events. Although discussion was necessarily limited by the medium, the invitation of readers' views gave the magazine the appearance of an open forum. The magazine also built community, or the illusion of community, in its familiar coverage of stories and people from around the nation. Short articles referred to individuals as if they were members of a small community, in spite of the fact that they came from all over the country and were probably unknown to the majority of readers. Details, such as Miss Eva Roosa's graduation from the New England Conservatory of Music, Mrs Dora A. Millar's presidency of the New York Colored Women's Business Club, or the speakers for a celebration at the A.M.E. church create the feeling of a tight-knit community, bolstering the sense of responsibility to others.[33]

The new black womanhood imagined and promoted by Hopkins appropriated the independence of the popular New Woman but, paradoxically, it used that independence in the service of the African-American community. As editor of *The Colored American*, Hopkins seems to have had great influence over the magazine's message, using it as an organ for this black New Womanhood. Hopkins left the *Colored American* in 1904 when it was bought and moved from Boston to New York. Although an editor's note would later claim that Hopkins left on account of poor health, most scholars attribute her leaving to a difference in philosophy with the Booker T. Washington acolytes who took over the magazine. She was accused of not being conciliatory enough.[34] Although there appears to be some evidence for this, there is also evidence to indicate that more than wishing for a more conciliatory voice in their editor, the new management wished for a more masculine one. With Hopkins's departure came some distinctly gender-marked changes in the magazine. Its covers stopped featuring portraits of race women and began promoting successful businessmen (figures 3 and 4). The magazine's content, although continuing to report events of interest to the race, offered far more profiles of successful businessmen than of exemplary women. The column 'Here and There' continued to appear, but it too featured men more frequently than women. A new column appeared entitled 'The Masonic Department,' edging out the regular reporting on women's clubs. This change in content influenced the readership, as indicated by the magazine's advertisements. No longer promoting beauty products such as hair straightener or skin lightener, the magazine ran ads for cigars, tailors, and real estate brokers.[35]

Whether these things are the cause or effect of Hopkins's leaving, we can say that with the withdrawal of Hopkins's influence, *The Colored American Magazine* no longer promoted the new black womanhood as it had under her leadership. Hopkins's work at this magazine, therefore, is important not only as an example of a woman of colour in a powerful literary position, but as an example of a woman using her literary position to promote the advancement of women and of her race.

8. 'Our Women and What They Think'

Amy Jacques Garvey, the New Negro Woman, and the Woman's Page of the Negro World

Barbara Bair

In September 1928, Amy Jacques Garvey (1896–1973) (figures 5 and 6) joined her husband Marcus Garvey in addressing an English audience from the podium at London's Century Theatre. Their respective speeches can be seen as representative of the political dialectic that had developed between nationalism and feminism within the Universal Negro Improvement Association (UNIA) or Garvey movement. The Garveys were on a public relations tour of London, Paris, Berlin, and Geneva on behalf of the UNIA, which had grown into an international Pan-African rights organization—then based in the United States and Jamaica (later, in the 1930s, it would be headquartered in London).

Amy Jacques Garvey spoke first, as the warm-up act for her husband. She began by pointedly noting both the time limitation set upon her and the cross-racial woman-to-woman intention of her message, observing 'I have been given 15 minutes to deliver a message from the Negro women of the world to the white women of England.' She proceeded to detail various forms of racial discrimination black women commonly experienced in London, and asked the white women listening to identify according to their gender and do what they could to end such acts of bias and shame. She concluded her speech with words directed expressly at the female members of the audience, forcefully implementing language of humanism, social justice, and equal rights:

> We appeal as black women and ask you to think twice and to remind your men that after all we are all human beings and, as the children of God, we deserve equal treatment, equal fairness, equal justice in common with all humanity.[1]

Marcus Garvey then rose. Building on the energy already created by his wife, he quoted from Shakespeare's *Julius Caesar* ('There is a tide in the affairs of men...')[2] and proceeded to give a lengthy oration—later released as a pamphlet—on statesmanship, the war, and racial oppression, outlining the basic principles of Africa for the Africans, the heart of the UNIA's anti-colonial platform, and criticizing American policy in Liberia.[3]

Back in New York, the UNIA's *Negro World* newspaper reported his speech as a 'classic' and said: 'Mrs Garvey also made a wonderful impression, and surpassed the English people in realizing that a Negro woman could speak with such force and conviction.'[4]

5. Portrait of
Amy Jacques Garvey, 1923

Originally founded as a benevolent society in Jamaica in 1914, the UNIA gained its political force out of the militant New Negro movement of the immediate post-First World War period, when black soldiers who had served the cause of democracy abroad were denied basic rights at home, and black people as a whole were subjected to repressive racial violence, including an upsurge in lynching and race riots. It took hold in Great Britain—in London, Liverpool, Manchester, and South Wales—primarily among men who had immigrated from West Africa and the West Indies to study or to work in the wartime shipyards and munitions plants. They enlisted as soldiers, merchant seamen, and labourers in the war effort. These black men found themselves, at war's end, facing long-term unemployment and discrimination as they were displaced from their work by the return of white soldiers, the postwar depression in the shipping industry, and the shift back to a peacetime economy. African repatriation, self-help, race pride, and the development of black business enterprise and Pan-African trade were major parts of Garveyism's widening appeal. Women as well as men were part of the movement. In the

6. Portrait of
Amy Jacques Garvey, 1925

United States and the Caribbean, women made up a large proportion of the membership of local divisions and were among its key officials.[5] But the masculine rhetoric and trappings of the war, and the concepts of sovereignty rights and empowered black manhood that the war had afforded, remained central to the dominant nationalist bent of the Garvey movement, and to the most radical aspects of its anti-colonial program.

When they made their 1928 tour of Europe, the Garveys were coming more or less fresh off their experience living in America. The year before, he had been released from prison and deported, and she had ended her stint editing the woman's page of the UNIA's newspaper in New York. They had come, by 1928, to embody closely related but distinct political stances within the Garvey movement. His was the dominant and highly masculinized 'race first' vision emphasizing militarism and nationalism, Pan-African unity, and colonial independence. Hers was a womanist perspective, emphasizing black women's ability and dignity and their partnership beside black men in the cause of racial advance. She vehemently shared the racial and anti-colonial militancy of her husband, but her politics were also deeply informed by a 'New Woman' appreciation of feminism and female potential that was largely missing from his world view. In her analysis of gender relations and the need for improvement of feminine status, she combined the liberal-individualistic premises basic to New Womanhood with older, more collective, social or domestic feminist perspectives. She applied these frameworks specifically to black women's experience and what she saw as black women's special callings in the cause of racial rights. Like many black women intellectuals and activists who preceded her, she—at least initially—emphasized black women's loyalty to and defence of embattled black men in racial uplift and advance, and the essential racial role black women played in giving birth to and carefully raising black children. Over time, as she accumulated experience as a woman activist within a male-dominated movement, she modified her perspectives, becoming more militantly feminist rather than less so. In the early 1920s, she honed her views for all readers to see as the editor of 'Our Women and What They Think', the woman's page of the *Negro World*. The first issue appeared in February 1924 and the page continued until April 1927. While Jacques Garvey used the page to present a full range of feminist-womanist and traditional perspectives, her own personal visions regarding the relative weight of race and gender in the push for greater freedom for women of colour underwent an evolution in the years that it appeared. She received support for her outspoken feminist analysis from other leading women organizers in the movement.

Conceptualizing a Forum for Women

Amy Jacques Garvey was decidedly a New Woman, one of the second generation of New Women who defied conventional private and domestic arrangements to follow their own pathways of self-actualization. Born and raised in a middle-class Afro-Caribbean family in urban Kingston, Jamaica, Jacques trained in stenography and accounting and worked as a legal assistant in a private law practice. At the end of the First World War, when she was twenty-two, she spurned her father's aspirations for her and emigrated as a single woman to New York. Soon after her arrival she attended a mass meeting of the UNIA at Liberty Hall in Harlem, and was swept away with enthusiasm as she heard fellow British West Indian Marcus Garvey deliver a rousing oration to a packed house. That meeting proved a turning point, showing Jacques a way to merge her desire for individual self-fulfillment with collective purpose by dedicating her abilities to the cause of racial rights.

Back home, the light-skinned, bourgeois, formally-educated Jacques would not have associated with the dark-skinned, working-class, largely self-educated Garvey. In America, she met him, she became his private secretary, his lover and close political confidante—and, in 1922, she married him. Their alliance was a powerful one, and it soon propelled Jacques Garvey into the public eye. She shifted quickly from being the supremely competent behind-the-scenes office manager of UNIA headquarters in

New York, to a place at the podium at UNIA meetings in Liberty Hall. She soon was the first woman on the editorial staff of the UNIA's influential newspaper, which at its height had an international circulation of 200,000, focused primarily in the United States, the Caribbean, Central America, and the British and French colonies of Africa. When her husband was convicted on politically motivated mail fraud charges in 1923 and incarcerated in Atlanta Federal Penitentiary in 1925, Jacques Garvey's fame and following expanded from New York onto the national arena. She went, somewhat reluctantly at first, and then with increasing determination and willfulness, from relative obscurity as the quiet, beautiful 'first lady' and loyal-wife figure behind the throne, into the direct limelight of public power and acclaim. Stepping in in the place of her politically martyred husband, she held no official office in the UNIA organization, but toughened into one of its leading organizers and proved an indomitable force in its affairs. Her broadbased influence as an editor began with her publication of the first of the two volumes of *The Philosophy and Opinions of Marcus Garvey*, which she compiled and edited in 1923, partly as one of many lobbying tools to use to win a federal pardon for Garvey. With the release of the second volume in 1925 (figure 7), she was recognized as the premier propagandist of the Garvey movement.[6] As she visited local divisions and lobbied federal officials on behalf of her husband's release from prison, she gained respect and was lauded by members of the UNIA at the grassroots level. Her voice was heard from stages around the country, as it would be later in the Caribbean and in England. By the mid-1920s, she was firmly accepted (and vilified) not only as a surrogate leader acting loyally on behalf of her husband, but as a leader in her own right.

A self-proclaimed feminist, Amy Jacques Garvey positioned herself early as a spokesperson for the women of the movement. In the same year that the *Negro World* became more multi-lingual, adding a Spanish-language and French page, Jacques Garvey introduced 'Our Women and What They Think'. The page was designed to serve as a forum for Garveyite women's thought and opinion, and as a clearinghouse to report women's activities in the hundreds of grassroots local divisions that had formed in the United States, Australia, Britain, West and South Africa, Central America, and the Caribbean. An advertisement that ran regularly on the page succinctly summed up the page's political intent while soliciting contributors: it urged, 'Women of [the] Negro Race! Let the World Know What You are Thinking and Doing.'[7]

Amy Jacques Garvey had multifarious political goals for the woman's page. She meant the page to display the importance of women's contributions within the movement (the 'doing'), and offer the opportunity for women to find their voices and express themselves with confidence in a way that would break boundaries of propriety, patriarchy, and secondary status (the 'thinking' for all the world to see). In a movement where women members made up the core if not the official leadership of local divisions, she wanted women's participation on the community level to be noted and recognized, rather than to go on invisibly. She asked women to report on what they and other women were doing on the grassroots level in their local divisions, hoping that these women would lend inspiration to one another and create an atmosphere of mutual sisterly encouragement for those female activists who might be working in relative isolation. She also wanted to generate greater general respect for women's minds, by emphasizing the value in revealing and sharing what it was ordinary women were thinking.

While maintaining certain standards for publication, she also hoped to move beyond the representation of a homogeneous, primarily middle-class, Anglocentric and neo-Victorian concept of the black woman activist to include the views and contributions of impoverished, rural, working-class, and non-English-speaking women of colour—whether they were UNIA members or not. 'Our Women' was designed in the abstract to be for Garveyites who were domestic and agricultural workers as well as urban office workers, teachers, or mothers, and for the hardworking immigrant labourer of Honduras or Nicaragua as well as the streetwise cosmopolitan girl of Harlem. The page, Jacques Garvey hoped, would reflect real debate, constructively incorporating disparate views among black women of various social statuses—including those who had been conventionally silenced through illiteracy, sexism, or poverty. By reprinting articles detailing a broad range of female achievements in careers, politics, and non-traditional walks of life, she would hearten women readers, especially young women, to follow their own dreams of self-attainment and recognize their responsibilities for working in their political and personal lives toward greater black empowerment, health, economic might, and self-esteem. And in the process of creating this forum of contributions and

7. *Negro World*, 3 January 1925, p.7

reprinted news, she and the women who participated would be tacitly demonstrating something about female intellect and female leadership ability to the men of the movement.

When Jacques Garvey outlined her goals for her readers, she detailed her vision that the page be simultaneously grassroots, multinational, cross-class, and multicultural in its scope. In doing so, she voiced a simple model of womanist political economy, or pan-womanist Pan-Africanism. 'It is our aim to encourage Negro women to express their views on subjects of interest to their communities, and particularly affecting our struggling race', she wrote. 'Our appeal is not only made to members of the UNIA,' she continued, 'but to all Negro women of all climes.' (figure 8) She encouraged contributions written in 'English, French, and Spanish' and she described the hoped-for secondary effect upon black men. 'By your expressions and opinions you will be able to help the race materially', she told potential women contributors. They would also help raise the standard of regard in which black men held black women. Utilizing the language of the black woman's club movement and religious and benevolent associations familiar to her readers, Jacques Garvey assured them that 'Our men will be inspired on reading our lofty ideals and aims; they will respect us the more when they learn of our activities for racial uplift, and our struggles and sufferings for the betterment and advancement of our children.'[8] She explained further that one of her primary goals for the page was the fostering of female empowerment, breaking boundaries between the domestic and public spheres:

> Usually a Woman's Page in any journal is devoted solely to dress, home hints and love topics, but our Page is unique, in that it seeks to give out the thoughts of our women on all subjects affecting them in particular and others in general. This pleases the modern Negro woman, who believes that God Almighty has not limited her intellect because of her sex, and that the helpful and instructive thoughts expressed by her in her home, with the aid of this page, could be read in thousand[s] of other homes and influence the lives of untold numbers.[9]

'Young ladies and old ladies, bobbed and unbobbed, we welcome your views'—she urged fellow black women of all ages and of either 'old' or 'new' persuasions—'and hope you will not hesitate to send in your copy.'[10]

Although the broad-based participatory goals Jacques Garvey had in mind in creating 'Our Women' were not realized in its three-and-a-half-year run, the page did prove to be a successful reader forum on gender within the movement. Jacques Garvey's husband voiced the dominant thrust of New Negro-era black nationalism when he told a Royal Albert Hall audience in June 1928, 'The negro is a man. We [the UNIA] represent the new negro.'[11] From the first inception of the woman's page, Amy Jacques Garvey made it clear to any who paid attention that the UNIA represented the New Negro Woman as well.

African Women Refuse to Hear Prince of Wales

PIETERSBURG, South Africa, June, 19—Prince of Wales attempted to deliver address here following review of assembly of natives, but was drowned out by protests of Zulu women. Native policemen, although threatening to beat them, if they weren't quiet, could not keep them silent.

8. *Negro World*, 4 July 1925, p.3

The New Negro Woman and the *Negro World*

As woman's page contributor Marie Trent put it, 'The Negro Woman of today truly represents the New Negro, with new powers of self-help, with new capacities, and with an intelligent insight into her own condition.'[12] Contributor Eunice Lewis observed that 'the New Negro Woman' is not a stay-at-home wife, but 'is bent on tackling those problems confronting the race.' She also signalled a change in gender relations. 'In a word,' Lewis wrote, 'the New Negro Woman is revolutionizing the old type of male leadership.'[13]

On the surface, 'Our Women and What They Think' had many things in common with woman's pages or editions of other black publications which had preceded or were contemporary with the *Negro World*, including Josephine St. Pierre Ruffin's *Woman's Era* and other writings associated with the 1890s black woman's club movement, and Pauline Hopkins's work for the *Colored American* in the first part of the century (see Sabina Matter-Seibel's and Jill Bergman's chapters in this collection). It was also not the only voice of New Negro womanhood among black radical publications of its time. In the summer before the woman's page began, an issue of A. Philip Randolph and Chandler Owen's socialist *Messenger* was dedicated to discussion of the New Negro Woman and her consciousness of

THE NEW WOMAN

In the Political World She Is the Source of All Reform Legislation and the One Power That Is Humanizing the World

9. Saydee E. Parham, 'The New Woman', *Negro World*, 2 February 1924, p.10

'her historic and noble mission of doing her bit toward the liberation of her people in particular and the human race in general.'[14] As Amy Jacques Garvey noted, 'Our Women and What They Think' had its recipe and home economics departments, and its scripture readings—standards of woman's pages and black women's religious newsletters elsewhere. More importantly, it served—through its contributed and reprinted articles, letters to the editor, poems, and organized reader forums—as a platform for cultural debates about race pride, new roles and relationships for black men and women, and revised definitions of black manhood and womanhood.

The page was fuelled through most of its run by Jacques Garvey's powerful editorials. Over time, her editorial focus shifted from the standard 'women's' intellectual territory of mothering and child welfare issues, much in evidence in her work in 1924, to more militant editorials on nationalist and anti-colonial topics, political economy, foreign policy, and international affairs. She wrote increasingly with no holds barred, and was often more hard-hitting than the men in these 'men's' areas. The reprinted articles she headlined on the page bolstered the radical slant of her editorials. She presented news of independence and sovereignty movements in Palestine, India, South Africa, and Ireland, highlighted advances for labour, and chronicled abuses under the British colonial system in the Caribbean and Africa. Articles profiled the status of women in Turkey, Greece, Japan, China, India, the Philippines, Latin America and the Soviet Union. The ancient civilizations of Egypt and Ethiopia were celebrated. Jacques Garvey also tenaciously tackled difficult subjects about the internal gender dynamics of the UNIA.

The inaugural issue of the woman's page, published on 2 February 1924, dealt explicitly with the phenomenon of the New Woman. The lead story, 'Labor at the British Helm,' on Ramsay Macdonald coming to power, appeared where Amy Jacques Garvey's editorial column would soon be located. It was matched by one about Macdonald's daughter, 'The New Mistress of 10 Downing Street', in which she was described as a New Woman more interested in science, physics, and social welfare than in housekeeping. An article entitled 'The New Woman' (figure 9) was written by New York Garveyite Saydee Parham, a young law student who was a frequent woman's page contributor. In it Parham argued that the New Woman was the natural outcome of human evolution toward an improved order of things, and had 'actually become the central figure of all modern civilization':

In the business world, she is the master of the clerical detail work; in the factories she is the dynamo of production; in the theatre she is the most magnetic form of entertainment; in the political world she is the source of all reform legislation and the one power that is humanizing the world. In all great movements for the redemption of the oppressed masses, she is always ready and responsive to the great appeal, and this power generated by this great civilizer of all future civilization is the new woman![15]

The banner article that ran next to the Parham piece countered the usual assumption that the equal rights emphasis of Alice Paul's National Woman's Party was necessarily alienating to black women. The story, entitled 'Women's Party Wants not Only Equal Rights, but Equal Responsibilities with Men', profiled bills introduced into the New York state legislature calling for the removal of legal restrictions upon woman and an end to her subjection in marriage and the workplace. The article observed regretfully that 'Only the poverty of the English language in the matter of pronouns with a dual gender made [makes] it necessary to use the pronoun "he" in referring to both men and women.'[16] Parallel to the National Woman's Party piece ran an article called 'Our Girls' by another New York Garveyite who would prove a regular contributor, UNIA clerk-stenographer Carrie Leadett. She pondered the future promise for educated New Negro Girls she saw all around her 'on Lenox Avenue with her [their] paint and powder', and worried that these girls, followers of fads and fashion, so eager to bob their hair and shorten their skirts, would become so self-absorbed in following that they would fail to develop the necessary skills for leading.[17]

In counterpoint to Leadett's critique, the next article, 'African Ladies are Leaders in Fashion', described the beautiful clothing found upon ancient Egyptian mummies recently discovered by archaeologists. Two of the five advertisements on the page featured women's clothing in 'The Very

Latest Style', one advertising the new pleated skirts, a must-have because 'Everybody is wearing them.'[18] The page wrapped up with the weekly scriptural reference, chosen to inspire from both a spiritual and a political perspective. Taken from the book of Zephaniah (*chap.2, v.1*) it was: 'Gather Together, O nation not desired.'[19]

This first page set the tone for the types of articles and the departments that would be featured alongside Jacques Garvey's editorials for the duration of the woman's page. Highlighted by their overall prevalence on the page throughout its run were stories of New Women entering public life, being elected for office or as delegates within political parties, and gaining access to male-dominated careers and professions. Historic black female role models such as Cleopatra, Harriet Tubman, and Sojourner Truth were profiled—'New' Women of their own ages. Regular news of England spotlighted white women running as candidates for Parliament, working in the Labour government, bobbing their hair to fit it more easily under their barrister wigs, and attacking the glass ceiling at Scotland Yard. Labour candidate Cynthia Mosley's trip to America and opinions on unemployment were covered, as was Margaret Bondfield's career, and Emmeline Pankhurst's views on suffrage, birth control and the 'de-sexing' of American politics.[20]

The page was filled with news of the attainments of individual women lawyers, doctors, dentists, politicians, business leaders, investors, inventors, scientists, engineers, and airplane pilots—even spies and explorers—all offered up for readers to emulate, as well as stories of women gaining power within their church governing bodies or access to the pulpit. The page carried news of struggles for women's legal rights and labour rights, and covered the issues of unionization of household workers, wages for housework, and discrimination against waitresses and wage workers. It addressed the potential power of black women as consumers in helping to dictate the success or failure of black-owned enterprises, their ability to start small businesses themselves, and their influence implementing the consumer boycott, or 'don't buy where you can't work' campaigns, against stores and restaurants that did not hire or serve black people.

The page also addressed the private sphere, and the ways that the racial politics of the UNIA intersected with personal choices. Marriage, motherhood, and child raising were popular topics. Contributors to reader forums debated such issues as whether women should be required to use the word 'obey' in the marriage ceremony or keep their maiden name, and whether men, like women, should wear a wedding ring.[21] Giving birth to and carefully raising black children was considered as a racial duty, part and parcel of other forms of racial activism that counteracted racial repression and genocide, and helped ensure black survival. 'The hand that rocks the cradle rules the world' perspective loomed large,—or, as Garveyite women liked to put it, 'the women make the nation.'[22] As one subtitle of a headline put it, 'Negro Women Should Encourage Motherhood and Let Their Race Live'.[23] Both women and men weighed in on the issue of whether women's participation in careers or public life compromised their roles as wives and mothers.

And readers emphasized that racial domesticity should not be seen as the New Negro Woman's only function. Lest women go overboard in idealizing home life, Garveyite Eunice Lewis of Chicago observed:

There are many people who think that a woman's place is only in the home—to raise children, cook, wash, and attend to the domestic affairs of the house. This idea, however, does not hold true with the New Negro Woman. The true type of the New Negro Woman is bent on tackling those problems confronting the race.[24]

Lewis went on to outline some of the proper roles of the New Negro Woman, including working 'on a par with men in the office as well as on the platform' and demanding 'absolute respect from men of all races.'[25] Lewis's letter was pointedly intraracial in its impact, implicitly challenging the men of the movement to reform their own attitudes to adjust to a revised model of womanhood. 'In a word', she concluded, 'the New Negro Woman is revolutionizing the old type of male leadership.'[26] The little poem she attached above her signature line ended with quite a *double entendre*:

We are women of the newer type,
Striving to make our Race sublime -
Conscious that the time is ripe,
To put our men on the firing linc![27]

WHAT WE BELIEVE

The Universal Negro Improvement Association advocates the uniting and blending of all Negroes into one strong, healthy race. It is against miscegenation and race suicide.

It believes that the Negro race is as good as any other, and therefore should be as proud of itself as others are.

It believes in the purity of the Negro race and the purity of the white race.

It is against rich blacks marrying poor whites.

It is against rich or poor whites taking advantage of Negro women.

It believes in the spiritual Fatherhood of God and the Brotherhood of Man.

It believes in the social and political physical separation of all peoples to the extent that they promote their own ideals and civilization, with the privilege of trading and doing business with each other. It believes in the promotion of a strong and powerful Negro nation in Africa.

It believes in the rights of all men.

UNIVERSAL NEGRO IMPROVEMENT ASSOCIATION
MARCUS GARVEY, Founder and President-General

10. Credo of the UNIA, *Negro World*, 27 November 1926, p.4

The gender dialectic that emerged over the years on the page mixed older, chivalric, visions involving the protection and idealization of women and the affording to them of certain privileges, with emphasis on the abilities and opportunities of women and their claim to certain rights. The first vision was the dominant line in the movement overall, most favoured in the rhetoric of Marcus Garvey. The latter vision emerged as the dominant one on the woman's page. There were liberal feminists primarily interested in individual attainments, and social feminists believing in women's special call to enter public life in order to purify the political sector and serve as advocates for social reform.

11. *Negro World*, 16 October 1926, p.6

In between these was what can best be described—as Elsa Barkley Brown, Alice Walker, and others have termed it—a 'womanist' vision, or companionate model, emphasizing women's racial partnership and unity with black men, and the empowerment and creativity that emerges among black women working in sisterhood with one another.

The womanist viewpoint was particularly strong among women who heralded Marcus Garvey as a leader-hero and who were attracted to the unifying 'race first' and Pan-African concepts of the Garvey movement and its Back-to-Africa platform (figure 10). Liberal feminists emphasized instead the parallel integrity, or equality, of women and men, the liberation this perspective promised for women, and the ways men's own lives could benefit from revised gender relations. The essential sameness of men and women, as expressed in the editorial 'No Sex in Brains and Ability',[28] rather than the belief in the essential differences between genders held by those of the social housekeeping point of view, was to these writers a plus rather than a liability—and one that did not diminish, but rather enhanced, femininity. For them, male and female members of the movement as well as wives and husbands could exist pragmatically side-by-side as complementary friends and companions rather than in any relative relation of hierarchy or service.

Carrie Leadett informed readers that 'Modern Men Want Sensible Pal-Wives'[29] and Amy Jacques Garvey also liked to use the word 'pal' to describe good gender relations between men and women. A contributor known only as 'Vera' wrote in about 'The Kind of Girl Men Like.' She contrasted modern and old-fashioned girls, and observed that while the last generation longed 'to be the mistress of a home...the modern girl's ambitions are not limited to home-making alone, but to law-making and every line of endeavor that tends to the betterment of humanity.' While the old girl planned for marriage, the New Girl had platonic friendships with men, and faced the world 'with a new spirit, a new determination.'[30]

The woman's page was often satirical and funny. Jacques Garvey reprinted, tongue-in-cheek, cautionary tales about the dangers of modern womanhood. Male experts warned of the New Woman turning 'mannish' as she flattened her breasts in order to wear the latest flapper styles or sought to challenge men in business or sports, and of bitter consequences for generations to come, as women driving motor vehicles instead of walking would warp their pelvises and thus increase the incidence of Caesarian deliveries, and women bobbing their hair would condemn their daughters to having beards and moustaches like men.[31]

There were also issues of class and cultural bias at work on the page, including in the reactions of old-style New Women against the modernism of the New Girl. While Jacques Garvey sought to make the page more than an outlet for middle-class positions, she was hampered by the fact that many Garveyite women had little education and their submissions were deemed unprintable. Although she encouraged these women to go to teachers in their communities for help drafting their contributions, the middle-class voice continued to predominate.[32] Both middle- and working-class proponents of Victorian propriety and dignified racial uplift disparaged the wanton black woman who danced and drank alcohol. Contributors chided mothers who left their children alone on doorsteps while they frequented dance halls, pool rooms, and movie houses flaunting their sexuality, and warned that they would do better to be home reading to their children of Harriet Tubman or Toussaint L'Ouverture.[33] To these women, who had long sought to countermand racism through fostering self-dignity, and had sacrificed many of their own personal ambitions for the good of the whole, the hedonism and self-centredness on display in the New Girl was disturbing because of what it did to black children, but also because it seemed to fulfil the very Jezebel-style white stereotypes about black female promiscuity that they had spent their lifetimes countermanding. The liberated dance hall life was also associated with race mixing, which was definitely anathema within the Garvey movement. At issue was racial as well as sexual purity.

Both the supposedly 'old' and 'new' models of womanhood debated on the 'Our Women' page were largely 'new' for the masses of black women, and indeed were radical in implication from a racial rights standpoint. The pedestal could look awfully good to a woman who has never been on one, and supporting one's man has a whole different meaning when one's man is being lynched or economically emasculated. While the privileged white woman might long to escape the limitations of home life or monogamy for sexual liberation or a career, the black woman often longed to escape the white woman's kitchen for a home of her own and the chance to devote her time to her own children. And while white New Women were interested in the freedoms of a more open sexuality and birth control, many New Negro Women were interested in the privileges of giving birth to and raising healthy black babies, and avoiding the sexual harassment of employers. Maternalism was not discussed as a limitation for them but a desire and a duty, part of their responsibility for perpetuating the race and circumventing white discrimination and violence.

A more liberated sexuality was seen by many New Negro Women, however, as part of young women's greater overall opportunities. 'Joy' was a word that contributors often associated with the greater options of New Womanhood, including sexual manifestations. Contributor Mabel

12. *Negro World*, 16 October 1926, p.6

Douglas's article 'Emancipated Womanhood: The New Woman Has Overstepped the Home Boundary and Is Serving All Humanity: The Toy-Wife Transformed Into the Joy-Wife' argued that the broader roles for the New Woman could prove uplifting for their men in all ways. The New Woman develops her body as well as her mind, Douglas reminded men, and 'refuses to be the "block-of-ice" type, as her predecessors have been typified.'[34]

Sex was related to beauty. Advertisements on the woman's page promoted various types of self-care and self-help, from dress and cosmetics, to chiro-practory, employment, or the purchase of a pistol ('accurate, hard hitting…a real woman's gun') for self-defence.[35] The page typically carried ads for treatments for hair and skin, alongside ads for flapper-style dresses. The largest long-running ad was for Society Face Beautifier, a cold cream lightener that promised to 'Satisfy your DESIRE for a brighter skin'—with the word DESIRE printed in big block letters. On the surface, these ads might be seen as promoting white concepts of beauty. One could see especially those of the 16 October 1926 issue that way, in which five of the seven ads that included illustrations featured pictures of seemingly white women. One ad was for a facial appliance that promised to 'reduce protruding, prominent, thick unshapely lips to ["]normal["]', and another, for Nelson's Hair Dressing, which showed a smoothly coiffed woman 'No Longer Ashamed of Her Hair' (figures 12–13). These ads implied that as the working-class black woman improved herself, her hair would become straighter, her clothing more fashionable, and her skin whiter. But they were also about something else. They were about caring for the self, and being cared for. These ads proclaimed that black women can be, and are, beautiful, elegant, and desirable, and that not just rich women, but poor women—women who laboured under hot sun in cotton fields, stripped tobacco in factories, or spent long hours bending and lifting over laundry tubs—deserved products that helped preserve the beauty of their skin (figure 11). They matched ads for pretty black—versus white—dolls and headlines of woman's page articles like 'Lovely Woman, Be a Goddess', 'Believe in Yourself', and Amy Jacques Garvey's 'I am a Negro—and beautiful' editorials.[36] They helped make the woman's page the forerunner of the self-love content of our present-day *Essence* or *Oprah* magazines, and they matched glamorous Liberty Hall events in which Garveyite women, as members of the Royal Court of Ethiopia auxiliary, paraded in elegant evening gowns and tiaras. They played in painful juxtaposition against articles decrying black men's penchant for white women and desertion of black wives as undesirable. And they contrasted to essays on the vulnerability of black domestic workers to white employers' sexual advances, and white society's daily stereotyping of black women as either outside the realm of desire—as bumpkin mammies in aprons—or all too desirable—as promiscuous seducers.

A closer look also reveals that these ads were often about women using their dollars as consumers to support women's labour and women's businesses (figure 14). The skin beautifier and hair ads were sometimes about recruiting women to work as agents for the products. Some included the addresses of local distributors and of women-owned beauty shops. Other ads featured women-owned businesses, including that of Dr Ethel May Brown, Chiropodist, who promised to bring relief to the aching feet of women who worked standing up all day, and whose lives contained little leisure.[37] An ad for Aunt Lydia's Wash Day Wonder, a laundry soap with bleach, was described as a 'colored washerwoman's discovery' which would decrease the amount of rubbing necessary to produce adequate results, and thus lessen laundry workers' physical labour.[38] These ads were all expressions of desire—sexual desire, desire for beauty and to be beheld as beautiful, desire to make a living in ways that did not involve working in white households, desire for fine things, and desire for relief, physical and emotional. They matched one of the favourite scriptural messages of Garveyism: 'I am black but comely, O ye daughters of Jerusalem' (*Sol. 1:5*).

Women Warriors

Most of the ambitious goals that Amy Jacques Garvey had for the woman's page were not met. She grew increasingly tired and frustrated—frustrated with women who did not contribute, and frustrated with the sexism of men who refused to let women enter the ranks of leadership or pay attention to what they had to say, who failed as breadwinners, and who did not have the gumption to keep up the militancy of the UNIA program. The early 'womanist' emphasis on companionate marriage as a model for political partnership between black men and women, or a surrogacy model in which black women stood in for black men hampered by restrictions and racism, gave way on the page to a more militant feminism in which the male side was largely stripped from the equation. Women UNIA leaders wrote angrily of being tired of waiting for men to step in to do their part, and of their intention of demanding their own rights, and of supplanting the men. The rhetoric of loving wives and friendly pals gave way to that of angry, armed Amazons and Woman Warriors.

Like the British suffragettes, the Garveyite women seized upon Joan of Arc as their model of the woman crusader, spearheading a wave of change.

'[I]f our men hesitate…then the women of the race must come forward, they must join the great army of Amazons and follow a Joan of Arc who is willing to be burned at the stake to save her country. Africa must be saved!', UNIA organizer Henrietta Vinton Davis wrote to the woman's page.[39] Davis was often referred to as a black Joan of Arc within the UNIA. Fellow female organizer M.L.T. De Mena, who later appeared like Joan of Arc atop a white horse, with sword in hand, at the front of a UNIA convention parade in the Caribbean, wrote in to the page that women were done politely 'lauding our men through the press, on the platform, and, in fact, from every angle' when 'in reality the backbone and sinew of the Universal Negro Improvement Association has been and is the real women of the organization.'[40] On the same page as De Mena's letter, Amy Jacques Garvey

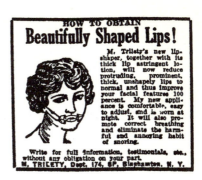

13. *Negro World,*
16 October 1926, p.6

14. *Negro World,*
17 November 1926, p.7

pointedly reprinted an article headlined 'Woman Suffrage' detailing the dates in which women had won the vote in countries around the world, beginning in 1893 with New Zealand and extending to Sweden and Turkey in the 1920s. Like De Mena, Amy Jacques Garvey had had it with the glass ceiling in the top echelons of the movement, and the narrow roles proscribed for women within the sexual division of labour in local branches. She served notice on the men that women were demanding equal opportunity to seize any position within the organization 'or anywhere else without discrimination because of sex' and apologized 'if it hurts your old-fashioned tyrannical feelings.'[41] Instead of conciliatory 'woman-the-vine' and 'man-the-oak-tree' models emphasizing male strength and female support, Jacques Garvey wrote of men clinging like 'barnacles,' serving as 'stumbling blocks,' and 'sticking like leaches', impeding the progress of women.[42]

Both the militant nationalist platform and the black feminist agenda with which it intersected within the UNIA were about hope in the new—a belief in upward cycles of civilization, in progress, and, as the name of the organization itself evoked, improvement, toward greater emancipation, independence, and more perfect social justice. The problem that Amy Jacques Garvey and the other women who contributed to the 'Our Women' page ran up against was what New Negro Women could do when their own evolution seemed to outstrip that of their men's.

III In a Different Voice

9. Elizabeth Robins, the 'New Woman' Novelist, and the Writing of Literary Histories of the 1890s

Sue Thomas

Elizabeth Robins's place in feminist theatre history of the 1890s has been carefully argued on grounds of her celebrated theatrical performances in Ibsen roles, her career as actress-manager, and her anonymous authorship, with Florence Bell, of the controversial play featuring infanticide *Alan's Wife* (1893).[1] In histories of New Woman fiction, however, Robins (1862–1952) is usually either ignored or positioned as 'vehemently, almost violently reactionary' against the New Woman[2] on the strength largely of *George Mandeville's Husband* (1894), published under the pseudonym C.E. Raimond. In this, scholars generally follow Elaine Showalter's lead in *A Literature of Their Own* (1977). During the 1890s *The New Moon* (1895), stories in *Below the Salt* (1896), and *The Open Question: A Tale of Two Temperaments* (1898) were characterized by a fair number of reviewers as New Woman fiction, *The Open Question* especially so as a belated example of its main genre, the problem novel. In this essay, I problematize the ways in which Robins as novelist and short story writer has been represented in histories of the New Woman, and detail of the narrative of radical 'rupture' which often structures literary histories of New Woman fiction. In this narrative the New Woman is characterized as 'a break with the past, with convention, and even with nature'.[3] I analyze here the manner in which the moral panic over the New Woman was played out in the reception of Robins's first published story 'A Lucky Sixpence', and her novels *George Mandeville's Husband* and *The Open Question*. I am particularly interested in where the modernity of Robins's texts is located by reviewers, how this is articulated in relation to standards of aesthetic value, and in the reviewers' address to particular moral constituencies. I work not only to extend and challenge historiographical placings of Robins,[4] but also to suggest that accounts of New Woman writing and the historicity of its radicalism are based on readings of too narrow a range of critical material from the 1890s.

My analysis is grounded in a conceptualization of the discourses that circulated around the 'New Woman' in the 1890s as a moral panic. The New Woman and New Woman fiction had become by 1895 stock and contested symbols of the modernity of the *fin de siècle*; '[b]y early 1897, the New Woman had faded as a contested icon in British culture'.[5] The naming of the New Woman, usually traced to Ouida in the *North American Review* in May 1894,[6] 'prised open a discursive space for her'. In her Foucauldian history of the figure Sally Ledger productively identifies a conservative dominant discourse and a more radical '"reverse" discourse' in which 'the New Woman began to speak on her own behalf', a speech with its 'own internal contradictions and limitations as well as…considerable feminist credentials'.[7] These discourses 'energiz[ed] and shap[ed]' a moral panic over the modernity attributed to the New Woman and its perceived cultural and sociopolitical implications. Simon Watney has argued that 'moral panics do not speak to a "silent majority" which is simply "out there" waiting to listen. Rather they provide the raw materials, in the form of words and images, of those moral constituencies with which individual subjects are encouraged to identify their deepest interest and their very core of being'.[8]

According to Arthur Waugh, who had been assistant editor of the *New Review*, the anonymous publication of Robins's 'A Lucky Sixpence' in the January 1894 number brought 'vehement protests from a number of subscribers' and he 'always believed that the *Review* never recovered from the shock'.[9] In inaugurating a new series of the journal with the January 1894 number, the editor Archibald Grove announced the desire 'to widen the scope, and in every way to modernize *The New Review*'.[10] This special announcement framed press comment on the inclusion of 'A Lucky Sixpence', a story that highlights the sexual and economic vulnerability of a servant, Hester, and her mistress Mrs Baily. The figure of modernity in the story is Mrs Baily, who is given to 'nervous rage' produced by anxieties over the effects of her husband's financial speculations on domestic income.[11] Her performance of her '*character role*' as respectable housewife[12] entails the conspicuous consumption of leisure and knowledge, reading 'books, French books' and an 'endless succession of yellow-backed novels'.[13] She also 'harr[ies]…a single callow girl whose life' is 'a chronicle of interminable labor',[14] withheld wages and threats to turn her out without money or a character reference—a situation Hester's experienced servant friend Sarah terms slavery, a violation of British birthright. The domestic alliance Hester forms with kindlier Mr Baily against her mistress renders her vulnerable to seduction and impregnation by him, and bullying to deny his paternity of the foetus. The 'fragments of low-voiced reconciliation' between the Bailys founded on Hester's 'poor little trembling lie' about paternity is metonymic of the fragility of modern middle-class marriage.[15] The *Illustrated London News* speculated, possibly on the strength of rumours about the soon to be published *Esther Waters*, that the author was George Moore and that the story was 'a chapter from a novel'; Robins's disclaiming of authorship was reported in the *Leicester Daily Post* on 19 March.

Ann Ardis argues that '[o]nly *after* 1894 will aesthetics be of primary concern in discussions' of New Woman fiction, that 'literary texts were evaluated in the 1880s and early 1890s as "agents of cultural formation", not as works of art whose formal complexity was to be admired'.[16] This is not borne out unequivocally in the reception of 'A Lucky Sixpence'.[17] The dominant aesthetic standard against which Robins's first published piece of fiction was measured was the affect the story produced in the reader. The most common descriptors for this affect were 'painful',[18] 'powerful',[19] and 'pathetic',[20] as in 'pathetic interest'.[21] The critical appeal is to an expressive realism, the ability of the author to convey her or his perception of the material;[22] the aesthetic register, pathos, invites sympathetic identification with Hester. The modernity of the story was located in its treatment of a 'delicate subject in a most tactful and artistic manner' and its being a 'fresh rendering of one of the oldest and saddest of stories', 'more powerful than pleasant', 'undeniably objectionable', 'nasty', and 'disagreeable'.[23] The number of comments that emphasize a negative moral affect is counterbalanced by reviews that praise the quality of the writing, with cleverness being emphasized.[24] In religious and some provincial papers it is the prospective cultural influence of the story's candour that is appraised. The *Church Times*, for example, acknowledged the story's morally educative function, describing it as 'dealing with that seamy side of life which must now and then be forced before the eyes of rich and poor alike'.[25]

'A Lucky Sixpence' was collected in Robins's volume of short stories *Below the Salt*, but it and the story ''Gustus Frederick'[26]—both potentially controversial—were dropped for the book's U.S. publication as *The Fatal Gift of Beauty and Other Stories* (1896). Reviewers of *Below the Salt* who commented on 'A Lucky Sixpence' used realism as more of a critical yardstick, which suggests that between 1894 and 1896 the moral panic over the candour of New Woman fiction became in aesthetic terms more narrowly localized. In the *British Weekly* the story was described as 'merely a hard, cruel photograph of vulgar sin', a view consonant with Arthur Waugh's severe reservations in 'Reticence in Literature' about the way in which the pursuit of 'an indomitable and damning sincerity' causes 'art' to be 'lost in photography'.[27] The *Pall Mall Gazette*'s reviewer found the story 'sustainedly cool, remorsely honest, unutterably cruel'; in *Vanity Fair* it was characterized as 'grimly realistic' (while James Whistler's cover design for the book, silver frigates in sail, was designated 'a model of good taste'). Arnold Bennett, writing as 'Barbara' in *Woman*, admired Robins's 'studies of servant life', commending both their 'high' 'artistic value' and their moral affect in extending 'one's sympathies' across class lines. In the first overview of Robins's development as a writer, 'Some Younger Reputations' (1898), he would concentrate on the artistry of the stories and their technical range.[28] The 'destabilising democratic tendencies' of the authorial voice[29] were thought to be outspoken enough in their 'almost brutal realism' to 'probably offend the fastidious' by the *Manchester Guardian*, a fastidiousness perhaps exemplified by the reviewer for the *Academy*:

> The constant petty dependence on the smaller wishes of other people is wearisome to study, and in this case this element is increased by the fact that the 'masters' and 'mistresses' are almost invariably stupid and vulgar; you are compelled to look at the characters of servants from the point of view of the narrow sympathies and underbred prejudices of the people who are made to discourse of them—people who are without the elementary qualification for the discussion, forgetfulness of class 'superiority'.[30]

Showalter characterizes *George Mandeville's Husband* as 'a denunciation of pseudointellectual women novelists and a satire on George Eliot';[31] for

Ardis the novel is dispiriting evidence of the fact that the 'delegitimation of female ambition was effected by women as well as men in the 1890s'.[32] 'George Mandeville' is the pseudonym of Lois Wilbraham, a mediocre, self-absorbed writer, who fashionably espouses 'the cause of Progress...the banner of Women's Emancipation'. The gap between her public persona and her domestic performance is exposed in indifference towards her 'exceptionally puny and ailing' daughter Rosina, who shows no signs of a 'precocious intelligence' that might have energized her maternal feeling.[33] *George Mandeville's Husband* was, for the most part, read as a satire not on Eliot, but on the 'lady novelist', the 'advanced woman' or the 'New Woman', but one that in terms of these horizons of generic intelligibility was wanting in artistic decorum and discrimination. Reviewers who speculated on the sex of 'C.E. Raimond' generally assumed that the author was male, citing as grounds the animus shown towards 'George Mandeville' or the perceived conservatism of the author's views on modern women's place. Ralph C. Elliott points out that the satirist's audience

> must share...commitment to certain intellectual and moral beliefs which validate his critique of aberration. Ridicule... depends on certain shared assumptions against which the aberrant stands in naked relief. The greatest s. [satire] has been written in periods when ethical and rational norms were sufficiently powerful to attract widespread assent, yet not so powerful as to compel absolute conformity.[34]

The satirical voice of *George Mandeville's Husband* did not strike a particularly common chord with the 'intellectual and moral beliefs' and aesthetic values of reviewers; nor, publication figures suggest, with reading publics of the day. By December 1900 2,140 copies had been sold; after 1 February 1895 no copies were sold.[35] Robins's satire was decried as 'overweight[ed]' against 'George Mandeville', partisanly 'caustic', 'too much exaggerated', exhibiting unjustified 'ferocity', and 'too powerful in places'.[36] The *Daily News* reviewer thought it 'exceedingly clever; but the vehement aversion of the author for the heroine mars it as a work of art'. In the *Speaker* the author was said to have weakened the 'blow struck at the modern woman' by the 'extravagance' of the satire. The *Bookman* critic complained that 'too much temper' was shown 'George Mandeville' 'and the situation is lop-sided'. In

Woman Arnold Bennett described 'George Mandeville' as 'much-mauled' by the author, and in this 'here and there' 'steal[ing] our sympathies'; in 1898 he said that the novel is 'marred, in point of art, by the ferocity of the satire with which "George Mandeville" was pursued and almost persecuted'. The *Christian Leader* was loud in denouncing 'New Woman' writers, 'these female novelists who have caught the public taste by their lack of literature and their lack of art, and who are doing their best to profane in the name of morality so much that is pure and simple',[37] but the critic's ambivalence about C.E. Raimond's authorial voice is evident in her or his labelling of its viscerality a 'venting' of 'his spleen'.[38]

In 'Reticence in Literature' Waugh vindicates the satire of Hogarth as an instance of 'drawing life as we find it, sternly and relentlessly, surveying it all the while from outside with the calm, unflinching gaze of criticism'. He juxtaposes this with 'yielding ourselves to the warmth and colour of its [life's] excesses, losing our judgment in the ecstasies of the joy of life, becoming, in a word, effeminate'.[39] His essay is now read as inaugurating '"the hale and hearty" school of literary criticism',[40] part of a 'reaction formation'[41] against the candour of New Woman writers.[42] His views on the effeminization of British culture are not representative of those of a wider intellectual community of critics and reviewers. Reviewers of *George Mandeville's Husband* identified excess in the novel's satirical voice, but did not process this excess emotion (causticity, 'ferocity', vehemence, 'temper') as effeminate. What is being violated by the satirical voice is an aestheticized standard of middle-class gentility and, for some reviewers, middle-class chivalry towards women. The voice is, given assumptions of the maleness of the author, operating outside the codes of 'moral' or 'domestic manliness' which developed in the nineteenth century,[43] and in this not exhibiting the fine sensibility prized in expressive realism.

The feminism of the novel is carried in Robins's treatment of Rosina and her relations with her parents. The indifference 'George Mandeville' shows towards her daughter challenges the assumption that 'all women possessed a "maternal instinct"'. In the generic register of pathos, Robins 'protests against the restrictive upbringing of girls and the inadequacies of their education' and the possible psychological consequences of 'ignorance about corporeal facts'—familiar concerns of pro-New Woman fiction.[44] A couple of reviewers highlighted originality in Robins's treatment of Rosina.

Jerome K. Jerome in *To-day*, for example, highlights a 'new *motif*—paternal affection takes the place of courtship and marriage'. Robins's ironization of Ralph Wilbraham's conservatism is carried principally in this plot. His denunciation of women's ambition beyond the home and playing the part of muse and scathing comments on George Eliot to his daughter are clearly motivated by his disgust at his wife, rather than being grounded in rational thought. The *Daily Telegraph*'s critic acknowledged that his 'so terribly masculine' views on female emancipation are 'his only kind of revenge' at his wife.[45] Ironically his love for Rosina is conditional on his ability to make her as different from her mother as possible. The chill that eventually kills Rosina, which compounds her distress at her mother assuming sufficient intimacy to tell her some facts of life, is exacerbated when she attends a rehearsal of an adaptation of one of her mother's novels for the stage. For all his protestations of concern for her health her father is easily distracted by a self-pitying vision of gender anarchy, in which new men take the part of oppressed Cinderellas with no fairy godmother in sight:

> 'the New Woman, if she has come to stay, will bear new men, who will sit in the chimney-corner while the girls go forth to war.' …In every quarter of this vast London were hordes of toiling, struggling women, waging the great economic war, to the peril of their bodies and their souls. Gods! What a spectacle, when one thinks of it!…He saw in imagination the woman horde advancing—taking by storm offices, shops, studios, and factories, each fighting with desperate success for a 'place', whether in a learned profession or on top of an omnibus. Competing with men in every corner of industrial life, jostling them in the streets, preaching to them, clamouring against them—crying 'Anathema!' at street corners, and 'Woe! Woe!' from the house-tops.[46]

The catastrophic outcome of this self-pity for Rosina retroactively points up her father's self-absorption in his larger relationship with her. The awfulness of the scope Ralph Wilbraham's sentimental vision of women's place allows Rosina is brought out in her deathbed fever. She anxiously raves that she could earn a living by her only clevernesses, plain sewing and jail-window darning. Ralph aroused the irked impatience of quite a few reviewers who found him unmanly in various ways: 'play[ing] the part of domestic acquiescence', 'passive', 'too weak', 'meek', 'rather invertebrate and weak-willed', 'very weak and somewhat of a maunderer', 'a despicable coward, who lacks the courage, not merely to preserve his own self-respect, but even to save his daughter from a heartless marriage'.[47] In the *Woman's Signal* his failings were held to signal the arrival of the New Man, whose 'only spirit' was 'the spirit of condemnation'.[48]

The several horizons of generic intelligibility in *The Open Question: A Tale of Two Temperaments* ground the mixed critical response to it. The novel was read principally as comprising a set of character studies, but also as a naturalistic family saga, a *Bildungsroman* with Val Gano as major protagonist (here on occasion inviting comparison with Sarah Grand's *The Beth Book* and *The Heavenly Twins* and George Eliot's *The Mill on the Floss*),[49] and as a problem novel. The 'problem-motive'[50]—consanguineous marriage in an U.S. family with hereditary tubercular tendencies, and the ethics of suicide—created controversy. The artistry of the character studies,[51] the narrative complexities of the saga,[52] and the *Bildungsroman* of childhood and adolescence earned extraordinary praise, artistic 'genius' being acknowledged frequently.[53] Robins's characterization of Sarah Gano, Val's stoic grandmother, was universally admired. The praise for the character studies often used portraiture art as a reference point, for example, the 'character-drawing showed fine psychologic insight'; 'the style is clear, precise, and cameo-like in its finish'; 'Mrs Gano is a living photograph'; a 'magnificent portrait'.[54] W. L. Courtney's complaint in attempting to produce 'a new, "virile" standard of aesthetic value'[55] that 'individual studies of character' were a sign of an inartistic 'feminine note in fiction'[56] was an isolated one. C. E. Raimond's development of the problem theme was generally described using the discourse of decadence familiar from earlier controversy over New Woman fiction, and was characterized as inartistic.[57] Morbid and morbidity[58] were frequent descriptors of this dimension of the novel; this discourse drew out, in particular, the ambivalence of critical response, as the 'living' qualities of the character studies were often emphasized. For Robins's contemporaries the novel 'lived' through five British editions by 1915. The novel's decadence was pointedly linked by the critic for the religious paper the *Guardian*, who praised Robins's 'flashes of startling genius and rare insight', with 'shallow commonplaces from the hackneyed répertoire of the eclectic agnosticism of literary London'. The implied reference point in the novel for the distinction between the originality of genius and the merely derivative artist is a comment the authorial voice makes about Ethan Gano, an aspiring writer who mixes with decadent artists in Paris: 'He had not originality enough to see that the cynicism was not his own'.[59] After Robins's pseudonym was revealed, this kind of distinction was often made, the cynicism or pessimism being traced to the influence of Ibsen and sometimes Nietzsche or Schopenhauer.[60] The baleful influence was identified as masculine and continental European.

Kate Flint observes in relation to the New Woman *Bildungsroman*:

> The reader's growth in knowledge is made to parallel that of the protagonist: as Rita Felski has put it,…'the feminist *Bildungsroman* is a didactic genre which aims to convince the reader of the legitimacy of a particular interpretative framework by bringing her or him to a cumulative and retrospective understanding of the events narrated in the text.' Such fiction simultaneously invites intimacy, particularly through its incorporation of telling details…and in its adherence for the most part to realist principles, it claims typicality.[61]

Robins's *Bildungsroman* accords with this pattern. Robins outlined in material printed in the review of her novel in *Review of Reviews* the temperamental oppositions that she elaborated through detailed study in her characters. She emphasized that her primary interest is in two fundamental and universal human types:

> we find in people's minds (morals apart) a determining balance in favour of light (joy and faith), or of darkness (pity and fear). It is not experience of life that makes men optimists or pessimists, so much as some subtle inborn tendency, some push in the one direction or the other, given to the soul before it was given consciousness.[62]

She implicitly draws on expressive realist assumptions, claiming '"authenticity" in describing the world of social relationships' and in 'conveying the inner experience (often seen as "universal") of the individual in quest of identity'.[63] Val's optimism, vivacity, and spirited conflict with her grand-mother invite the intimately sympathetic identification of readers; Ethan is a pessimist, for whom Val is a figure of redemptive American inno-cence. The disappointment of reviewers over the problem theme in *The Open Question* was tied to their repugnance at the narrative closure, cousins Val and Ethan carrying through the suicide pact that initially sealed the progress of their love to marriage. The pact is that before a child can be born of their marriage they will commit suicide as a duty to racial health, 'race' being understood principally as family, and secon-darily 'socialist' community, in which 'mental and moral health' is founded on health of the body.[64] John Gano, Val's father, expounds this view of socialism, arguing that capitalist competition in the U.S.A. produces ill health, which will be transmitted cross-generationally. W. T. Stead wrote of Val: 'She is an intensely natural human girl, so natural and so real that one feels almost a personal grudge against the authoress for dooming her to be the victim of the problem which she poses in the book'.[65] The *New Age* critic remarked, alluding to Aubrey Beardsley, a key figure of British decadence: 'A story is told of an insane painter who used to spoil his most beautiful pictures by painting a small grinning devil in the corner of his pictures. "C.E. Raimond," and for the matter of that, certain of her talented sister writers, remind us of this painter, for they find it impossible to keep out of their pictures some particular little problem-devil of theirs'.[66]

The romance plot that draws together the threads of the 'problem' was frequently but not universally[67] located as the novel's site of monstrous modernity and pathologized. Morbidity was located in Val and Ethan— as in 'There is no limit to the morbid ideas which two diseased minds may generate in each other'—and in the authorial voice—'eccentric and perverse'.[68] W. T. Stead decried the potential cultural work of the 'prob-lem': 'The tendency to suicide at the present day is quite strong enough without having the suggestion of self-murder pressed upon the mind in such a fashion as to make it appear almost a virtue'.[69] In a letter to the *Daily Chronicle* published after her pseudonym had been revealed, Robins herself denied the perceived modernity of the thematic of suicide and its Ibsenism, arguing that 'the question of the value of life' had been 'opened' in Ecclesiastes and The Book of Job.[70]

The thematic provided the sensational element in the plot and in the novel's reception; processing the thematic as being of the problem genre characteristic of New Woman fiction, reviewers mobilized a very familiar dismissive discourse appealing to a ready-made conservative moral constituency. This categorization, though, signally failed to highlight Robins's demonstration that the thwarted energies that drive Val's childhood and adolescent artistic ambition—she wants to be a diva, and has untutored singing talent—become redirected in a self-enclosing manner towards Ethan. Her ambition is belittled, sometimes patronizingly, and in several ways by her grandmother, father, and Ethan. Her grandmother destroys and mocks the secret magazine written by Val and her sister Emmie, describing it as 'young girls ruining their figures, and their eyesight, and their prospects, bending over stuff like this', a 'wasting' of 'youth' in a 'pernicious fashion'.[71] The narrative of Val's artistic ambition is offset against and underlined by two other embedded narratives of thwarted female creativity: that of her aunt Valeria, a would-be sculptress, and of Mary Byrne, who leaves her marriage and pursues a career not only as an artist, but as an advocate of suicide for those who cannot 'live *worthily*'.[72] Being male, Ethan has had opportunities to exercise his literary ambitions in London and Paris. Robins alerts readers to the 'unconscious and societal factors'[73] that contribute to Val's suggesting a suicide pact to secure, against vehement parental and grandparental disapproval, the object of her erotic ambition.

Robins took particular exception to reviews which stated or implied that *The Open Question* had a 'pessimistic design or a pessimistic moral'.[74] This is apparent in an annotation on a letter from Stead dated 28 December 1898: 'I *do* wish the F.nightly article *had* been out this month'.[75] She is referring to William Archer's essay 'Pessimism and Tragedy', published in the March 1899 issue of the *Fortnightly Review*, in which he challenges charges of 'intellectual pessimism'[76] against *The Open Question*, in an argument covering the career of Shakespeare and Selma Lagerlöf's *Gösta Berling's Saga*. Archer was Robins's lover and literary mentor; their relationship and her annotation suggest that she approved his essay.

What was at stake in debating whether the novel was pessimistic? Firstly, there was a sense that the aesthetic status of the romance plot as tragedy (a high art form) was being diminished by being read as an endorsement of a particular philosophy (pessimism), that typically brought with it characterization of a work 'in a stereotyped set of adjectives of which "morbid" is the least denunciatory'. Archer implied that such characterization produces a lazy, superficial reading of a piece of literature. Secondly, Archer challenged aspersions on the potential cultural work the romance plot might do by attempting to explode the assumption that 'tragedy is intended to beget, or does necessarily beget, a pessimistic mood in the spectator or observer'. In discussing Robins's novel in relation to this assumption he emphasized the vitality of Sarah and Val Gano, arguing that '[a]bstract beauty and psychological probability (given Ethan's character and the family circumstances) demanded that *The Open Question* should come to a tragic close'. The '[a]bstract beauty' seems to be, in his reading, Val 'hold[ing] death preferable to a life of disloyalty and shrinking compromise'.[77] Given the particular reviews and commentaries to which Archer is responding, thirdly, there was a perceived need to challenge the ways in which some readings of Val as an exemplar of the New Woman led to morbidity falsely being associated with her and her character type being misidentified as pessimistic rather than optimistic. In one commentary in *Literature*, probably by editor H.D. Traill, Val was identified as a type of

[t]he newly 'emancipated' young woman, with her feverish mental activity, her thirst for 'experiences,' her desire to 'live her life,' her moods of reckless gaiety alternating with fits of depression and despondency, [who] is not only an unmistakable product of the times, but one which a whole series of modern 'movements,' educational, economic, and other, is tending to send forth in ever-increasing numbers into the modern world.

This view of a 'morbid and creedless' Val[78] was explicitly criticized by Archer through quotation from the novel and analysis of Val. W.L. Courtney's reading of Val and the implications of the pessimism of the novel in the *Daily Telegraph* (slightly reworked for his chapter on Robins in *The Feminine Note in Fiction*)[79] also seems to be within Archer's sights. Robins's letter of complaint about his review in the *Daily Telegraph* was apparently not published; she implicitly defended her novel against some of his charges in a letter published in the *Daily Chronicle*. For Courtney, Val, 'being a modern young woman, has gone through that dreary round, first of disbe- ~~lief, then of amateur philosophizing, finally of pessimistic despair, which~~ at the present day seems to be changing the whole nature of growing and developing womanhood'. He described the book as

> a nightmare begotten of a perusal of Nietzsche's philosophy. From beginning to end the burden is the burden of a querulous and unsat- isfied egoism, and that way, as we know from many prevalent exam- ples, lies madness....Nearly every one of the characters is painfully travailing over the welfare of his or her soul, a problem which, for reasons that are tolerably obvious, is always connected with a sick and green-hued pessimism.[80]

In the *Daily Chronicle* Robins claimed that the suicide of Val and Ethan is altruistic: 'Their altruism may be as morbid, as cowardly, as reprehen- sible as you please, but is altruism, not egoism'.[81] The commentary in *Literature* described pessimism as the '*maladie du siècle*', the 'predisposing conditions' for which are the challenge posed to 'a comfortable middle class' by the 'advent of Democracy', 'the vast, mixed, fluctuating, emotional public of the present day'.[82] In terms of the 'tradition/modernity oppo- sition as elaborated in dichotomies of authenticity and alienation, nature and culture, timelessness and history',[83] Archer and Robins worked to distance the novel from the temporality of modernity invoked by review- ers in characterizing the novel as pessimistic or egoistic in its philosophy. Archer, whose essay gave him wider scope than Robins's two brief public comments, tried to give the romance plot a more 'universal appeal'[84] by arguing for its credentials as tragedy, a form with a long genealogy in European culture and aesthetics.

The manner in which the moral panic over the New Woman was played out in the reception of Robins's 1890s fiction qualifies several aspects of recent feminist literary histories of New Woman fiction in the 1890s. By 1898, when *The Open Question* was published, the feminist *Bildungsroman*, as it dealt with childhood and adolescence, had achieved cultural legitimacy, a legitimacy the novel itself might have enhanced further, given the extra- ordinarily high critical acclaim Robins earned for her treatment of this narrative thematic. Even Courtney described it as 'beyond praise'.[85] Literary historians who elaborate a 'reaction formation' against the rupture New Woman fiction seemed to represent to the aesthetic aspirations and standards of 'new realists'[86] and critics supportive of them draw on a minute fraction of the critical cultural production of the period. Measured in the critical reception of Robins's fiction, Waugh's account of the effeminization of British culture to justify a 'hale and hearty' school of criticism[87] or Courtney's effort to articulate a '"virile" standard of aesthetic value', for example,[88] are by no means representative or particularly influential. Courtney's use of *The Open Question* to press his case through a newspaper review was not uncontested. Archer's and Robins's reverse discourse against this and other shallow invocations of morbidity, however, was not a defence of *The Open Question*'s feminism but of its artistic credentials, evincing the expressive realist assumptions characteristic of criticism of the day. 1890s reviewers of Robins's fiction judged it against aesthetic criteria based on these assumptions. Ardis argues that after 1894 critics 'tried to discredit the cultural work of New Woman novels by focussing on their aesthetic limitations'.[89] I have demonstrated that this is not unequivocally the case in the reception of Robins's work. In the critical response to the satirical voice of *George Mandeville's Husband* aesthetic limitations are used to discredit the cultural work of an attack on the lady novelist or New Woman.

10. 'Der Mensch als Weib'[2]

Lou Andreas-Salomé's Literary Response to the Woman Question in Turn-of-the-Century Germany

Christa Zorn

> For one of the paradoxes of this most paradoxical question is precisely that, with all our literature about *La Femme*, and all our violent discussions, economical, physiological, psychological, sociological…we do not really know what women are. Women, so to speak as a natural product, as distinguished from women as a creation of men...
>
> *Vernon Lee, 'The Economic Parasitism of Women'*[2]

Lou Andreas-Salomé's psychoanalytical essay on femininity, 'Der Mensch als Weib' (1899), appeared during a period which was marked by a multitude of new psychologies and the post-Darwinist debates on woman's nature.[3] The urge for a new definition of womanhood occurred at a time when women entered into public space and the established relationships between individual and society, self and other, were challenged by what has been called a crisis of subjectivity. In Western society, the extended professional possibilities for women created among themselves political momentum and a new consciousness. Since traditional concepts of femininity could not encompass women's increasing visibility and changing profile, images of the New Woman were often conjured up in a masculine iconography based on a dualism which could conceive of an alternative female existence only as male. Contemporary creations like the 'mannish', 'unwomanly' or 'deviant' woman (used by such diverse critics as George Bernard Shaw or Havelock Ellis) reveal the male-invested control mechanism of the symbolic systems in literature and science.

Lou Andreas-Salomé (1861–1937) lived through the epoch-making intellectual and social developments which saw the beginnings of the women's movement, psychoanalysis and modernism. A New Woman, more through her independent lifestyle than through political advocacy, she ranked among the most influential women writers of her day who associated with the intellectual and cultural elites of Germany, Austria, Russia, and France. Born into a bourgeois-aristocratic family of the German-speaking community in St. Petersburg, Lou Andreas-Salomé, like most daughters of the Russian upper class, received a cosmopolitan education in Zurich, one of the few places where, in the early 1880s, women could attend university lectures.[4] She established her reputation as a writer through several pieces of short fiction, such as the first book-length studies of Nietzsche (1884) and Ibsen (1886) and numerous essays on religion, philosophy, and literature for such acclaimed journals as *Zukunft*, *Neue Deutsche Rundschau* and Freud's *Imago*. Today, she is often remembered by her relationships with leading figures of the intellectual avant-garde, from Nietzsche to Rilke to Freud. Ironically, her association with 'great men' more so than her writing has kept her in our literary histories.[5]

Salomé's phenomological exploration of what it means to be a woman emerges from her fiction and prose of the 1890s, but most intensely and provocatively from her pre-psychoanalytic essay, 'Der Mensch als Weib'. This text not only reflects the era's complex and often contradictory discourses on sex and gender but also has relevance for our modern feminist debates on identity and subjectivity. It contains the groundwork for her later studies in psychoanalysis, especially her alternative versions of the Freudian notions of drive, narcissism, and the unconscious.[6] In the 1890s, Salomé tried to find an aesthetic form for her religious, psychological, and erotic experience, in search of a female role which could accommodate her desire for autonomy and self-fulfilment without placing unwomanly demands on herself. She repeatedly conceptualized her experiences of a woman seeking self-preservation in an environment where men were becoming interested in female ways of knowing while still assigning to women ancillary or subservient roles. Salomé's encounters with Nietzsche exemplify this ambivalence. Nietzsche, fascinated with her 'heroic soul' and ability to transform personal experience into transcending theory, toyed with the idea of making her his disciple, even to marry her—if only for two years.[7] Nietzsche, like Freud later, admired Salomé's extraordinary intellectual power, but otherwise remained rooted in hierarchical traditions which generally depreciated women as deficient. Still, Nietzschean philosophy had great relevance for Salomé and the New Woman writers of the period, who adopted his affirmative concepts of the *Übermensch* and the Will to Power for their new images of a powerful female 'eros'.[8]

Lou Andreas-Salomé's 'Der Mensch als Weib' was a reaction against male-centred metaphysics but, paradoxically, saddled her with the reputation of being anti-feminist. She was sharply attacked by leading figures of the German feminist movement, especially the labour-oriented Hedwig Dohm[9] and the political activist, Rosa Mayreder, a key figure in the bourgeois women's movement in Austria. What most offended feminist reformers was Salomé's claim of essential difference between man and woman at a time when the women's movement in Western Europe had become organized around doctrines of political, legal and economic equality. Their political project was contested by the distinctly anti-feminist medical and biological research aimed to confirm the superiority of maleness and to justify women's exclusion from intellectual or political work. The effect of this doctrine was particularly pervasive among the bourgeois middle classes, where it was believed that an education in discursive reasoning would corrupt women's intuitive judgment and therefore their 'natural' femininity.[10] As a consequence, German women remained 'undereducated, undertrained, underutilized victims of the so-called gender characteristics that saw them located in a particular realm of domestic responsibilities'.[11]

Although feminists like Dohm and Mayreder welcomed Salomé's female-centred subjectivity because it challenged conservative assumptions about woman's inferiority, they condemned the grounding of her discourse in the misogynist biological parlance of the day. Her style too closely resembled the anti-feminism in Emile Durkheim's anthropological or Paul Möbius's medical polemics which propagated that woman (like a child or savage) was less evolved than man and that, because of her undifferentiated nature, she was more suited for motherhood than the more demanding tasks outside the home. Salomé was well aware of these prevailing prejudices. She discussed her own understanding of an autonomous femininity widely with the important feminists of her time—among them Ellen Key, Laura Marholm, Helene Stöcker, and Helene Lange.[12] Yet she did not see herself as a political advocate in the feminist movement. Her interest in the woman question derived from religious and philosophical concerns, especially after her 'loss of God' at an early age. In her writing, she translated this loss into a search for selfhood which she increasingly voiced in the psychological terms of sex/gender and their significance in constituting the human subject.[13]

Salomé's philosophy of self made her highly suspicious to collective thinkers like Dohm whose reactions have had a lasting effect on the reception of Salomé's work, especially by feminists. Today critics are still debating whether we should read Salomé's essay with the provocatively archaic title as an anti-feminist piece or as a philosophical fable of a new (female) consciousness which the referential mode of contemporary feminism could not accommodate.[14] Avoiding the feminist collectivism of her day, Salomé propagates a form of female individualism which strikingly anticipates an autonomous female consciousness advocated by women writers of the modernist generation, such as Dorothy Richardson or Virginia Woolf. What links Salomé especially with Richardson (and less with Woolf) is her rhetorical detachment from material social conditions which feminist critics have seen as inextricably linked with the development of female autonomy.[15] The question is whether Salomé's concept of the autonomous woman helped shape a modern female consciousness that escapes external ideological constraints *because* of its socio-economic detachment. A brief summary of the most salient points in 'Der Mensch als Weib' can help us understand why Salomé's position has been ambiguous and not readily accessible to modern feminist thought.

Contrary to nineteenth-century views of clearly divided sex and gender characteristics, Salomé envisions 'woman' as bearing masculine and feminine traits in a reciprocal relation, a form of 'two-way' narcissism she later developed in her influential treatise, 'Narzissmus als Doppelrichtung' (1921). To lend her female subject scientific relevance, Salomé borrows from molecular biology the important assumption that cells develop towards maturity in different ways. Based on Wilhelm Bölsche's well-known account of the increasing complication, differentiation and specialization of organic functions, she claims that the self-content female cells are less in need of coupling and therefore more indolent than the smaller male cells, whose partition and increasing fragmentation require them to stay mobile and restless. Woman's comprehensive and complete sexuality, Salomé argues, is already determined at her natural origin in a more indolent cell. At the

beginning of human life, the larger, more serene and complete cells determine the feminine; the smaller, more frenetic ('vorwärtsstrebende') cells
constitute masculine character. Quoting contemporary scientists from Ranke
to Virchow to Claus, Salomé demonstrates that early on, the female cell
remains less differentiated, capable of reproduction and innovation even
before fertilization. As such, the female element is at home in its native
sphere, self-sufficient, and yet in immediate touch with the infinite whole.
The tiny male cell, by contrast, is predestined for progress. Driven out of
itself with ever greater division and specialization of its forces, it reaches out
constantly for new tasks and new goals, only to find them receding indefi-
nitely. Needless to say, the biological model here mirrors the division of
labour between the sexes in contemporary middle-class life: men at the
competitive work front—women in the secluded space of the home. However,
in Salomé's version of home, woman is not reclusive but like a snail carries
her 'house' with her, always ready to gather new experiences and incorporate them into her being. This redefinition of home eliminates the traditional
distinction between domestic and public spheres without denying that male
and female still command two different modes of existence—albeit not
necessarily in a hierarchical relationship: 'It is meaningless to argue which
one of the two modes is the more valuable one or summons a mightier effort
in strength.'[16] Salomé validates the female subject through a scientific explanation but at the same time removes from scientific discourse the underlying ideological assumptions which would have reinforced traditional gender
inequality. She dismisses the widely accepted electro-vitalist model of male-
female polarity, which defined the male as the positive (active) force and the
female as the negative (passive) receptacle:

> Misconceptions of the feminine are always based on the same mistake,
> no matter whether woman is defined as man's passive appendage or
> whether she is predominantly seen as the pure motherly type, so long
> as femininity is being framed in terms of passive reception, germi-
> nation and bearing. Such misconceptions lead to wrong conclusions
> and are prevalent even among the advocates of the woman question.[17]

The understanding of woman as man's other, Salomé argues, ignores
the female potential to embody an all-encompassing human subject.

Woman's intact, undifferentiated nature ensures the continuity of the whole species, while the masculine drive leads to greater diversification and therefore generates the individual formations of the species within the evolutionary pattern. In fact, Salomé finds the two sexes so unlike each other in their regulatory schemes that they command different modes of expression. 'Individual and general life…shapes the two sexes in their different and characteristic ways depending on their essence and relationship to each other, giving each sex its special force in life'.[18] To recognize these differences, Salomé calls for a revision of the metanarrative that defines human subjects by a single notion or only one explanatory model. She contends that woman cannot be reduced to the objectified and objectifying forms of male culture without deforming her distinct character. Woman has not come into her own yet because she has modelled herself on the fragmented and specialized male. Instead of losing herself in competitive battles with man and losing her potential of an all-encompassing femininity, Salomé argues, woman should put her own stamp on the world. Different from man's culturally productive agency, woman's creativity cannot be measured in outward signs since its value is internal and integrated into her whole life.[19] Her art has to be conceived in the service of the human species as enactment of an original, comprehensive life principle, different from the highly specialized, outwardly directed male who is yet compelled to return to the feminine centre for his survival: 'For his composure, recreation, and zest for life, he needs to find the peaceful union he desires and which has already been completed in the realm of woman'.[20]

Salomé develops a narrative that is both critical and mimetic of the prevailing languages on sexual difference; or as Biddy Martin puts it, 'The essay works within and against the terms of biological and evolutionary thought'.[21] Combining biological description with the non-realist mode of parable and fairy tale, 'Der Mensch als Weib' first reads like another version of Bölsche's popular scientific treatise, 'Das Liebesleben in der Natur' (love life in nature), an account of human behaviour according to the laws of evolution. Like Bölsche's extension of bio-chemical principles into the social sphere, Salomé's fable of 'woman' is invested with an epistemology of wholeness which echoes romanticist ideas of pre-capitalist harmony. Opposing the fragmented view of humanity in contemporary science, Salomé deliberately remythecizes its rational and analytical discourse. Her poesis of 'das Weib' turns biology into an imaginary chance for woman to represent the vital centre of a holistic human subject: self-supportive and a positive category in itself.[22]

'Der Mensch als Weib' challenges contemporary thinking about gender hierarchies which reached greatest exemplary significance in Otto Weininger's *Geschlecht und Charakter* (1903). Weininger identified the masculine with the transcending force of the intellect against an essentially sexual and therefore inferior feminine existence. In the post-Darwininian climate, biological determinist models by Ernst Haeckel, Paul Möbius and Emile Durkheim described woman's developmental inferiority as having been manifested in her social role. Salomé questions the inherently misogynist value judgments in their theories. In her redefinition of the feminine as a complete, self-supportive and active unit, Salomé constructs for her audience other possible readings of femininity in which masculinity may be dependent on and in need of the feminine. As Biddy Martin has pointed out in *Woman and Modernity*, the subtlety of Salomé's formulation here is crucial. In sexologist and biologist discourses it had become customary to speak of the female as a passive principle. Salomé makes plausible that, instead of calling the female passive, one could speak with equal or even greater 'appearance of legitimacy of the greater need and dependence of the masculine'.[23] She denies that there is any inherent biological meaning in sexual difference nor in such derivatives as activity versus passivity. In her own text, then, the abundance of metaphors alludes to the fictional character of explanations derived from scientific facts. Accordingly, she treats science as 'a set of stories she can use to her own ends'.[24] Thus, Salomé can create her own version of the conventional practice that defines women first by their sex (which in her philosphy means 'being') and second only by their work or social activity.[25] Her female subject is not sexual but erotic, which implies in contemporary idiom that she integrates body and soul, sexuality and personality into one being. Woman's self-directed eroticism pervades her whole existence and does not enter her consciousness as a specialized, localized drive like man's, whose (almost mechanical) sexuality can be separated from his personality. She draws symbolic significance from the biological autonomy of the female egg to show that woman is her own independent self and does not need the established forms of proof that underscore male achievement. Indeed,

woman's lack of this need is her strength, whereas man's highest endeavours cripple his humanity, and this fragmentation ironically constitutes
manly greatness:

> Even the most highly developed male relinquishes harmonious growth
> achieved by balancing all of his powers for the purpose of staying
> attractive, cheerful and healthy, as soon as he can reach his goals
> through the specialization of his strengths. What he elevates as his
> goals can actually disfigure him, and the very fact of being capable
> thereof affords him greatness.[26]

Having a dig at the German feminist movement, Salomé contends that
woman has yet to understand the full extent of her femininity. Her ignorance has made her leave her 'house' and fight with the same relentless-
ness as man so that instead of gaining autonomy she has reinforced her
dependence, a development which is contrary to real emancipation.
Salomé's warning not to limit woman's identification to male-defined social
or economic conditions aroused suspicion among progressive German
feminists. Hedwig Dohm is the first among a number of critics to casti-
gate Salomé for compromising the emancipatory goals of the German
women's movement: women's right to paid work, legal equality, and the
right to vote. Dohm believed that in the contemporary climate, Salomé's
biological essentialism would reinforce the prejudices against women's
professional and public endeavours. Although she acknowledged that
Salomé shared the feminists' demand for women's rights and liberties, she
saw a crucial difference between feminists and 'anti-feminists' like Salomé
in their views on women's economic independence. According to Dohm,
the 'anti-feminists'—among whom she also counted Ellen Key and Laura
Marholm—accepted economic independence only so long as it did not
diminish their femininity: 'The representatives of the reactionary side
demand these rights only if they benefit their private lives or their roles
as mothers. To them, the right to freedom is conditional only in so far as
it does not adversely affect their female characteristics'. [27]

Dohm perceived Salomé's allusiveness as a mystic veiling of real problems and practical solutions which she rebuked as elitist and insincere. She
was frustrated by upper-class intellectuals like Salomé who argued against

women's professional ambitions while using their own artistic or intellectual talents and privileged positions to influence the cultural debates:

> By God! If these dear and highly gifted poetesses so vehemently
> oppose women working and entering into competition with man,
> why don't they themselves stay within the boundaries of femininity,
> away from any kind of employment, and why do they produce such
> autumnal fruit or similar stuff?[28]

Mocking Salomé's flowery style, Dohm exposes the idealist metaphor
of the 'noble female' in her 'aristocratic castle' as unrealistic and elitist. If
Salomé's metaphors were taken at face value, she argues, woman could
only lead the self-indulgent aristocratic life that Salomé evidently envisions
through considerable support from the government. For Dohm, rationality and science, not poetics and erotics, carried the promise of equality for
women.[29] In an earlier essay, 'Reaktion in der Frauenbewegung' (1899),
she admits that she was at first seduced by Salomé's style but, upon a
second reading, 'the charm was broken' ('und der Zauber war gebrochen').
She accuses Salomé of elevating herself as the universal feminine ideal,
an act which denies women's diversity: 'There are Amazons and sacrifi-
cial lambs, Hypatias and gentle, simple Angels of the House'.[30] For polem-
ical reasons, Dohm rebukes Lou Andreas-Salomé, Ellen Key and Laura
Marholm collectively for their conservative stance on the female role, but
only in her criticism of Salomé does she focus repeatedly on language issues.
True, in the midst of real social and political injustices Salomé's symbolism was bound to appear as a form of reactionary escapism, and ardent
reformers like Dohm assumed its effect to be politically paralyzing. After
all, Salomé's metaphors resembled too closely some of the most conservative, misogynist or paternalist assumptions about women.[31] Is Dohm
spelling out the dangers of reading the metaphorical language of 'Der
Mensch als Weib' all too literally? Salomé seems to have anticipated this
effect since she warns her readers not to take her at face value: 'I know
full well that such catchy phrases, which apply only to the basest structures,
must not be taken literally'.[32]

From her fiction and prose essays of the period, we know that Salomé
was not opposed to female education.[33] But she was concerned about

contemporary feminism remaining dependent on the dominance of masculine principles: 'The traditional ideal of manhood seems to be haunting exclusively women's minds. However, for woman it ought to be less important to be doing something significant than to be steadily doing it as a woman'.[34] Her skepticism of women's desire to enter men's professional world and to partake in cultural production did not only result from her struggles with feminism but also from her involvement with contemporary 'Lebensphilosophie' reform movements. For instance, the sociologist and philosopher Georg Simmel, who offered an anti-capitalist, anti-patriarchal critique of the division of labour, saw the fragmentation of the individual as a correlative of maleness. Like Salomé, Simmel claimed that 'man' can easily engage in all kinds of activities without integrating them into his whole personality: 'However, as the entire history of work demonstrates, it is obvious that the division of labor is incomparably more congruent with the male nature than with the female…It seems as if the man has more opportunity to allow his energy to flow in a unilinear direction without threatening his personality'.[35] In his study *On Women, Sexuality, and Love* Simmel conjures up the feminine as a timeless, pre-modern concept, a position from which to attack human fragmentation in capitalist male culture. Since the female existence 'is more closely connected with the center',[36] woman cannot engage in the same externalized and fragmented activities without destroying her self-contained repose, that is to say, her irreducible femininity. It is obvious where Salomé's and Simmel's models of the male and female overlap: both focus on the fragmentation and objectification of masculine culture, its state of restlessness as opposed to woman's more content, harmonious state of being. Like Simmel, Salomé maintains that human life cannot be reduced to a single form or a single model of explanation. In contradistinction to Simmel, however, she does not use 'woman' as one example of the pluralism of forms but positions her in the very centre, as the site for a new, more comprehensive form of human subjectivity which even accommodates the contradictions posed by current epistemological models.

All that which makes woman appear less capable than man is defined by her habit of integrating only such things as nourish, assimilate, vitalize and revitalize her…Hence woman's innate understanding of

what cannot be grasped by the mind alone. She is capable of receiving and organically digesting such contradictions as man must dissect
first through theoretical processes before gaining greater clarity.[37]

This paragraph illustrates that 'Der Mensch als Weib' involves more
than the woman question. Throughout the essay, Salomé seeks to dismiss
the boundaries between secular and sacred (rationalistic and mystic) epis-
tolary modes, a project which from a rationalist Enlightenment standpoint—like Hedwig Dohm's—had to appear reactionary since it obfuscated
social reality.[38] Indeed, the question of Salomé's anti-feminism appears to
be intertwined with her opposition to the dominance of rational and analytical modes in the emerging scientific discourses which split objective reality from subjective consciousness. Such practice, she believed, prevented
thinking in terms of the human subject as a whole. Salomé deplored the
dominance of rationality in scientific discourses and the speed with which
these had emerged without being assimilated by a humanist language.[39] Her
own message is delivered in an ambivalent poetic style which transposes
naturalist terminology into a mystic union of soul and body to avoid the
alienating effect of the conceptual language by which her contemporaries
tried to categorize men and women.[40] She alternates between psychological precision and poetic ambiguity, which creates the perplexing effect of
familiar terms appearing in unexpected connections, the kind of recasting
of values that she had seen in Nietzsche. For instance, her image of undifferentiated, less developed womanhood at first seems to reinforce traditional
gender hierarchies. At second glance, we realize that she construes her
undifferentiated woman without the underlying stereotype of female passivity so that the concept of 'woman' is opened up for reinterpretation.
Similarly, she dislodges woman from the prevailing notions of sexuality
('das Geschlechtliche') to present traditional (and often constraining) virtues
of woman in a different light. By removing allegedly feminine virtues such
as purity and chastity from their dependence on male sexuality, she can
reclaim them as positive feminine values: 'Therefore, words like "purity"
and "chastity" and such not only have a negative meaning, but at the same
time, they embody the radiance and magnificence of a world which we view
from the all too one-sided perspective of human sexuality.'[41] Salomé uses
so-called 'essentials' strategically, signifying a new, feminized context. She

transforms the conventionally negative role of the female in binary opposites into a positive one by placing it in a system organized by an alternative (female) subject. Her curiously archaic style serves as a kind of
masquerade in an attempt to produce cultural forms of femininity within
the masculine discursive conventions in which the self-reliant woman may
not be recognized.

Few of Salomé's critics understand her mystic symbolism as woman's
undisclosed possibility, a conjecture that requires expression beyond the
realist mode of actuality. In a recent study, Lorraine Markotic has demonstrated that Salomé's rhetoric parallels Irigaray's innovative language to
circumscribe an identity that still has to be created.[42] Irigaray's ambivalent reception by feminist critics has shown that any exploration of woman's
otherness is a Scylla and Charybdis-like dilemma: 'it is not easy to depict
a non-essentialist woman and to avoid both archetypes and stereotypes: it
is difficult to delineate a new image, one that does not inevitably fall into
familiar categories, or at least one that is not perceived as so doing'.[43]
Despite its problematic ideological implications, Salomé's poesis of the
female body can be understood as a prophetic vision which transforms reality back into possibilities so that femininity can become 'more than its hegemonic social definition allows'.[44]

Recent scholarship from Martin to Markotic to Gabler converges on the
conjecture that 'Der Mensch als Weib' figures as an early psychological
study of human (provocatively named 'woman's') identity formation from
within. More precisely, it is an investigation of what Foucault has called
'the forms and modalities of the relation to self by which the individual
constitutes and recognizes himself *qua* subject'.[45] While contemporary
political feminists concerned themselves with the way women as external
empirical subjects negotiate their place in public and professional life,
Salomé points to internal subjectivity, that is, the relationship between
discursive positions and inner psychic processes as more specifically developed in her later text, 'Zum Typus Weib' (1914), in which she describes
the process of subjectification in more psychological terms. Subjectivity
here is defined as individual experience, which recreates or conceives
outside reality without becoming a part of that reality and thus keeping
a certain amount of individual liberty. Such inwardly (re-)constructed reality is a less visible but highly effective part of the human subject.[46]

In 'Der Mensch als Weib' Salomé ascribes to the female an unalienated and undivided form of subjectivity which commands an alternative identification process. To emphasize that the female constitutes a subject of a different order, Salomé compares women to a gang of thieves who follow a strict code outside the law—'as we follow ours within'—which is based on their own unique form of existence.[47] Arguably, Salomé is concerned with the inner potential to build subjectivity, the imaginary process of aligning the individual with the 'rudimentary levels of psychic identity' and the 'discursive formation and practices which constitute the social field'.[48] To circumvent the reductionism of both analytical science and political realism, Salomé employs the (equally reductionist) language of contemporary biology and anthropology, most notably Bölsche's evolutionary myth. She attempts to create in woman a site for a reconceptionalization of subjectivity at a time when scientific and political discourses were competing in shaping a dominant concept of humanity.

Salomé carries philosophy and psychology beyond their contemporary scope, not simply by adding the female perspective but by suggesting that the different ways in which men and women view themselves and each other command different epistemological structures. As Markotic puts it in a succinct summary of her intricate argument:

> But even if 'woman' symbolizes otherness as such to both sexes, this may mean something different for each sex....Andreas-Salomé maintains that men and women should not be understood as two halves designed to fit together; each constitutes a world of her or his own.[49]

In her literary and theoretical texts around the turn of the nineteenth century, Salomé repeatedly discounts the place assigned to woman by dominant scientific, social and sexual norms. 'Der Mensch als Weib' goes beyond the woman question by making visible the exclusionary and provisionary nature of scientific and philosophical narratives even as they profess to define truth—which can only be 'narrative truth', i.e. an explanation that defines its own conditions. As Lorraine Markotic has convincingly argued, Salomé questions such truth claims, but she may have pushed her post-structuralist argument too far by implying that Salomé, in an 'almost Derridean manner', suggests that there are 'no extra-discursive characteristics to read'.[50] Salomé does not deny that woman has certain 'natural' characteristics; she only reinterprets what these characteristics have been taken to mean. In response to *fin-de-siècle* demonization and disdain of the female, as Renate Weber and Brigitte Rempp have argued, Salomé redirects the image of the feminine into an erotic (rather than sexual) reservoir of at-homeness and self-sufficiency.[51] During a period which projected cultural anxiety in images of restlessness and fragmentation, woman's association with harmony and at-homeness could harbour positive values. It is obvious that from this position Salomé cannot logically encourage women to partake more equally in a progressive but fragmented male culture.

It has not been sufficiently emphasized that the metaphors of sex and gender in 'Der Mensch als Weib' represent different epistemological styles; that is, Salomé construes the scientific-particularizing mode as masculine and the mythic-synthecizing mode as feminine. To her, contemporary philosophy and science totalize the partial and the fragmental, a principle associated with the male body whose more aggressive sexuality is directed outward in a single, particularized act. Salomé's positioning of woman in 'natural' harmony was meant to serve her larger philosophical program in an attempt to adapt Nietzsche's vision of the affirmative man for her holistic, woman-centred definition of humanity. In language which reveals her indebtedness to Nietzsche and to nineteenth-century iconography, she created a pre-Freudian subject but without dissecting it into analyzable fragments. Her synthetic approach, which Freud acknowledged with respect, offers interesting insights into alternative subject theories at the inception of modern psychoanalysis and of the discourse of modernity.[52]

At the same time we cannot absolve Salomé entirely from the criticisms that have accompanied her work from the beginning. Although her feminization of human subjectivity opens up interesting possibilities for recent feminist theories, her text reveals the problem of all biocentric models: she assumes the body's unmediated existence while constructing it in the linguistic and cultural terms of contemporary discourses. This is risky argumentation in an historical context at a time when imperialist ideologies placed 'higher' developed (meaning European, industrialized, male) life forms and organizations at the top of the evolutionary hierarchy and at the bottom all other forms (meaning uncivilized, primitive, female). Thus we should not be surprised by tongue lashings of frustrated feminists to whom Salomé's text appeared to reflect the most notorious anti-liberal arguments. We may agree with Hedwig Dohm that Salomé locks woman up in an essentialist sanctuary from which only she (Lou) herself can escape. Salomé universalizes her individual embodiment of femininity in an idealistic discourse that corresponds to her upper-middle-class background, a discourse which takes for granted and thus is silent about the prevailing social or political circumstances. Although she dislodges maleness from the universal subject and gives it a feminine face, she does not question the notion of universality itself, presupposing the same timeless female nature underlying all cultural and historical variations. In this respect, we need to ask whether her metaphorical womanhood does not simply reproduce the underlying epistemological structures of Western metaphysics.

Beyond these qualifications, Salomé's text offers a hypothesis for rethinking traditional models of human subjectivity and the individual processes of identification attached to them. Her concept of autonomous femininity bears striking parallels to modernist concepts of female consciousness and more recent feminist conceptualizations of the formations of subjectivity, from Luce Irigaray to Julia Kristeva and Judith Butler. If we read Salomé's metaphor of femininity not as an escape from reality but as an alternative philosophical possibility, 'Der Mensch als Weib' enables us to review the limitations of modern feminist discourses which sometimes merely update a preconstructed patriarchal order. For this purpose, the design of an abstract subject position of woman may lead (as Salomé suggests) to an investigation and discovery of 'the ways in which the interests of feminism as a political movement for social change are entangled in the hierarchical structuring of racial, class, sexual, and gendered subject positions'.[53] After all, Salomé's 'false' essentialist abstraction does not have to lead back to a more conservative model of thinking. On the contrary, as Judith Butler would have it, we sometimes consciously have to adopt false and painfully generalizing notions in our methodologies to bridge a temporary impasse or to mark a period of transition.

Salomé's ambivalent psycho-philosophical approach to womanhood and her search for unusual metaphorical connections do not fit into the empirical categories we have established to define woman from the outside. Could we say, then, that her tale of autonomous femininity was meant to present woman internally and metaphorically; and more to herself than to man? She re-invents female identity on a new conceptual level which illuminates the inner, less visible process of subject identification: close to the body, philosophic and poetic at the same time. How useful her psychological myth can be for postmodern thought depends on the extent to which 'Der Mensch als Weib' can function as a vantage point for feminist (and other) theories to look at themselves. As such, Salomé's fable of 'das Weib' is a persuasive opportunity to re-evaluate the epistemological ground of our own terms and to maintain the liberating dynamics of critical theory across the disciplines.

11. 'Female Consciousness'

Aesthetic Concepts and Feminist Thought in Dorothy Richardson's Writing

Eveline Kilian

Dorothy Richardson's notion of 'female consciousness' is an idea that takes up a prominent place in her thought. It is defined as a mental property that influences an individual's perception in a certain way and that also plays a central role in artistic production. I will analyse the aesthetic and philosophical implications of this concept in a first step, and place it in the context of Modernist and Romantic poetics, the two dominant areas to which it can be linked. Richardson's specific view of female consciousness also raises questions as to its positioning with respect to the contemporary discourses on the emancipation of women and the social opportunities gained by the New Woman. This point will be dealt with in the second part of my article. The sources I base my argument on are both Richardson's journal articles and her series of novels *Pilgrimage*, where some of her tenets expounded in her articles and reviews can be seen operating in a self-contained fictional universe.

Richardson's views about writing have variously been seen as prefiguring some of the tenets of the New French Feminist thinkers of the 1970s, notably Hélène Cixous's concept of *écriture féminine* and Luce Irigaray's *parler femme*.[1] Critics often attacked these positions on account of their aloofness from the sphere of political action and because of their inherent essentialism or biologism, which runs the risk of playing into the hands of the ideology they set out to subvert.[2] As we shall see, Richardson's position, especially her idea of 'female consciousness', exposes itself to the same kind of criticism.

Dorothy Richardson (1873–1957) clearly distinguishes between male and female modes of consciousness and perception. Men, in her opinion, think in propositions and rely on an 'overpowering collection of facts'.[3] They construct 'theologies, arts, sciences, philosophies' in order to give the world a clearly defined and manageable shape. These systems only 'become the battle-ground of conflicting theories,'[4] however, interlocking in endless controversies far removed from any direct access to reality. This urge 'to fix life'[5] in one-sided positions has a deadening effect on one's perception and fails to grasp the nature of reality, which, in Richardson's view, reveals itself in moments of astonishment and privileged awareness that transcend the knowledge provided by pre-ordained patterns of seeing. Miriam Henderson, the protagonist of Richardson's *Pilgrimage*, characterizes a man's consciousness in the following way: 'the hard brutal laughing complacent atmosphere of men's minds...men's minds, staring at things, ignorantly, knowing "everything" in an irritating way and yet ignorant'. She considers such an attitude disturbingly limited and comes to the conclusion that it would be 'awful to have nothing but a man's consciousness'.[6]

In contrast to this, Richardson puts forward her notion of 'the synthetic consciousness of woman'.[7] Women are able to move beyond the partial and compartmentalized view of men. In that sense they are closer to 'the rich fabric of life'.[8] They can guide their thoughts 'in all directions at once', they can see 'life whole and harmonious'.[9] Rachel Blau DuPlessis explicitly takes Richardson's idea of synthesis as the basis for an anti-hierarchical, anti-dualistic mode of perception and presentation which she terms 'both/and vision', and which, in her view, constitutes an essential characteristic of a 'female aesthetic'.[10]

It is rewarding to have a closer look at the aesthetic and philosophical implications of what Richardson calls female consciousness. It especially calls to mind contemporary concepts of *impersonality*, and it has a clear connection to Virginia Woolf's notion of the androgynous mind, which she developed in *A Room of One's Own*. In *Pilgrimage*, Miriam Henderson's decision not to take sides any more, an important precondition for her own writing, can be linked to 'a release from wrath', a step towards a position of disinterestedness.[11] This connection evokes Woolf's distinction between literary texts written 'in the red light of emotion' and those written 'in the white light of truth'.[12] Woolf considers the emotional charge maiming certain texts more specifically as a result of what she calls 'sex-consciousness',[13] i.e. an awareness of the gender conflict, which in male authors is often expressed as a stance of condescending superiority with respect to women, and in female authors as a noticeable resentment of and indignation at the social oppression of their own sex. But it is only when these gender-specific mental positions are overcome and when the male and female components are fused and a state of neutrality is reached that the mind can make use of all its faculties.

So we can say that the characteristics which in Woolf's poetics result from an androgynous mind are attributed to a female consciousness in Richardson's conception. When, to use Woolf's words, the mind is 'unimpeded' and 'undivided',[14] it is free to think of things in themselves. To achieve this kind of impartiality, Richardson's protagonist withdraws from all dogmatic positions, in particular her involvement in debates about the nature and value of socialism. She decides against writing socialist tracts and other 'argumentative articles'[15] her journalistic pursuits had included, and instead turns to an exploration of her inner life that is to become the subject of her literary project. Such an impartial outlook enables her to see '[t]hings as a whole', 'from all angles at once,…one's mind gliding over the whole, alighting nowhere'.[16] Although she does not exclude men completely from this type of sensibility and knowledge, Richardson comes much closer to an essentialist view than Woolf, which is reflected in her statement about the few exceptions: 'the great male synthetics, the artists and mystics, are three-parts woman.'[17]

Richardson's notion of *impersonality* is defined by a high degree of distance from one's own self and, at the same time, by a stance of extreme subjectivity.[18] Like Woolf,[19] Richardson draws on Romantic concepts of the imagination. When she qualifies female consciousness as 'synthetic',[20] she takes up an epithet used by Coleridge to describe the imagination.[21] For him it is synthetic because it brings together the subject and its object of contemplation in a flash of insight that partakes of the divine and reveals the unity of all things.[22] For Richardson such intense moments of heightened awareness lead to the perception of an 'ultimate reality',[23] an experience for which she uses terms like 'enchantment', 'magic' or 'transfiguration',[24] and which serves to make everything appear 'new and strange'.[25] Here we are directed to *deautomatization* or *defamiliarization*, a concept prominent in Russian Formalism and developed by Viktor Shklovsky in his 1917 essay 'Art as a

Device'.[26] According to Shklovsky it is one of the major functions of art to counteract our automatic perception and instead to 'make strange' familiar objects by casting them in unusual and unexpected linguistic forms. This correponds to Richardson's concern to see something new and wonderful in the habitual and everyday:

> [D]istance *is* enchantment. It is a perpetual focus. And escape from the obstructive, chronic discontent we are considering the state of deadness to the habitual...is possible only to those who by nature or by grace have the faculty of ceaseless withdrawal to the distance at which it may be focussed.[27]

Richardson attributes this potential of a higher knowledge to 'the womanly woman'.[28] In her article 'Leadership in Marriage' she characterizes her in the following way: 'Ceaselessly within her is a small gleam of the infinity men seek to catch within the shapes of systems of religion, of philosophy and of science.'[29] Here we can see that Richardson's 'womanly woman' is not synonymous with the 'womanly woman' described by some of the defenders of the New Woman in the 1890s, and should not be confounded with their attempts to stress the New Woman's traditional feminine qualities in order to counter critics decrying her as 'masculinised', or to contrast her real nature with an artificial womanliness.[30]

Richardson's differentiation between female and male modes of consciousness corresponds to another dichotomy, that of 'being' versus 'becoming'. 'Becoming' implies a dynamic, horizontal movement, a ceaseless striving towards some goal, 'being' is a vertically oriented concept that characterizes a state of being at one with oneself, resting in oneself and reaching down to 'one's own deep sense of being'.[31] Man believes that 'being' and 'becoming' can be entirely separated, and he has a clear 'passion for becoming': 'Humanity, the civilizations, look to him like a series of becomings.'[32] For woman, on the other hand, 'being' and 'becoming' are intextricably linked. By moving from one experience to another, one gradually develops a feeling of one's immutable identity, what Richardson calls 'the unchanging centre of being in our painfully evolving selves'.[33] But for her, 'being' is by far the most important component,[34] because being in touch with one's core of self means having reached a position of disinterestedness, the precondition for impersonality, for 'being simultaneously in all the warring camps'[35] without having to take sides.

This difference in attitude accounts for 'man's incomplete individual-ity'[36] and his marked ambition, which Richardson calls 'a form of despair'[37] and which holds him in an endless process of doing and producing. As a further consequence Richardson observes two types of selfishness. '[M]asculine selfishness'[38] is linked to man's ambition and the relentless pursuit of his aims, ideas and systems of thought. '[F]eminine egoism'[39] is most pronounced in the 'womanly woman' and is, paradoxically, equated with utter unselfishness: 'Only completely self-centred consciousness can attain to unselfishness—the celebrated unselfishness of the womanly woman.'[40] This seeming contradiction can be explained in the light of what has been said before. Egoism here is the quality of 'a complete self'[41] and means giving precedence to the state of 'being' over that of 'becoming', retreating from external circumstances into the deepest layers of one's consciousness, towards the centre of one's self where a stance of impar-tiality or disinterestedness is reached. This '[d]escent into impersonality'[42] couples a high degree of subjectivity or self-centredness, with a maximum of unbiased and hence unselfish perception.

This implies two things: first of all the ability to free oneself from one-sided, selfish interests bound up with a particular ideological position, to distance oneself from any emotional involvement in the matter considered, and instead to see things with a clear and 'distant focus'.[43] And, secondly, this kind of impersonality also affects interpersonal relations, because it is bound up with the 'gift of imaginative sympathy',[44] also referred to as 'sympathetic imagination',[45] a faculty that allows the subject to identify with another person completely and experience reality from their point of view. This intersubjective component can be developed into an aesthetic dimen-sion, too, if we consider the affinity between Richardson's sympathetic imagination and the Romantic concept of *negative capability*,[46] more specif-ically, Coleridge's and Wordsworth's characterization of the poet as a 'myriad-minded'[47] being. This means that for short spaces of time the poet can 'confound and identify his own feelings' with 'those of the person whose feelings he describes.'[48] In *Pilgrimage* Miriam Henderson tries to cultivate this ability as a basis for her own literary production. It is a quality which is transmitted in the texture of an author's writing and which in turn enables the reader to take up a similar stance of impersonality *vis-à-vis* the text. Miriam comments on this experience in the following way: 'you *felt* the writing, felt the sentences as if you were writing them yourself'.[49] In Richardson's own writing this effect is achieved by the use of a narrative technique that completely dispenses with an omniscient narrator and mainly consists of a presentation of the characters' consciousness—in *Pilgrimage* it is Miriam Henderson's—by means of internal focalization. Richardson sees herself in the tradition of writers employing impersonal narration, a technique specifically associated with Flaubert.[50] But Richardson criticizes Flaubert in two respects. Firstly, she calls his method of 'statement without commentary' a 'stylistic dogma'[51] that becomes an exercise in pure form and detracts the reader from becoming one with the text and the characters by implicitly demanding his or her appreciation of the *author's* brilliant execution.[52] And secondly, she reproaches him for his condescension and ironic distance with respect to his characters that plainly contradict his claim to narrative impartiality.[53] And it is in this context that we have to understand Richardson's own attempt in Pilgrimage 'to produce a feminine equivalent of the current masculine realism'.[54] It is a type of realism that is impersonal in its fullest sense, that operates from the centre of being, that is '[d]etached, in order to be able to focus'[55] and that is engendered by a female consciousness.

To sum up our findings so far: Richardson's idea of female conscious-ness is linked to the concept of impersonality, a concept which is deeply individualistic and intersubjective at the same time, and which has psycho-logical, perceptual, social and aesthetic implications. Impersonality involves related issues such as defamiliarization and sympathetic imagination; it is cleary resonant of the poetics of Romanticism and it forms an integral part of Modernist aesthetics.

Against this background of a gender-specific aesthetics Richardson's refusal of certain tenets of contemporary feminism, especially, as she puts it, to 'regard women as potential men',[56] becomes clear. The notion that equal-ity between the sexes means women's identification with men's ideas and imitation of men's pursuits leads to 'a growing army of man-trained women' obediently parroting men's formulas,[57] a phenomenon that Richardson increasingly observes in her own time. She characterizes such women as 'brisk, positive, rational creatures with no nonsense about them, living from the bustling surfaces of the mind; sharing the competitive partisanship of men.'[58] Many apparently well-meaning men, as Richardson states, see modern women in exactly that way, making sure, however, that they submissively follow suit rather than take precedence in any matter: 'Women, they say, are beginning to take life like men; are finding in life the things men have found.'[59] But these women are tacitly expected to take their place 'behind the vanguard of males at work upon the business of reducing chaos to order'.[60] Richardson here shrewdly exposes the rhetoric of subtle difference in a seemingly egalitarian discourse, which in fact envisages a scenario of active (male) shapers of the world and passive (female) followers of causes not their own. Her reference to these women 'living from the bustling surfaces of the mind' makes it sufficiently clear that in her view such a behaviour would mean forfeiting the most valuable quality they have, i.e. their female consciousness, and becoming advocates of one-sided theorems instead of striving for a holistic view of things.[61] She pleads for a cultivation of that female consciousness instead of its substitution with male concepts of existence. The problem to be solved in Richardson's view is 'not the problem of "woman"...but of man the specialist' who, in her opinion, has become an outmoded species.[62]

It is worth while to consider the implications of Richardson's argument. Like other essentialist positions it comes dangerously close to traditional gender discourses postulating fundamental differences between the sexes that finally serve to cement women's traditional place in society.

An example that illustrates this problem is John Middleton Murry's and Dr. James Carruthers Young's article on 'Modern Marriage' published in *The New Adelphi* in 1929. To them the partners' awareness of their respective roles is as an essential condition for 'a true marriage': 'It is the man's business to lead in married life; and it is the woman's business to know and to demand that the man should lead.'[63] The reason for this division of duties between the sexes lies in their difference of orientation towards reality: 'The man is the adventurer in the world of objects, the woman has the knowledge of the inward world. Man is centrifugal, woman centripetal.'[64] This assumption recalls Dorothy Richardson's distinction between 'becoming' and 'being'. The difference between their views, however, lies in the conclusions they draw from their findings. Whereas Murry and Young evoke a model of complementarity reminiscent of Victorian ideas of man-and womanhood—a man needs a woman 'to renew him, to give him courage, and to restore his faith', while a woman needs a man 'to give direction…and to insert design into her life'—[65] Richardson refutes any such functionalizing. In fact, their ideas are taken up critically in *Pilgrimage*, when Miriam Henderson distances herself from Hypo Wilson, who lectures her 'with the air of a demonstrator intent on directing a blank and wavering feminine consciousness'.[66] And Miriam declines several suitors in the novel because of their views on marriage, which echo Murry's and Young's points.[67]

Furthermore, Richardson's sympathy with feminism shows clearly in her review of *Feminism*, a book written by H. A. Wieth-Knudsen, a Danish professor of jurisprudence. She takes issue with his thesis that female frigidity is a direct result of the progress of Western civilization, notably of the upsurge of contemporary feminism, as well as with his claim that women 'are immeasurably inferior to men'.[68] She reads his onslaught as the result of an 'uncontrollable fury'[69] that leads him to draw wild conclusions from insufficient evidence. Such an emotionally tainted view is a common feature detectable in many books written by men, as Miriam discovers in *Pilgrimage*. They reproduce current prejudices about woman's nature disguised as scientific facts, classifying her as '*inferior*, mentally, morally, intellectually, and physically…her development arrested in the interest of her special functions'.[70] Here we recognize Virginia Woolf's criticism of those books produced by 'innumerable schoolmasters, innumerable clergymen mounting their platforms and pulpits and holding forth with loquacity'[71] their emotionally charged views about women. And it calls to mind Richardson's criticism of H. G. Wells's writing, whose 'women are all one specimen, carried away from some biological museum of his student days'.[72] They are types of one 'rather irritating dummy',[73] representations that obstruct the direct 'rapport between himself and his readers',[74] the way that Flaubert's ironic distance to his characters or Aldous Huxley's sarcastic commentaries act like 'a screen interposed between the reader and the presented realities'.[75] In short, these authors lack the quality of impersonality.

And yet it is difficult to claim Richardson as a clear advocate of the women's movement. For her, both anti-feminist and feminist positions are ultimately one-sided and therefore to be avoided. As Miriam realizes in *Pilgrimage*: 'Anything that can be put into propositions is suspect. The only thing that isn't suspect is individuality'.[76] Such a stance of uncompromising individuality becomes problematic, however, when it comes to the question of social change. Richardson's claim that the synthetic consciousness of woman 'has always made its own world, irrespective of circumstances'[77] seems a rather dubious assumption, since it is blatantly obvious that the chances of development of this particular faculty can at least be considerably enhanced by the provision of appropriate opportunities. This is a point she herself explicitly concedes in her essay 'Women in the Arts'. Like Virginia Woolf in *A Room of One's Own*, she attributes the lack of female excellence in the arts to the lack of a female tradition[78] and to the fact that the external and domestic contexts in which women live are not conducive to artistic production. And this applies to the absence of the necessary 'conditions of artistic achievement', i.e. quiet, solitude and the 'freedom from preoccupations',[79] encapsulated in Woolf's image of the 'room of one's own',[80] as well as to the lack of emotional support that men usually receive from their wives or mistresses.[81] Consequently Richardson infers that '[a]rt demands what, to women, current civilization won't give.'[82]

In other respects, Richardson is aware of the necessity of greater freedom for women, too. In an autobiographical sketch she describes the restricted job opportunities for women and her own attempts to earn her living. Just like Miriam Henderson in *Pilgrimage*, she starts out as a teacher, '[s]ince in those days teaching was the only profession open to penniless gentlewomen'.[83] Later she takes on a secretarial job in London, clerical work being another area offering employment to women. In the capital her own sense of adventure in exploring new spaces becomes apparent, the liberating effect she experiences when immersing herself in the urban landscape and the rich and varied life of London.[84] She becomes friends with a number of writers and makes contact with different religious and political groups, and these activities form the backdrop for the exploration of her inner life and the journey to her centre of being.

In conclusion we can say that in Richardson's notion of freedom two intimately connected dimensions became apparent. For one thing it is an inner condition, a state of mind that is free of preconceived patterns and systems and can therefore 'act as a focus for divergent points of view',[85] and that we have called *impersonality*, a quality she associates with a female consciousness. But, secondly, freedom also applies to the external context. It means freedom from material constraints and freedom of movement. And this kind of autonomy is by no means automatically granted to women. In fact, a gradual expansion of this liberty must be attributed to the struggle of the women's movement to achieve equal rights for women on a par with men. We have seen that Richardson rates these two components differently. For her, the concern with impersonality clearly takes precedence over more worldly matters. And this leaves us with an unresolved paradox in Richardson's thinking. It is the very definition of female consciousness, its core quality of disinterestedness, that excludes the subject's direct involvement in specific political causes, but on the other hand, as we have seen, the restricted conditions of women writers and women in general can severely hamper the development of a female consciousness in the first place, and would therefore call for more direct action to improve them.

IV The Voyage Out

12. 'Nature's Double Vitality Experiment'[1]
May Sinclair's Interpretation of the New Woman
Laurel Forster

The trope of the New Woman is a persistent theme in May Sinclair's fiction: independent female secretaries, spirited women, sexually uninhibited women, all appear in her novels and short stories.[2] It has been variously argued that Sinclair (1863–1946) portrayed the New Woman as a decadent and as a figure of female chivalry.[3] However, in this paper, I want to discuss a different type of New Woman in Sinclair's writing; an idealised, theoretically-constructed notion of womanhood; to use Sinclair's terminology: 'nature's double vitality experiment'. The 'double vitality' refers to strength and ability of both mind and body, a powerful combination of the physical and intellectual aspects of woman: a sort of super New Woman. This intellectualized interpretation of the New Woman provides a means for Sinclair, over the early part of the twentieth century, to discuss her cultural, social-philosophical and evolutionary views, and aspirations for womankind.

In order to achieve this formula for the New Woman, Sinclair draws heavily on evolutionary theory and philosophy, in particular the work of Jean-Baptiste Lamarck and Herbert Spencer. In addition, Sinclair interjects her own personally-held views about Idealism and self-realisation.[4] No stranger to combining quite disparate philosophies, Sinclair wrote *A Defence of Idealism* (1917), an engagingly eclectic work which expounds her multifarious views concerning Idealism and reality.[5] Whilst *Defence* reveals the undisciplined approach of the self-taught scholar, it also demonstrates Sinclair's lively ability to appropriate the ideas of others and incorporate them into her own systems of thought.

As already mentioned, Sinclair drew on theories of evolution and biological determinism, but her concept of the New Woman also encompasses related ideas of eugenics, degeneration and decadence. In addition, her belief in Idealism and Mysticism can be traced in a number of ways: in general terms through the sense of aspiring to a spiritual ideal of woman-hood; and in specific terms through Sinclair's strong interest in education for women, both formal schooling and through life experiences. This array of theoretical and cultural ideas, I suggest, provides the foundation for Sinclair's heterogeneous New Woman, and there is much to be said about the various ways Sinclair combines theory with fiction within the malleable concept of the New Woman.

This process of appropriation is central to Sinclair's version of the New Woman which I want to discuss in this essay. It has been argued that the New Woman is not an easily identifiable or even stable category of woman-hood, but rather is a site of contradictions and disputed claims.[6] Precisely because of this diversity and flexibility of the trope of the New Woman, Sinclair was able to develop her formula for womanhood and project it into the New Woman debate. Sinclair's New Woman is characterized not so much by the usual physical or external attributes of bobbed hair, ratio-nal dress and a career as a typist (although such stereotypical New Women do exist in her fictions), but is more significantly determined by her consciousness of herself and her role in the future of civilised society. Sinclair's New Woman can therefore range from a nineteenth-century woman breaking free of domestic constraints, to a suffragette, or to a war heroine. But external circumstances remain less important than an inter-nal mind set. As with many of Sinclair's constructs, the Sinclairian notion of the New Woman is a complex figure, moulded from a range of her intel-lectual interests.

This chapter will discuss only a few of these complex ideas in detail. I will initially consider Sinclair's pamphlets *Feminism* and 'A Defence of Man' (both 1912), which respond to Sir Almroth Wright's now infamous anti-suffrage letter to *The Times* and also outline her own theorised view of the future of womankind.[7] Then the discussion will move back to the turn of the century to consider one of Sinclair's fictive examples of the New Woman, in this case rooted in ideas of teleological evolution and educa-tion for women.

Sinclair's intervention into the debate about modern woman in the periodical press at this particular moment is interesting. As a successful single woman writer and sometime suffragette herself, it is natural that she would want to argue against Wright's conclusions about suffragettes being pathologically unbalanced. Perhaps it was the medical, pseudo-psychoanalytical tone of Wright's letter that enraged her and compelled her to reply. Always interested in psychoanalysis and psychotherapy, Sinclair was one of the earliest women novelists to follow Freudian ideas in her novels and was, around this time, involved in the inauguration of one of the earliest clinics in Britain to specialize in psychotherapy: the Medico-Psychological Clinic of London.[8] This and her extensive reading on psychology as well as a whole range of other intellectual subjects lent Sinclair sufficient authority to argue against Wright's conclusions. She took this opportunity to give voice to her own central tenets for a New Womanhood: a double experiment of nature superior in both body and mind.[9]

In March 1912, Sir Almroth Wright, Professor of Experimental Pathology at the University of London, wrote a letter to *The Times* about the militant hysteria of the suffragettes, resting his argument on a number of psychological, social and cultural reasons why Englishwomen should not be given the vote. His three column sustained polemic against women's suffrage in Britain sees mental disorder at the root of the suffrage movement.

Wright develops his argument along the lines that women are naturally prone to 'phases of hypersensitiveness, unreasonableness and loss of the sense of proportion' and to 'serious and long-continued mental disorders'. He implies that this distortion of the female mental equilibrium is related to women's 'physiological emergencies' of menstruation, childbearing and the 'change of life'. Consequently, 'the mind of woman is always threatened with danger from the reverberations of her physiological emergencies.'[10] Wright's anti-feminist invective continues to range round various other unenlightened anti-feminist arguments, detailing the evils of women's suffrage and propounding his belief in female inferiority.

Wright extrapolates his theory to the women's movement, arguing that 'there is mixed up with the women's movement much mental disorder'. Suffragette recruitment, he claims, comes from the half million excess women who should long ago have been sent overseas to mate. From this surplus quotient of women, Wright identifies various types: the physically violent, the 'sexually embittered', those whose personalities have atrophied, and those who have misplaced self-esteem. He pinpoints colleges and schools as the source of such burgeoning militant hysteria. Here, unmarried suffragists are teaching young girls to have much higher expectations and, most intolerably, to become feminists![11]

There was a small flurry of varied responses in *The Times* over the following weeks: some agreed with Wright, some repudiated his points, and some tried to apply reason. That this diatribe elicited any serious response at all is indicative of the insecurity of the feminist position at the time.[12] Sinclair responded to *The Times* within days, referring to herself as a 'looker-on' who 'sees most of the game', and arguing against Wright's unrepresentative sample and '*pseudo*-scientific' findings.[13] Seemingly on the same day, 31 March 1912, Sinclair also wrote *Feminism*, a much extended reply to Wright, expanding on her letter and adding many other points. This forty-six page pamphlet, written for the Women Writers Suffrage League (WWSL), discredits Wright's unscientific approach and countermands his claims that female hysteria, degeneracy and neurosis are the norm in the suffrage movement. To begin with, the tone of Sinclair's response is oppositional, remonstrative even, its occasional irony revealing her deep irritation:

> As far as can be made out in the confusion of his onrush, his hypothesis is that what we may call journalistically the 'hysteria bacillus' is present as the pathogenic agent in every case of what the journalists are calling 'Suffragitis.'[14]

However, as the pamphlet progresses, a certain level of disguised complicity with aspects of Wright's argument can be detected. For example, early on in the pamphlet Sinclair mocks Wright's views on sexual inequality,[15] but later on, when discussing female education, she comes close to expounding her own theory of inequality between men and women. She argues that the feminine brain has been exploited by misguided and over-zealous educationalists who have produced two types of intellectual: the natural and the artificial.[16] Because of the excessive demands on the brain of the 'artificial intellectual', so goes Sinclair's argument, her 'mental overwork' can lead to bodily degeneration, physically and reproductively. This overtly biologically-deterministic argument confirms Sinclair's interest in late nineteenth-century anxieties about the detrimental effects of over-education on women's reproductive capacities.[17] Ironically, at this point,

Sinclair's biologically-based arguments seem just as negative and unsup-
portive of the female cause as Wright's socially-reasoned letter.

The way Sinclair resolves this problem of over-stretched female minds
is through 'nature's double vitality experiment'. The duality of the experiment refers to the twin aspects of body and mind, resulting in a heightened physical and intellectual capability for the New Woman.[18] This model
of womanhood will evolve in the future, so Sinclair argues, when girls of
'artificial intellect' are extinct. Sinclair rests her case on a teleological view
of the evolutionary forces of nature to answer the problem of the 'artificially intellectual' woman. At the heart of the matter is the optimistic
belief that 'nature', once her way is cleared, will produce a woman strong
of body and mind, and who is equipped with this 'double vitality':

> Nature, mindful of the Race, tends to adjust this formidable disturbance
> of her balance, and the Artificial Intellectual is often sterile; and her
> numbers will tend to become more and more so, until, if she were left
> to Nature, and not produced artificially, she would soon be weeded out.
> And with her, the enterprising female educationalist, the amateur in
> evolution, would become extinct. And when she is extinct, Nature will
> have a chance for *her* double vitality experiment again.[19]

In this passage Sinclair conflates the idea of 'nature' as a positive,
progressive evolution, with nature as a catalyst for evolutionary progress.
In Sinclair's terms this progression is towards nature's 'double vitality
experiment.' Female over-education, as engineered by women educationalists, is seen to have inhibited this progress. There are four elements to
this remarkable view that I would like to comment on briefly: vitality,
evolution, education, and nature.

Vitality is an essential aspect of Sinclair's programme for the development
of woman through this double experiment of nature: Sinclair terms it the
'Life-Force'.[20] Here, Sinclair borrows but does not acknowledge Bergson's
Élan Vital (which she discusses more fully in her later philosophical work).[21]
In *Time and Free Will* (1910) Bergson wrote about the *Élan Vital* as a sort of
unified conscious thought.[22] In *Feminism*, Sinclair utilises this concept, arguing that it resides predominantly within the female sex as a moral consciousness and, furthermore, that it is this element of life which will be transformed,

sublimated even, into the 'increased energies of the body and the brain'.[23] Thus the metaphysical concept of the 'Life-Force', as explained in this pamphlet, affords Sinclair the opportunity to conjoin Bergson's *Élan Vital* with her own philosophical idealism, making them central to her concept of the New Woman. This essential and powerful 'Life-Force', rather than Wright's restrictive 'physiological emergencies', argues Sinclair, is the true 'reverberation' at the heart of the Suffrage movement.[24]

Sinclair's 'double vitality experiment' rests on a particular view of evolution: teleological rather than natural selection. Jean-Baptiste Lamarck (1744–1829) was an evolutionary biologist whose major contribution to evolutionary debates was the idea that an organism could acquire new characteristics as a result of use and environment, from one generation to the next, in a steady teleological progression.[25] Like others, Sinclair adapted Larmarckian ideas into more general writings.[26] What underlies her idea of the 'double experiment' is an improving model for womankind, which responds directly and individually to the environment. In Sinclair's case the environment is interpreted as a cultural shift towards sexual equality. Thus Sinclair is able to promote a generation of women, younger than herself, in whom she can see (or at least optimistically predict) a greater physical (and reproductive) strength alongside an enhanced intellect. These women will have acquired new characteristics to meet the demands of the changed social climate.

Of equal importance to Sinclair were the ideas of Herbert Spencer (1820–1903), an influential English philosopher-scientist whose belief in theories of evolution and scientific progress underpinned most of his work. Perhaps his most important work was his *Principles of Psychology* (1870–72), but his *Essays on Education* (1854–59) also had a significant impact on Sinclair with regard to providing a cultural context for the New Woman.[27] These essays are wide-ranging in their scope and above all suggest an organic approach to the subject and delivery of education. Advocating a broad approach, Spencer calls for an education which is more relevant to modern life: to family duties; to citizenship; and to careers in business and science. As part of this holistic approach to education, he expounds his 'economy of nature' theory, whereby the prematurely forced development of an individual (particularly intellectually), may well cause nature to allocate her energies unevenly or sparingly to other characteristics of that person. Sinclair makes use of this theory in her article 'A Defence of Man'. Here she expands on the idea of balance and economy of nature to explain the inequality between the sexes in the past. Her article addresses the question of man, raised in the wake of the ubiquitous 'Woman Question',[28] arguing that man's difference does not necessarily imply his inferiority, rather, his difference is due to the balance and economy of nature. Familiar Victorian arguments of female superior spirituality and sexual morality are invoked as part of this imbalance. Such imbalance should, according to Sinclair, now come to an end with modern woman who values both herself and her race. Sinclair deploys the concept of 'nature's economy' to explain that up until now one sex has had demanded of it 'an endurance, a devotion, and capacity for self-immolation', resulting in a 'suicidal tax upon the other'. While women have been acting as moral guardians of civilisation, men have been worked nearly to death by 'the struggle and labour of getting'.[29] In using Spencerian ideas concerning the economy of nature to bolster a feminist argument, blame for women's inferior position in society is diplomatically shifted onto nature rather than the male sex. With the shift in balance of cultural roles, namely man's new social and racial conscience, combined with the New Woman's ability to enter the professions and shoulder some of the burden 'of getting', Sinclair envisions not degeneration but an almost utopian egalitarian society.

By countermanding concerns about the degeneration of the female sex with the concept of 'nature's double experiment'—both physical and intellectual advancement—Sinclair negotiates her own answer to Wright's *Case Against Woman Suffrage*. She achieves this by deploying evolutionary and biological discourses for rather than against the New Woman. Thus Sinclair's New Woman is both a New Woman and an answer to the problems suggested by the critics of the New Woman.[30] Sinclair has achieved a feminist position of inclusion here: Lamarckian notions of teleological evolution are combined with Spencerian ideas of nature's economy. In addition, Sinclair emphasizes a more spiritually-based equality, with the Life-Force residing within women, and heightened responsibilities for the self and the race now pertaining to both women and men.[31] In this way Sinclair fuses evolution, nature and vitalism with spirituality, racial responsibilities and New Woman equality.[32] With its suggestions of selectivity and improvement, her argument, although focused on individual responsibility, has eugenicist undertones. Sinclair suggests that in this transitional time the evolutionary balance is altering. However, the fight for survival is conceptualized not in purely biological terms but placed within a moral and spiritual framework which complies with her own interpretation of Idealism.[33] This spiritual evolution, Sinclair continues, will lead to the essential balance of the sexes. Women's value in the workplace, combined with their moral superiority in the home, constitutes a feminism without de-feminizing women.[34] Sinclair reaches an all-encompassing position in the sense that her version of the New Woman is not just a significant social force but holds the future of humankind in her palm.

Feminism and 'A Defence of Man' articulate ideas Sinclair had already expressed in her fiction over ten years earlier in 1901. Her journalistic pamphlet and periodical publication bring to sharper social attention the ideas of vitality, evolution, education and nature explored in her *fin-de-siècle* fiction. Some of her earliest fictions investigate ideas of decadence and degeneration, demonstrating Sinclair's wide-ranging interest in issues surrounding women at the time, such as motherhood and racial responsibility; inherited characteristics; the vacuity of feminine decadents; financial dependency and degeneration; and the 'wild woman'. Sinclair wrote over forty short stories spanning almost three decades from the late 1890s to the 1920s. Two of the early ones were published together as *Two Sides of a Question* and can be seen as her fictionalized response to the dichotomies involved in the 'Woman Question' of the time.[35] The first of these, 'Cosmopolitan', is a tale of female liberation; it suggests the idea of the Wild Woman (the precursor of the New Woman).[36] The heroine, Frida (meaning freedom) is unfettered from all the normal parental, marital and class-based restrictions, and in place of these, physical fitness, life-force energies and personal philosophies are her defining characteristics. She has chosen a more bohemian lifestyle, sailing around the world with a female companion, free from the cultural and sexual restrictions of society.[37] In this figure Sinclair combines ideas of both the decadent and the New Woman.[38]

The other story, 'Superseded', is set, significantly, in a girl's school, and is the tale of an ageing spinster schoolteacher, Miss Quincey, who is indeed superseded by a new type of female—the dual experiment of nature—the concept used to argue against Wright's anti-feminist claims. Issues of biological determinism, female biological and spiritual roles, and female education are all raised in this short fiction. The new model for womanhood, Rhoda Vivian, has both vitality (as indicated in her name) and intelligence. She is younger, more able, more attractive and more modern than the prototype of teacher-spinster.[39] Whereas Miss Quincey is an 'artificial' intellectual, having struggled to maintain her position and authority as a mathematics teacher, Rhoda is a 'natural' intellectual. The familiar figure of a young doctor is used to voice a view of biological determinism in opposition to women's liberation, along the lines of the 'intention of nature' theory.[40] Rhoda's suitor, Dr. Cautley, aware of Rhoda's personal superiority in physique and intelligence, and also her potential to bear offspring of the same calibre, simultaneously admires her looks, her mind and her potential fecundity. Cautley is a problematic figure: he is a committed scientist-materialist, whereas Sinclair usually favours more spiritual psychical healers. And yet here she uses his voice and authority to describe Rhoda in terms of the balance of nature, comparing her favourably to Miss Quincey:

> It struck him that Nature had made up for any little extra outlay in one direction by cruel pinching in another. It was part of her rigid economy. She was not going to have any bills running up against her at the other end of the universe. Nature had indulged in Rhoda Vivian and she was making Miss Quincey pay.[41]

In passages such as this it can be seen just how closely Sinclair is using ideas from Spencer's *Essays on Education*. The accountancy metaphor with the notion of achieving an equal balance is taken directly from his work, as is the idea that female qualities can be weighed and measured in this way:

> For Nature is a strict accountant; and if you demand of her in one direction more than she is prepared to lay out, she balances the account by making a deduction elsewhere. If you let her follow her own course, taking care to supply, in right quantities and kinds, the raw materials of bodily and mental growth required at each age, she will eventually produce an individual more or less evenly developed.

If, however, you insist on premature or undue growth of any one part, she will, with more or less protest, concede the point; but that she may do your extra work, she may leave some of her more important work undone. Let it never be forgotten that the amount of vital energy which the body at any moment possesses, is limited; and that, being limited, it is impossible to get from it more than a fixed quantity of results.[42]

However, where Spencer discusses 'balancing the account' of an individual woman, Sinclair has extended this to a sense of women as a whole, and 'Superseded' expands Spencer's description of the individual balance into a more global form of accounting for women as a total body. Still using the voice of Cautley, this socio-political view of nature is changed into a more evolutionary-metaphysical view. As the story goes on, the scope of the balance of nature's account is extended to successive generations of women, one generation being debited in order to credit the next generation: 'Nature had indulged in Rhoda Vivian and she was making Miss Quincey pay.'

Rhoda is a certain type of idealised New Woman: she is educated, beautiful, modern, and able to earn her own living. She is also deeply heterosexual, looking forward to marriage and children with the rather unenlightened young doctor, who has learned all he needs to know about women from his own specialism—gynaecology. Despite her evolutionary superiority, Rhoda is no revolutionary: she demonstrates kindness towards the older woman, but no more. She accepts her powerlessness against the combined forces of evolution and advancements in the educational system which have made her the surviving type of New Woman. The contradictions apparent in this New Woman echo competing discourses of the time, such as evolution and degeneration, female spirituality and women's emancipation.

Evolutionary and other *fin-de-siècle* discourses continued to be important to Sinclair and to her concept of the New Woman. However, the 'double experiment of nature' explored in her realist fiction of her middle period of writing is portrayed with less conviction than in her earlier New Woman writings. For example, her novel *The Creators* (1910) quite overtly rehearses issues surrounding women's emancipation, particularly those of biological determinism, this time as an argument for motherhood to the exclusion of other more self-fulfilling creative work. The author Jane, or Jinny, the central character, remains an exhausted mother, only able to write effectively when she is removed from the domestic environment; she cannot perform both functions simultaneously. Others come to regard Jane's creativity or 'genius' as 'a malady, a thing abnormal, disastrous, not of nature; or if normal and natural—for Jinny—a thing altogether subordinate to Jinny's functions as a wife and mother.'[43] In *The Creators* there is no idealised resolution to the problematic of the 'dual experiment of nature'. Similarly, another novel, *The Combined Maze* (1913), could be said to explore this 'dual experiment' from the perspective of physical and moral strength.[44] This novel uses an anti-degenerate athletic metaphor as an organic model for life as a whole. Ultimately, however, physical fitness and a moral conscience prove insufficient resources in the face of fate and social determinism. Perhaps Sinclair's increasing understanding of the complexities and complications facing society and the individual made this 'double experiment' less viable.

The First World War might have seemed to offer suitable conditions to reconsider the 'double experiment'. In this time of enormous cultural upheaval, when huge pressures were put on men and women to perform to their best ability, Sinclair pursues the notion, in her war journalism, of women having dynamic dual capabilities. Most of her articles about women emphasize the two-fold role of women in war: their knowledgeable capability (strength of mind), and their capacity for hard work (strength of body).[45] The tone of Sinclair's war articles, however, both fervently patriotic and feminist, seems to belong to a different era:

> It is not that this extraordinary war has brought forth an extraordinary race of women-athletes; it is that the race of women-athletes was there, absolutely prepared for the tests of an extraordinary war. Hospital work to-day may at any moment turn to an affair of rapid and sustained athletics.[46]

This extract highlights the incongruities between the idea of the 'double experiment'—suggested by the article's reference to public girls' school athletics—and the brutal realities of war work for men and women at the front. In such a practical application, the 'double vitality experiment' appears anachronistic.

Sinclair's 'double vitality experiment' enabled her to encompass many disparate, even conflicting, theories into her rationale for sexual equality, and to adapt this image of New Womanhood across her writing. The duality of body and mind within the 'Woman Question' underlies much of her enquiry into real and fictitious female characters. Like other first-generation New Women writers such as Sarah Grand and Olive Schreiner, Sinclair understood that evolutionary politics, motherhood, female spirituality, education and social roles all had a part to play in defining the New Woman. Like Sarah Grand, Sinclair believed that spiritually-superior woman had to assist men to adapt to their new morally-conscious roles in society.[47] Like Olive Schreiner, Sinclair believed in women's work ethic.[48] However, there are important ways in which Sinclair differs from these first-generation New Women writers. First, Sinclair deploys the figure of the New Woman not as a site of political or social activism but as a solution to the current transitional state of sexual inequality. Sinclair's New Woman seems passively to accept her given role rather than proactively to demand a new place in society. Generally speaking, in Sinclair's New Women, consciousness is portrayed not through the developing, enquiring character of the New Woman herself, but through a more indirectly-narrated social investigation. Sinclair's New Woman does not explore the 'Woman Question'—she answers it.

Second, whilst many other early New Woman writers born in the mid-nineteenth century ceased writing after the *fin de siècle*, Sinclair's career had only just started. Sinclair was almost forty at the turn of the century, her mother's death in 1901 leaving her free to commit herself solely to her writing career. In contradistinction to most other first-generation New Woman writers but like Elizabeth Robins, Sinclair's writing developed from, rather than peaked at, this point. Sinclair went on to embrace literary Modernism,[49] in terms of style and subject-matter, and indeed is famous for coining the phrase 'stream of consciousness' about Dorothy Richardson's work. One of the many complex aspects of May Sinclair (and she is not alone in this) is the way her writing embraces her present and yet both draws on the previous century and anticipates the future: in short, she is both modern and old-fashioned. She engages with the idea of the New Woman in her contemporary setting, but does not let the matter rest there. She continues to rehearse and adapt her 'double experiment' model for womanhood over the next decade and a half, through the figure of the suffragette, the woman war worker and other characters. Meanwhile, she attempts to bring her vast philosophical reading of Idealism of the previous century to bear on this 'new' New Woman figure. Thus when Sinclair argues, in *Feminism*, that 'Not until the Millenium will you wholly eradicate the "Social Evil"' [*sic*],[50] we can comprehend that in her scheme, the New Woman is not a revolutionary of the moment but a more considered resolution, taking the best part of two centuries to come into her own.

13. 'She in her "Armour" and He in his Coat of Nerves'

May Sinclair and the Rewriting of Chivalry

Leigh Wilson

Chivalry is a useful framework through which to see the shifting debates around sexual politics during the late 19th and early 20th centuries. Although its rhetoric acted as ideological glue in the construction of English masculinity, in delimiting the terms of sexual difference, and in justifying England's imperial mission, many feminists challenged not the monolithic nature of chivalry as a belief system, but rather its practice as being exclusively masculine. One of the ideas repeatedly critiqued in New Woman fiction was that women needed to be protected, most usually from certain kinds of knowledge. The New Woman writers argued that innocence was ignorance and, as such, profoundly damaging to women. Instead, women too should be able to occupy a place of duty, courage and honour. Again, during the pre-war suffrage movement, women's militancy was justified as an assertion of their own chivalry and as an exposure of the hypocrisy of the chivalry of men. However, in both these cases, the use of chivalric rhetoric precluded a place for female desire. Femininity and integrity, moral, political or corporeal, could only be brought together if women were seen as outside or above or beyond being determined by sexual desire.[1]

As Catherine Belsey argues, the chivalric worlds of Chrètien de Troyes and Malory were far less stable than late Victorians and Edwardians assumed. In both writers, it was exactly desire which conflicted with chivalry. In Malory, while protection of and courtesy towards women are compatible with what really matters in the world of chivalry—that is, '[w]hat is at stake in the fellowship of the Round Table is a relationship between men'[2]—passion and desire outside of the homosocial are incompatible with it. The Round Table is, in the end, destroyed by a passion in excess of the chivalric code—more particularly, the chivalric world is destroyed by the active desire of a woman. When Launcelot and Guenevere are finally exposed, it is because the Queen has requested that he come to her chamber. Her expression of desire has made Launcelot's courtly treatment of her and his loyalty to the King impossible to reconcile. Arthur's agony at the end is caused not by sexual jealousy but by pain at being estranged from his best knight. A delicately balanced, harmonious rhetoric of chivalry makes necessary the exclusion of desire.[3]

The work of the novelist May Sinclair (1863–1946), one of the most successful and respected British women writers, has been read as an important transitional link between the concerns, themes and aesthetics of the late nineteenth century and those of Modernism.[4] However, her work is central to exposing the struggle to re-situate the New Woman within a different cultural moment. Sinclair's novels of the First World War were written during the same period as her modernist experiments in form. In these latter novels, *The Three Sisters* (1914), *Mary Olivier: A Life* (1919) and *Life and Death of Harriett Frean* (1922), her models for a renewed femininity are primarily concerned with interiority, subjectivity and consciousness. The successes and failures in the lives of her female characters in these novels do indeed display the concern with the 'double vitality experiment' discussed by Laurel Forster in this volume. However, my interest in this chapter is the difference the war made to Sinclair, especially given that her war novels have been criticised as reactionary and propagandistic by a numer of feminist critics.[5] In comparing Sinclair's responses to these issues in her non-fiction and fiction, her novels attempt a radical resolution of the competing claims of chivalry and desire. In particular, the ambiguous symbolism of Joan of Arc in the context of the First World War allows the novels to present a harmonisation not possible in non-literary forms.

The anti-suffrage uses of chivalry before the war are demonstrated in Sir Almroth Wright's infamous letter to *The Times* in 1912, in which he suggested that militant suffragettes were suffering from a form of mental disorder. The middle section of the letter is dominated by a discussion of violence. Wright's statement of his position within this debate is interesting both for the connections it makes between women's desire, the law, citizenship and representation, and for the light it throws forward onto the reconfiguration of these during the war. The real 'law' against women committing physical violence, he says, is not statutory but an 'unwritten and unassailable' chivalric code:

> Up to the present, in the whole civilised world there has ruled a truce of God as between man and woman. That truce is based upon the solemn covenant that within the frontiers of civilization…the weapon of physical force may not be applied by man against woman, nor by woman against man. Under this covenant the reign of force which prevails in the world without comes to an end when a man enters his household. Under this covenant that half of the human race which most needs protection is raised up above the waves of violence…And it is this solemn covenant, the covenant so faithfully kept by man, which has been violated by the militant suffragist in the interest of her morbid, stupid, ugly, and dishonest programmes.[6]

Wright's letter attempts to maintain a coherent rhetoric in which violence and chivalry are differentiated. Violence can only be honourable between equals—it then becomes chivalry. Otherwise it is merely violence and therefore illegitimate. Violence, then, is not a single concept; it comes to mean very different things depending on who commits it and against whom it is committed. The less powerful—the colonised and women (and these examples are from his letter)—only have a relation to violence in that they should be protected from it. The 'legitimate' act of violence is a marker of social and political power. Violence belongs to men. Women's relation to the world should be mediated by men. By assenting to this, their bodies can be protected. Crucially, what Wright sees as illegitimate sexuality 'unprotects' women as much as their acts of violence do. So the desire for knowledge shown by women has destroyed 'some of the modesties and reticences upon which our civilization has been built up',[7] and 'the very kernel of the militant suffrage movement is immorality'. These destroy the chivalric system and give Wright licence to imagine these women being 'crushed under the soldiers' shields like the traitor women at the Tarpeian rock'.[8]

The response provoked by Sir Almroth's letter included, in May 1912, a pamphlet by May Sinclair, entitled *Feminism* and published by the Women Writers' Suffrage League. In it, she attempts a recovery of female sexuality, what she calls 'the Life-Force', from Wright's 'physiological emergencies'. Through the veiled language of mysticism Sinclair is able to justify sexual energy in women beyond the polar opposites of either maternity or extra-marital behaviour (which was still conventionally lumped together with prostitution):[9]

> The physiologist will tell you further that there is voluptuousness in a man's chivalry and in a woman's tenderness, in her very rapture of self-immolation for her lover, her husband, her child. He will show you, hidden deep-down in the sexual life, the roots of the mystic Rose of Love itself.
>
> It is little wonder, therefore, and little shame, if he tells us that the sublime enthusiasm and self-devotion and self-sacrifice of the suffragists spring from the same root. They will join with the lovers, the musicians and the saints...in praising God for the wonderful root, deep-hidden that bears the mystic flower.[10]

All positive human activity has the same source; male chivalry and female suffrage activity are motivated by the same thing. And this is, for Sinclair, not an atavistic or bestial remnant, but evidence of divinity and of the transcendent. Sinclair challenges the sexual division of labour implied by Wright's chivalric structure. For Wright, chivalry *is* sexual difference. Women threaten to drag men down to the sexual, whereas men have the ability to distinguish between chivalry and violence. Sinclair's pamphlet enacts a repudiation of this in the language she uses to write about both sex and violence. Through a critique common to many in the suffrage movement, Sinclair's example of the dynamic of violence challenges the assumption that state violence operates according to separate rules or codes:

> It was the nursery rule when I was a child that you were not to hit your big brother because he could not hit you back. But I remember that, if your big brother broke the pact and hit *you*, retaliation on your part was invariably condoned by the authorities.[11]

The chivalric construction of femininity was used by pre-war feminists in their justification of militancy. Here I want to look at what happened to the chivalry debate when state violence, duty, honour and action reconfigured after August 1914. In Sinclair's non-fiction written during the war, she continued to argue for the propriety of women's presence in the public world, but in this context, it seems, female desire had to disappear. An article appeared in the August 1917 edition of *The Medical Press* under the heading 'Women War-workers and the Sexual Element'. The author, a Dr Burnet, alerts his readers to the dangers inherent in women's increased involvement in public life through war work. The war, he says, has 'slackened our moral tone', as women wear shorter skirts and smoke and drink in public. For many women, he argues, this laxity is not an unforeseen result of war work, but its very purpose:

> That the object of many of these war-workers have in undertaking such work as they are now engaged in has a sexual basis must be recognised. I grant that many of these women are unaware of the fact, but a fact it remains nevertheless. There is undoubtedly a certain glamour, if nothing more, in the wearing of male attire; and these women war-workers seem to thoroughly enjoy what to them is obviously a source of genuine satisfaction.[12]

The 'amateur' nurse, too, has a 'golden opportunity' in her proximity to 'officers and soldiers at a time when the latter have leisure'.[13] The integrity of the martial world is threatened by female promiscuity and its supposed consequence, sexually transmitted diseases.

Two weeks later, *The Medical Press* published a letter by May Sinclair in response. She has read Burnet, she says, 'with amusement', and goes on to challenge the evidence on which his views are based. War work, she argues, prohibits rather than provokes passion:

> Let him ask the conductress of the first motor 'bus he gets into how she feels at the end of the day's work. She will probably say, as one girl said to me: 'Well, we don't want anybody to sing us to sleep at night.'[14]

Five years after Sinclair's *Feminism*, a mystical recuperation of female sexuality no longer seems appropriate. The emphasis is on women's work, suggesting that desire must indeed be absent from the public world of duty and honour. At the beginning of 'Women's Sacrifices for the War', published in *Woman at Home* in February 1915, Sinclair is keen to establish a distinction between 'sacrifice' and 'service'. The former implies both loss and a claim to special moral status, while the latter is no more nor less than would be expected given women's equal claim to the fullest citizenship: 'For the British woman at her best is very like the British soldier.'[15] Crucially, it is women's relationship to work that established this equality. In Sinclair's journalistic writing, then, the desire to secure what she saw as women's 'proper' place within the context of the war leads to a closing down of the tensions between violence, passion and work. In the novels, however, these tensions are explicit, are indeed what provide the dramatic tension, and a different, more complex, kind of resolution is attempted through the figure of Joan of Arc.

For the pre-war suffrage movement, Joan of Arc—that is, a woman's body, self-possessed, inviolate and almost completely covered with armour—represented claims for a woman's ownership of her own body and her full subjectivity. Femininity could be disentangled from its associations with contagion, dirt, disease, excess and triviality, its synonymity with loss of order and boundaries.[16] In two of May Sinclair's four war novels, however, the figure of Joan of Arc is used to explore explicitly the tensions between a corporeality through which women's entry into the public world of war is made safe *and* active female desire.

Tasker Jevons: The Real Story, published in 1916, is the story of Jevons, a highly successful working-class writer, narrated by his friend Furnival, less successful, but urbane, upper middle class and cultivated. Jevons is rejected by the army on health grounds so, in his desperation to see action, he joins an ambulance corps. He is followed to Belgium by his estranged wife, Viola, and Furnival. The various journeys to the front are focused around discussions of the ownership of the war, chivalry, sexual passion and sexual difference. Before his departure, Jevons had already asked Furnival to make sure that Viola does not follow him across the Channel. He says:

> You've got to stop her if she tries to get out. They're all trying. You should just see the bitches—tumbling, and wriggling and scrabbling with their claws and crawling on their stomachs to get to the front— tearing each other's eyes out to get there first. And there are fellows that'll take them. They'll even take their wives....

It ought to be put a stop to.
The place I'm going to—the things I'm going to see—and to do—aren't fit for women—aren't fit for women to come within miles of.[17]

Jevons' words begin to make problematic the line between chivalry and misogyny. Which needs to be protected and which will be contaminated by proximity—women or the trenches? An ambiguous link has already been made in the novel between sexual impropriety and desire, and journeys to Belgium. Before their marriage, Viola and Jevons disappear together. Furnival, as a favour to Viola's scandalized family, tracks them down in Bruges and travels there to bring Viola home. The impossibility of knowing whether Viola remained inviolate following her trip dominates the narrative for some time. As her father says to Furnival: 'That's it, my dear fellow. We can't prove it.'[18] What these two moments of anxiety around who should and should not go to Belgium have in common is questions around the propriety of a woman's body and its relation to notions of chivalry.

When the three of them eventually meet up, in order to persuade Viola to return home, Jevons recounts what one wounded Belgian had told him: 'he didn't mind his wounds and he didn't mind the Germans: what worried him was the lady being there when he wasn't able to defend her.'[19] Viola in turn defends herself by talking about her work, about her duty to the wounded. I quote the remainder of their argument in full. When Viola says she doesn't want to be protected, Jevons replies:

'Men aren't made like that—if they are men. You can't have it both ways.' And he said something about chivalry that drove her back in sheer self-defence on a Feminist line.

She said that nowadays women had chivalry too.
'And *our* chivalry is to go down before yours?'
'Can't you have both?'
'Not in war-time. *Your* chivalry is to keep back and not make yourself a danger and a nuisance.'
'Come,' she said, 'what about Joan of Arc?' And that was too much for [Jevons]. He jumped up off the bed and walked away from

her and sat on the table as if it gave him some advantage.

'No, no,' he said. 'I can't stand that rot. When you're a saint—or I'm a saint—you can talk about Joan of Arc. If you want to be Joan of Arc go and be it with some man who isn't your husband—who isn't in love with you. Perhaps *he* won't mind.'[20]

The figure of Joan of Arc, for the pre-war suffragettes 'not only a perfect patriot but a perfect woman',[21] is rejected as 'rot' by Jevons precisely because of the presence of desire within the context of war. The entry of her figure into the conversation is 'too much' for him, and his impulse in response is to put more distance between Viola and himself. Jevons's rejection of his wife's argument suggests that what causes anxiety and repudiation is the presence of sex, of desire, on the battlefield. Jevons's passion and war work cannot co-exist without danger. But what the use of Joan of Arc at this point does is to make it clear, in a way that Sinclair's response to Burnet avoids, *whose* passion it is. Jevons refuses to admit that Viola can compare herself to Joan of Arc, inviolate, chaste, passionate only about her mission, because of *his* love, because he is in love with her. Sinclair's central character speaks out for the centrality of male subjectivity and male work, and projects onto women the responsibility for the chaos of passion.

However, what is extraordinary about the novel, what finally shifts the way these passages can be read, is its resolution. Rather conventionally, the final lines speak of the healing of the Jevons' marriage, but what allows this healing is the resolution of Jevons's fear; the fear, it is revealed, which has motivated him throughout the novel. His enthusiasm for the war is an explicit claim for masculinity; but the climax of this comes, not in a reappropriation of the inviolate body away from women, but as wounding and a strange redefinition of masculinity. When Furnival and Viola arrive in Belgium, they come across Jevons in a hotel, limping from a leg wound. He says, 'I like my wound. It—it makes me feel manly.'[22] Jevons's final wound, his loss of his right hand when saving someone from a burning building, cures him of his fear, re-unites him with Viola, and cancels out the effects of his class position with both his wife and her family.[23]

These questions of masculinity, femininity, passion and integrity that cluster around the figure of Joan of Arc are present in another of Sinclair's war novels, *The Romantic*, published four years later in 1920. Here, the confrontation between female chivalry and male wounding is more stark. The two main characters, John Conway and Charlotte Redhead, meet before the war and fall in love, but John refuses to have a sexual relationship because, he says, at any hint of sexual desire in a woman, his love turns to hate. Charlotte is created through familiar tropes of the New Woman: she is a typist, has a room in Bloomsbury and bobbed hair, and is open and frank in sexual matters. Early in their relationship John tells Charlotte that she looks like Joan of Arc: 'Her sight was second sight; your sight is memory. You never forget things…I shall call you Jeanne. You ought to wear armour and a helmet.'[24] In contrast to *Tasker Jevons*, in this novel the epithet takes the form of an ambivalent tenderness that allows it to slip between marking sexual desire, and martial strength and physical integrity. This occurs early on, before the war, but structures our reading of the rest of the novel in terms of a challenge to the meanings of sexual difference. The figure is repeated a number of times when Conway calls Charlotte 'Jeanne', making it even clearer than the use of 'Joan' would that it is the feminine form of his own name.[25]

Once in Belgium, the couple's different responses to the wounded soldiers they meet begin to reveal exactly what motivates Conway. He professes commitment to them, but is perfectly willing to abandon them if he feels himself threatened. Charlotte feels love for her wounded, but this is explicitly within a framework of integrity and strength. Seeing her at one point in an ambulance in the firing line in her uniform, John 'looked at her and smiled. "Jeanne," he said, "in her armour."'[26] Eventually, as the 'truth' of John's secret becomes clear, that is, his impotence, Charlotte moves from worrying about his attitude to the wounded to figuring him as wounded:

> And who was she to judge him? She in her 'armour' and he in his coat of nerves. His knowledge and his memory would be like a raw open wound in his mind; and her knowledge of it would be a perpetual irritant, rubbing against it and keeping up the sore…And if she gave John up his wound would never heal. She owed a sort of duty to the wound.[27]

John becomes a wound, and one, at this point, that she can heal. What protects Charlotte, what constitutes her 'armour', is her knowledge, her awareness, her ability to face the truth. This assertion of her vision, her version of 'second sight' as John calls it at the beginning of the novel, is what enables her to act with propriety, to act chivalrously, on the battle-field. However, it is this clear-sightedness that, at the beginning of the novel, allows her frank and guiltless sexual relationship with her first lover. Sex, she believes, gives 'The clear reality of yourself.'[28] At the end of the novel, though, John moves beyond her protection; he is killed, shot in the back while trying to run away. Finally, in the explanation of this illness from the psychotherapist who leads the ambulance corps, a most extraordinary reversal is effected. The doctor tells Charlotte: '[Conway] sucked manhood out of you. He sucked it out of everything—out of blood and out of wounds.'[29] Conway, then, is a vampire, and on him are focused the dangers usually associated with women. This feminization of Conway has been seen as part of the novel's propaganda, a rejection of the 'unmanly man' because of the damage he does to the war effort.[30] But *The Romantic* was written after the war when the understanding of such responses to the war had shifted. More than this, though, the proliferating associations of vari-ous types of wound with John is interesting in its implications for a read-ing of Charlotte. At the end of the novel, she contains 'manhood', that is bravery, a commitment to her work, a place in the public world. And yet, at the same time, she is allowed sexual desire. What the novel is struggling towards, in particular through the figure of Joan of Arc, is a vision of wholeness for a woman—an integration of work and passion, of the public and the private, of being both protector and protected.

Both during and after the war Sinclair was experimenting with narra-tives which concerned themselves with the interior lives of her female characters, and produced novels which were innovative in terms of both form and the possibilities of female identity. In particular these novels considered the nature of female desire, and the destructive consequences of its suppression. While it has often been seen as conservative, her war writing, while more formally conventional, continues to chart the trajec-tory of the New Woman. These novels imagine a place for women's subjec-tivity and active participation in the public sphere, and for a desire which is both confident and unapologetic. Within the context of the First World War, female chivalry, a mixture of the deeply conventional and the new, creates possibilities for a radical re-thinking of desire and sexual difference.

14. Elizabeth Banks

An American on Fleet Street

Jane S. Gabin

The story of Elizabeth Banks (1870–1938) is the American 'luck and pluck' saga with a transatlantic twist. As she herself stated, she loved both Britain and America, and felt free to criticize them both. But as a journalist she had a greater loyalty to truth and human rights than to one political identity. She exemplifies the New Woman journalist: risk-taking, bold, taking decisive action to carve out an unusual career for herself. Though the life of Elizabeth Banks is at present almost unknown to contemporary readers and scholars, it should be a life rediscovered.

Banks is a bit of an enigma. As a young woman, writing about herself and her adventures as a journalist, she is outspoken, courageous, brash and independent—and at times a bit self-important. As an older woman, though, she chose silence. She apparently published nothing during the last decade of her life, and requested that after her death all personal items be sold or destroyed. In her will, she mentioned letters, papers, and photographs in particular—all to be destroyed. Therefore, because we have nothing from Elizabeth Banks other than her will and what was published by and about her during her lifetime, I have had to reconstruct her life and cobble it together from a variety of sources. We can begin by using her autobiographical works as guides, corroborated by other sources. Her name is recorded in newspaper articles, her college's alumnae records, directories and lists of writers, and rosters of English suffrage groups. Interviews and reviews provide some additional information. We can also look at changes in self-reported information—for instance, in thirty-seven successive entries, each a mini-vita, in the annual British *Who's Who*—to track the development of her career and personal interests. But the lack of a body of personal papers adds an element of mystery and perhaps sadness to her story.

Elizabeth Banks was an American journalist who lived in London from 1893 until her death in 1938. Frustrated by the lack of opportunities for women at the Midwestern and Eastern newspapers where she first worked, she decided to try the challenges offered in England. She arrived there with no connections and very little money, yet through determination, brashness, and a compelling writing style soon had a recognized byline. Within a few years she had a large audience devoted to her regular columns in several well-known newspapers and magazines, including the *Referee*, *Strand*, *London Illustrated*, *Fortnightly*, *Pall Mall Gazette*, *Punch*, the *Daily News*, and the *St James's Gazette*. She may not have received the 'press' of her flamboyant American contemporary, Nellie Bly, but she also had an outstanding career and made a significant impact upon her readers, particularly through her exposés of social iniquities.

By the turn of the century, Elizabeth Banks had made herself well-known through her free-lance work. The 'In Cap and Apron' and 'Almighty Dollar' series had made her name famous, and she worked hard to keep her name in front of the public by contributing to many different publications. She had also published an autobiographical work, *Campaigns of Curiosity: The Adventures of an American Girl in London*. Published in 1894 in Chicago and New York by the firm of F. Tennyson Neely, it was a reprise for American readers of 'In Cap and Apron' and 'The Almighty Dollar' along with her account of arriving in London and trying various ways of earning a living. In 1902 her *Autobiography of a 'Newspaper Girl'* was published in New York by Dodd, Mead. Here she related her life leading up to her decision to go to London, her initial work for English periodicals, a return to New York for a brief foray into 'yellow journalism', and going back to London, where she resolves to give both American and British editors what they want so that she can continue to live independently.

Elizabeth Banks was successful because she wrote well, she was spurred on by idealism, and because she had assessed her market well. She wrote what she knew and she learned how to give periodicals what they wanted. When she arrived in England at the age of 23, what did she know about? Being American, working her way through college, her first jobs, and coming to England. These subjects provided the grist for many articles.

In 1895, for instance, she published an article in *Cassell's Family Magazine* titled 'Some Differences Between English and American Homes', and to *Nineteenth Century* she sold 'Some American "Comparisons" and "Impressions"'. *Cassell's* liked her work; it published several other of her works including a two-part article on 'Paying Occupations for Gentlewomen'.[1]

Around 1897 she returned briefly to the States,[2] trying to make a living with freelance work in New York while maintaining her contacts with the magazines in London, giving her English readers glimpses into life in the States. The Cassell firm in London also published a journal called *Quiver*, an 'Illustrated Magazine for Sunday and General Reading.' *Quiver* featured articles on religion, missionary work, moral tales, favorite hymns. So Banks gave them articles on American religious traditions: 'American Country Parsons and Their Wives' and 'The Story of Thanksgiving Day in the United States'.[3] She also contributed an article to *Nineteenth Century* on 'The American Negro and His Place', basically a study of racism in the States.[4]

The trend of 'yellow' journalism, at its height in New York, had little appeal for her, but she had to write for some of these papers in order to support herself. Additionally, it provided her with the opportunity to sell a disapproving article on 'American "Yellow Journalism"' to *Nineteenth Century* and another a month later to a Boston magazine, *Living Age*. The only good thing she could say about yellow journalism was 'its tendency to recognise the equality of the sexes so far as the matter of pay is concerned.'[56] The work was disheartening and disillusioning. And the pull of London was stronger. Banks felt she was actually better known there than in her native country. In 1900 she sailed back to resume her career in London.

By 1901 Banks was prominent enough to rate a listing in the British W*ho's Who.*[6] She continued her freelance career, contributing articles to *Quiver*, *Nineteenth Century*, *Longman's*, *Fortnightly*, *Temple Bar*, and *Women's Home*. She maintained some of her New York contacts as well, publishing articles in *The New York Times* and in American magazines whose readers were interested in her English experiences. For instance, she published 'Maid-Servant in England and America' in a Chicago magazine, *World To-Day*, and 'Window Boxes of London' in *Good Housekeeping* (the latter under the byline of 'Mary Mortimer Maxwell', one of her two pseudonyms).[7]

Elizabeth Banks was a versatile writer, producing short stories as well as articles on a variety of subjects. Although many of her articles were written as straight observation, most had some element of social criticism. For the *London Illustrated Magazine*, she contributed a first-person account of flower-selling to a series called 'How the Other Half Lives.'[8] Her subjects were often working-class or middle-class people, both British and American. Probably one of the reasons Banks could look at America critically, and at the British status quo critically, is that she was not a typical expatriate, and she kept herself at a distance from the moneyed Americans in England, writers or otherwise. A number of the wealthy and prominent American women writers living in London during Banks's day (e.g. Pearl Craigie [John Oliver Hobbes], Jennie Jerome Churchill, Louise Chandler Moulton) mention each other in their writings; but among all the names they mention, they do not refer to Banks. Nor does she mention them.

Elizabeth Banks was a working woman from a working-class family. Though she sometimes moved among the financial elite, she never lost her detachment from them. 'I am not the sort of person', she wrote, 'that rich Americans who live abroad generally "take to," nor do I seem particularly to "take to" them. Most of my friends on this side are British.'[9] Because we do not have a body of correspondence to and from Banks, we really cannot know who these friends were. We do know that Banks had a very good professional relationship with the crusading editor W. T. Stead, and she admired him tremendously. In *Remaking of An American* she wrote:

> I know that W. T. Stead was looked upon as 'yellow' when he did his big work in the old Pall Mall Gazette. That was some time before I went to London and had the honor of counting him as one of my best and most helpful friends. I look upon him as the greatest journalist who ever lived, and I believe that he will so be recorded in history. Let us hope the fact that Britain produced Stead and some of his great contemporaries will be remembered when later panderings to journalistic sensationalism for the mere sake of sensation and big sales have been forgotten, or, at least, forgiven.[10]

In 1911 Banks's career reached a pivotal point as she was offered a regular staff position on a weekly paper called the *Referee*, where she remained for five years. This paper was an unusual but highly-regarded weekly published in London every Sunday from 1877 to 1928. It billed itself as 'The Paper that makes you think', and consisted mainly of articles on politics, sport, and the theatre. The paper addressed its public as the 'Refereaders', and there seemed to be a strong rapport between them. The most unusual feature of the paper was that all writers had pen-names taken from stories of the knights of the Round Table, presumably as a way of indicating that they saws theirs as a mission for truth, chivalry, and patriotic valour. The editor was 'Pendragon', and regular columnists were 'Vanoc', 'Percival', 'Tristram', 'Lancelot', 'Gareth', 'Boris', 'Launvel', 'Balin', and 'Dagonet'. The identity of the last gentleman was well-known, however; he was George R. Sims, a prominent writer of drama, ballads, sentimental stories, and muckraking articles and books on the condition of London's poor.

When she joined the paper in the spring of 1911, Banks, the lone woman on the staff, became 'Enid', and originated a series called 'The Lady at the Round Table.' The fact that Banks could write under an assumed name was probably less appealing than the fact of having a regular paid position. And while having a *nom de plume* gave Banks a certain freedom in expressing her opinion, she really made no secret of her identity (e.g. one of the little stories she published in support of the war effort had Enid printed in parentheses below her name on the title page).[11] Each author, it seems, had a set place in the *Referee*; the paper was always fourteen pages long, and Enid's column appeared, with few exceptions, on page seven. Very soon, she was receiving as much correspondence as the older, more established columnists.

Banks noted that until about 1910 the *Referee* was known as a 'man's paper' and a conservative one.[12] An examination of numerous issues of the paper reveals an assortment of attitudes—male supremacist, jingoistic ('England for the English'), anti-Semitic, xenophobic—that characterized the 'traditional' educated Englishman. But the paper also supported good causes, such as a children's home, and eventually its politics even veered to the liberal. Banks knew she was hired because the editor realized the practical need for a 'woman's column'. But this suited Banks for, as she said, 'I was looking for a Sunday pulpit from which I could preach the Gospel [of women's suffrage] to every creature.'[13]

The editor warned her that the paper was 'dead against Votes for Women...You don't happen to have turned suffragette, do you?'[14] Actually, Banks sympathized with the constitutional suffragists;[15] so she could, in all truth, say she was not a suffrag*ette*. She also promised not to mention the word 'vote' without the editor's instructions. This pleased the editor mightily and posed a creative challenge for the new writer.

Banks found that gentle but pointed preaching to men in her column had its results. She wrote for the men indeed not mentioning suffrage as she had promised, but talking around it, trying to awaken men to its importance. It was as if she wrote in a sort of code. She was so effective at this task that at one point a member of Christabel Pankhurst's branch of the suffrage movement called her to say she was going to write a letter to the *Referee* thanking it for its change of stance. Banks begged her to refrain, for the paper had no idea that it had a pro-suffrage writer on its staff. Banks wrote for suffrage, advertised meetings, and helped sell copies of the newspaper *Votes for Women*.[16] And while she personally would not engage in any of the violent tactics, such as window-smashings, she wrote about the militant suffragists in a sympathetic light. By 3 November 1912, the 'Lady at the Round Table' column is headlined 'WHERE THE VOTE IS "THE THING"' and describes how chic the suffrage issue is considered in the United States. Of course, Enid is simply reporting what the 'Smart Set' is doing in America, but in doing so she manages to use the phrases 'Votes for Women' numerous times. The 6 April 1913 issue prints some of the results of a verse-writing contest addressing both sides of the suffrage issue. These verses are given the entire eye-catching right column of page 5, which is headed, in bold print: VOTES FOR WOMEN. Enid's name appears nowhere, but it is safe to assume that she had a hand in arranging this.[17] The evolution of the *Referee* from an anti-suffragist newspaper which wouldn't even mention women's rights to one calling attention to these issues has to be due in large part to the efforts of Elizabeth Banks.

And the *Referee's* prohibition against her using the word 'suffragette' did not apply, of course, to what she might write for other publications under a pen name. Therefore, 'Mary Mortimer Maxwell' could publish 'In Jail With the Suffragettes' in *Harper's Weekly* in 1912, while serving at the same time on the *Referee* staff.[18] This article describes the conditions in prison for her friend Henrietta, who also appears in the first chapter of *Remaking of An American*.

During her tenure at the *Referee* she again moved, this time to a building with historic and literary significance. Her new address was 5 Robert Street, The Adelphi WC1. Two blocks east of Charing Cross Station and just off the Strand, the Adelphi was only a few minutes walk to Fleet Street or the theatres. The Embankment Gardens, where Cleopatra's Needle had been set up in 1878, was only a few steps away. In the 18th century, when the buildings were new, J. M.W. Turner used to come to the Adelphi Terrace to paint views of the Thames.[19] These terraced houses built by the Adam brothers were, from all accounts, a desirable and fascinating place to live; and residency there symbolized, for Banks, the fact that she had 'arrived' as a writer in England.

Among her neighbours were George Bernard Shaw (Banks called him the 'Dean of the Adelphi'),[20] John Galsworthy, Thomas Hardy, and J.M. Barrie. Several suffrage groups and other progressive 'anti' organizations[21]—the Freedom League, the Actresses' Franchise League, the Tax Resistance League—had their headquarters on the street, and Banks recalled that she had only to lean out of her window to read the new placards in the opposite windows to learn the latest news.[22] Only a few of these houses still survive, most replaced in 1938—the year of Elizabeth Banks's death—by a large block of Art Deco offices. Some of the buildings in John Adam Street, however, retain the elegance of their origins, including No. 8, currently the home of the Royal Society of Arts.[23]

The Adelphi years seem to have been the golden ones of Elizabeth Banks's career. She was now a well-known figure in newspaper and other literary circles. Even if she herself were not recognized on the street, almost every English reader knew 'Enid' or Banks's other persona, 'Mary Mortimer Maxwell'. One time during the war, Banks travelled to Devon—an area off-limits to aliens—for a break. She had unluckily left London without her identity papers, and was detained by the police. When she convinced the officer of her identity and that she was 'Enid', he was astounded, so certain was he that 'Enid' was thoroughly English. She was released.[24]

When the Great War broke out, Banks had another reason to dissociate herself from her wealthy compatriots. She was sympathetic with tourists caught overseas by the war:

But the people who had lived on this side for years and then suddenly found they were such good Americans that they could not stay away from their own country — those who had built homes here, paid taxes here and none at home, made their livings here and lived here on the money they had made in America, educated their children here, were rearing them as English boys and girls, had fallen into English ways and made sport of the tourists who, as I often heard them say, came 'a culture-hunting'—all these angered me. England at peace they loved. England at war they forsook.[25]

Her love of both America and England shaped her writing and activities during the war years. Although she could have left Britain, she stayed to do her part as a journalist and keep British morale high. She organized a highly successful fund-raising campaign on behalf of the Belgian relief. This was the 'Authors' Christmas Belgian Fund', and for it she enlisted the aid of every writer she knew, asking them to autograph copies of their works, which would be sold for the cause.[26] First she recruited her neighbours, the Adelphi authors, then others whom she knew, and soon her kitchen was crowded with famous authors and stacks of their books. H.G. Wells came to sign his novel *The Passionate Friends*, followed by Sir Arthur Conan Doyle. Other writers who obligingly sent signed copies of their books for Banks to sell for the cause included Hardy, Galsworthy, Kipling, Masefield, Alfred Noyes, and Arnold Bennett.

This charitable effort seems to have been one of the highlights of Elizabeth Banks's life. Every year after 1914 she included in her *Who's Who* entry: 'Originator, Hon. Organiser and Hon. Secretary of the Authors' Belgian Fund and Dik's Fund for the Allies.'[27] Banks seems to have gone about the mobilization of this effort in a most organized way. She realized that having some 'names' as patrons would attract attention, and enlisted the aid of titled people and celebrities. Ultimately she obtained autographed books from over seventy authors, including many of the best-known writers of the day: Rudyard Kipling, Thomas Hardy, John Galsworthy, Israel Zangwill, Sir Owen Seaman (the editor of *Punch*), William Archer, Arnold Bennett, H.G. Wells, May Sinclair, Beatrice Harraden (like Banks, Sinclair and Harraden were members of the Women Writers' Suffrage League), Sir Arthur Conan Doyle, and George R. Sims ('Dagonet' of the *Referee*). Although, for Banks, a certain amount of self-promotion was inevitably involved in the Authors' Belgian Fund, her motives were altruistic and she was careful to demonstrate that the Fund was run in a businesslike way. According to records in the Imperial War Museum, about £300 was raised in 1914 and a similar sum in 1915. Banks reported that the author with the most books sold for the Fund was Sir Arthur Conan Doyle, with sixty-four volumes. 'The next largest number autographed and inscribed were by myself. The next largest in number were by Mr. Kipling and Mr. H.G. Wells.'[28] The concerted efforts of all involved in the Fund resulted in a demonstration of both patriotism and solidarity with a national ally, and a not-inconsiderable sum donated to the children of Belgium. But for Banks it must have been much more than that. Chapter 9 of *The Remaking of An American* practically glows with the excitement of having literary celebrities come to her flat with their offerings for the Fund. She describes Sir Arthur Conan Doyle, 'come to autograph and inscribe six dozen big and little books....When he had finished what he laughingly called his "stint," he, too, looked about the kitchen and declared himself to be in glorious company...celebrated authors climb to my kitchen, writing their names in the books I have gathered there ready for the Authors' Belgian Christmas Fund'.[29]

Some curious ironies come out of this. From Banks's writing we get the impression that she was at the centre of a lively writers' village, enjoying the comradeship of other authors and marshalling them into pleasurable patriotic activity. Yet none of the writers whom she knew as a neighbour and/or as a contributing member of the Authors' Fund mentions her in their own letters or reminiscences. Neither does George R. Sims in his 1917 autobiography, *My Life: Sixty Years' Recollections of Bohemian London*, although he had worked on the *Referee* with Banks from 1911 to 1916. Clearly these men did not value Banks's work and friendship as seriously as she valued theirs. Perhaps Banks's perspective on the Authors' Fund made the project sound grander than it was. At the least, it was more important to her than it was to participating authors. Having Sir Arthur Conan Doyle auto-graph books in the kitchen of her flat was a major event for Banks; but to Sir Arthur it was relatively minor.

Banks must have been on cordial terms with her literary neighbours at the Adelphi, else she would have not have mentioned them so warmly in her autobiography. But why did they not mention her at all? In a letter of

26 October 1917, Barrie describes an evening of German air raids against London and searchlights sweeping the skies for invading airplanes. Thomas Hardy was visiting that night, and 'he and Wells and Shaw and Arnold Bennett and I sat up one night watching the strange spectacle.'[30] Was the American woman from around the corner ever invited to a vigil such as this? Or to any social gatherings among the literati in the neighbourhood? Probably not—first of all, if she had been, this surely would have been included in *The Remaking of an American*. So why was she excluded? Not because she was a woman, or an American—Barrie was a great friend of the American actress Mary Anderson de Navarro, and used to visit her home in the Cotswolds regularly for parties and cricket matches. Shaw and Wells also enjoyed wide social circles. Perhaps Elizabeth Banks just wasn't notable enough, and, as a freelance journalist rather than a writer of *belles lettres*, never made it to the inner circles of any literary groups.

It also may be that although she enjoyed a certain readership in London, first as 'the American girl' and then as 'Enid' and 'Mary', she may not have been a very social person. She was a member of several London clubs, and she was active in suffrage efforts—but did she have any close friends? Aside from Henrietta Marston, whom she mentions in writing about suffrage—assuming Henrietta is a real person, not an invented character[31]—Banks does not mention specific close friends. Perhaps she was a rather solitary person who lived a full life professionally but a quiet one personally. In her *Who's Who* entries she usually listed as her recreations 'playing with children, dogs, and kittens.'[32] Whose children? Did she have friends with families, who invited her to dinner on the weekends? Did she work with children after she retired from journalism? Without the evidence of any journals, diaries, address book, or letters we can never know about this aspect of her life.

The first part of the Great War was a time that greatly tested Banks's patriotism. She was impatient for America to enter the conflict and could not understand its stance of neutrality. This section of her reminiscences she called 'The Alien', for while she was considered, politically, an alien in England, she now felt emotionally alien in America.

Banks was back in London when America did decide to enter the war, and described her reactions to the sight of the first American troops marching through the city. She confessed that 'their features rather took me by surprise, but something held me back from commenting aloud.' Living in London all these years, she had missed the great waves of European immigration into the United States, and it was logical for the new American troops to reflect the new ethnicity of the country. Banks admitted that at first she expected 'a British-looking contingent,' but then realized that so many people she met in Canada and America were not what she considered 'British-looking'. However, she was incensed when another onlooker, an American woman, an expatriate of long standing, declared: 'Why! They're not Americans! they're foreigners!' An expatriate American man also reacted: 'What does it mean? I tell you they're not Americans!'[33] Banks was angered that her compatriots were so unwilling to accept the idea of these 'new' Americans as their representatives in uniform.

Banks's postwar transatlantic attitude was paradoxical. She remained devoted to England, but became increasingly critical of it, disillusioned especially by its rigid and persistent class system. And while she asserted the superiority of the American way, she ultimately chose to remain a resident of Britain.

In the mid-1920s, Banks travelled again to the United States, this time to examine the phenomenon of the 'new Americans'. She wrote,

> Years ago I talked with Israel Zangwill about his play, 'The Melting Pot,' and I remember he expressed surprise that I seemed to have so little knowledge of what went into the pot and what came out. I, a free-born citizen of the United States, living much of my life abroad, knew little of what my country was doing in the way of creating a new race with a great destiny.[34]

Now, after having travelled through the country meeting the newest Americans she observed: 'My native land became a land of delight and a place of enchantment. So much was new to me, the returned native.'[35] This was the beginning of Bank's 're-Americanization'.

She loved England, where so much had been exciting and lovely—but so much had been separate as well. Banks had always been put off by the 'upstairs/downstairs' physical separation of the classes. This separation was emphasized by the educational system, whereas she saw the system in America as bringing people together. Banks was inspired to begin, in 1922, a study of what she called 'The Trail of the Serpent of Caste'—how the English educational system conspired to keep classes separate and prevent poorer children from attaining a better position in life. Her study was published in 1924 as *School for John and Mary: A Story of Caste in England*.[36]

Banks's final published work was her third autobiography, *The Remaking of An American*, originally published in 1928, and only in the U.S. In contrast to her two earlier autobiographical books, *Campaigns of Curiosity* and *The Autobiography of a 'Newspaper Girl'*, this book presents the maturer woman's perspectives on change, not only in herself, but in the two countries to which she is most closely bound. The book is not a straight narrative, but rather a compilation of reflections and anecdotes from three periods in her life: 'The Expatriate' covers 1912–1914, when Banks worked on the *Referee* and organized the Belgian Authors' Fund; 'The Alien', covering the Great War, when Banks was legally classified as an alien in Britain; and 'The American', documenting her disillusionment with England and her 'reconversion' to American values. Throughout, she mentions well-known people and places, and events with clear historical context. As a narrator, Elizabeth Banks is still the brave and headstrong woman she was in her earlier years of muckraking journalism, but with more experience and literary acquaintance to expand her views. In only one area does she remain dogmatic, and that is in the recounting of her 'reconversion' to American ideals.

While Banks seems to have enjoyed the brash, bold activities and writing adventures of her youth, she also seems to have become rather reclusive and self-effacing in her later life. After *The Remaking of An American* appeared in 1928, she published nothing else. She suffered from arthritis, and that may have kept her from writing. She seems to have retreated almost totally from public life. By the 1920s she had moved from central London to the 'suburb' of Hampstead, where she lived first at 104 Sumatra Road and later a few blocks away in Broadhurst Gardens, a street of comfortable redbrick homes, some of which were multiple dwellings. A 1934 post office directory in the London Library lists the Broadhurst Gardens address as a boarding house. Banks was independent but she was never affluent. Indeed, in her last years she may have had financial difficulties. As she published nothing—based on the complete lack of evidence in any periodical index or book search—she would have had no earnings. How had she managed? The Probate Registry listed the value of her estate at the time of her death as just a little more than £97. In the London of 1938, that would have been enough for about a year's rental of a small flat, so it was not a negligible amount; but neither was it a financial cushion, and Elizabeth Banks must have had to live very frugally during the last years of her life.

Although she never gave up her American citizenship, Banks also never gave up living in London. And while she always proudly proclaimed herself an American, socially she did not identify with her compatriots. Her friends and associates were, for the most part, British. She had not joined American organizations, such as the American Women's Club, which had been founded just a few weeks after her arrival in London. The only organization of which she remained a member for many years was the English-Speaking Union;[37] in fact, for the last eight years of her life, she listed her address in care of the ESU headquarters in Charles Street, near Berkeley Square. Her last residence was in Braden Street in Maida Vale, a quiet neighborhood not far from the Regent's Canal.

Elizabeth Banks's most active professional years were those early in her career, from her arrival in London in her twenties through her wartime activities in her forties. When she died in the Surrey County Hospital on Monday, 18 July 1938, the Associated Press obituary, wired from London and appearing in the next day's *New York Times*, concentrated in its six paragraphs on her early journalistic experiences and the Authors' Belgian Fund.[38]

It is ironic that Banks's death was listed in the leading American newspaper but seems to have gone unnoticed in the British press. Although Banks had lived in London for forty years, her passing seemed to be ignored there. But actually it was just eclipsed by other events. The day of her death, an eloquent plea appeared in the London *Times*, written by a number of Christians alarmed by reports of what was happening to the Jews of Vienna. This letter, so chilling in retrospect, was relegated to a small inside column.[39] The paper much preferred to concentrate its attention upon the King's upcoming visit to Paris, and almost every page of the paper was devoted to French history, art, cuisine, landmarks, fashion, and hotels. Francophilia bubbled from the pages like a happy vintage.

These were modern times, and the news of an earlier day— what life was like belowstairs in 1894, how Americans used to be able to buy presentations at Court during Victoria's day—was irrelevant. But perhaps the readers of 1938 would have been intrigued by Elizabeth Banks's account of her travels in the United States in 1915, in which she anxiously probed the psyche of a nation that was trying, desperately, to stay out of a world conflict.

To frustrate any future biographers, Banks wrote in her will: 'I earnestly request my Executors to remove all inscriptions from my jewelry and to destroy all private papers and photographs.'[40] Her executors were Jemima Steevens and Denys Kilham Roberts. The latter was a writer and editor and served as secretary of the Incorporated Society of Authors, Playwrights and Composers, a predecessor of the Society of Authors. We can assume that her executors carried out their instructions faithfully, for there are no original Banks papers in any library or archive, and we have no photographs of her other than those appearing in her early books.

How ironic that a woman who had been so independent, bold, and adventurous had become self-negating to such a final degree. Someone who, over the course of thirty-four years, published three autobiographies had to have a very strong sense of self. Therefore her wish to erase herself— her possessions, her pictures, even her ashes—is beyond the analysis of this essay. What happened? We can speculate, but we cannot know.

Perhaps Elizabeth Banks wanted anyone who might remember her, or who might learn about her, to focus on the earlier and probably happier woman. In her 1902 book she thanked

> the fate that endowed me with a certain kind of reasoning power that helped me to distinguish between what I could and could not do, as a 'yellow journalist,' and still retain my womanhood and self-respect, and I can especially thank the fate that endowed me at my birth with a particularly prominent self-assertive and combative disposition that enabled me to recognize my rights and then to fight to the death, if necessary, to maintain them.[41]

And so she remains for us—the young woman with serious eyes, who set out with her typewriter to survive in London.

——— *Notes*

Introduction
Ann Heilmann

1. Lyn Pykett, 'Foreword' to Angelique Richardson and Chris Willis (eds), *The New Woman in Fiction and in Fact*: Fin-de-Siècle *Feminisms*, Basingstoke, Palgrave, 2002, p.xi.
2. Virginia Woolf, 'Mr Bennett and Mrs Brown', 1924, in Rachel Bowlby (ed.), *A Woman's Essays: Selected Essays*, vol.1, Harmondsworth, Penguin, 1992, p.70.
3. See Sally Ledger, *The New Woman: Fiction and Feminism at the* Fin de Siècle, Manchester, Manchester University Press, 1997, p.1, and Ann Heilmann, *New Woman Fiction: Women Writing First-Wave Feminism*, Basingstoke, Macmillan, 2000, p.4.
4. Radclyffe Hall, *The Unlit Lamp*, London, Jonathan Cape, n.d. [1926], pp.300–1.
5. Virginia Woolf, *A Room Of One's Own* (1929), Harmondsworth, Penguin, 1945, p.63.
6. Gillian Kersley, *Darling Madame: Sarah Grand & Devoted Friend*, London, Virago, 1983.
7. Susan Standford Friedman, 'Women's Autobiographical Selves: Theory and Practice', in Shari Benstock (ed.), *The Private Self: Theory and Practice of Women's Autobiographical Writings*, London, Routledge, 1988, p.40.
8. For a brief outline of (Eleanor Rathbone's) New Feminism see Susan Groag Bell and Karen M. Offen (eds), *Women, the Family, and Freedom: The Debate in Documents*, 2 vols, Stanford, Stanford University Press, 1893, vol.2, pp.317–8.
9. Mona Caird, 'A Defence of the Wild Women', *The Morality of Marriage and Other Essays on the Status and Destiny of Women*, London, George Redway, 1897, pp.173, 171, repr. in Ann Heilmann (ed.), *The Late-Victorian Marriage Question: A Collection of Key New Woman Texts*, 5 vols, London, Routledge Thoemmes Press, 1998, vol.1.
10. Mona Caird, *The Stones of Sacrifice*, London, Simpkin, Marshall, 1915, p.378. The protagonists Claudia and Alpin conduct their marriage in two adjoining flats with a shared living room.
11. See Lisa Ganobcsik-Williams's discussion of Allen's concept in the concluding parts of her essay.
12. Abstract submitted to 'Feminist Forerunners' conference. Subsequent unreferenced quotations in this chapter refer to contributors' abstracts.
13. Sui Sin Far, 'Leaves from the Mental Portfolio of an Eurasian', *The Independent*, vol.66, no.3138, 21 January 1909, p.132; Virginia Woolf, *Three Guineas* (1938), London, Hogarth Press, 1986, p.125.

14. Alice Walker, *In Search of Our Mothers' Gardens: Womanist Prose*, London, Women's Press, 1984, pp.xi–xii, emphasis in original.
15. Ledger, *The New Woman*, p.10.
16. Lyn Pykett, *Engendering Fictions: The English Novel in the Early Twentieth Century*, London, Edward Arnold, 1995, p.13.
17. Abstract, 'Feminist Forerunners' conference. Salomé's and Egerton's concepts of femininity offer intriguing parallels with Hélène Cixous's 'The Laugh of the Medusa' (1976), in Elaine Marks and Isabelle de Courtivron (eds), *New French Feminisms*, Brighton, Harvester, 1981, pp.245–67. See also George Egerton, letter to Ernst Foerster, 1.7.1900, and 'A Keynote to *Keynotes*' (1932), repr. in Heilmann, *The Late-Victorian Marriage Question*, vol.5.
18. For *fin-de-siècle* meanings of the 'womanly woman' see Heilmann, *New Woman Fiction*, pp.15–22, 30–34.
19. Sarah Grand, 'In the Days of My Youth: My First Success', *M.A.P.*, 22 May 1909, repr. in Ann Heilmann and Stephanie Forward (eds), *Sex, Social Purity and Sarah Grand*, 4 vols, London, Routledge, 2000, vol.1, p.201.

1. Fatal Attractions?
Gillian Kersley

1. Sarah Grand, *The Heavenly Twins* (1893), Ann Arbor, University of Michigan Press, 1992.
2. Gillian Kersley, *Darling Madame: Sarah Grand & Devoted Friend*, London, Virago, 1983.
3. Elaine Showalter, *A Literature of Their Own: British Women Novelists from Brontë to Lessing*, London, Virago, 1977, p.209.
4. Ibid.

2. Alternative Wifestyles
Andrea Peterson

1. Britta Zangen, *A Life of Her Own: Feminism in Vera Brittain's Theory, Fiction, and Biography*, Frankfurt, Peter Lang, 1996, p.33.
2. Alan Bishop, 'Introduction', in Paul Berry and Alan Bishop (eds), *Testament of a Generation: The Journalism of Vera Brittain and Winifred Holtby*, London, Virago, 1985, p.30. Copies of all the published articles and unpublished manuscripts written by Vera Brittain and referred to in this chapter are held in the Vera Brittain Archive (VBA), McMaster University, Hamilton, Ontario, Canada. In the case of published articles, I provide details of the newspapers and periodicals in which they originally appeared; since most of the articles have been preserved as cuttings, it is not possible to provide page references. For clarity I also provide the VBA catalogue number, as published in *McMaster University Research News*, vol.4, no.4, 1978 and vol.4, no.5, 1999.
3. Berry and Bishop, *Testament of a Generation*, back cover.
4. Vera Brittain, *On Becoming A Writer*, London, Hutchinson & Co., 1947, p.73.
5. Vera Brittain, 'Semi-Detachment. A Modern Solution of the Marriage Problem', *Evening News*, 4 May 1928 (VBA, G107). There are several versions of this article, one of which appears as '"Semi-Detached" Marriage' in Berry and Bishop, *Testament of a Generation*, pp.130–2.
6. Brittain, *On Becoming A Writer*, p.180.
7. Vera Brittain, *Testament of Youth: An Autobiographical Study of the Years 1900–1925* (1933),

London, Fontana, 1979, p.72.

8. Brittain, *On Becoming A Writer*, p.180.

9. Vera Brittain, 'The Age for Marriage', *Manchester Guardian*, 25 March 1927 (VBA, G37); 'Marriages That Last', *Daily Chronicle*, 12 February 1929 (VBA, G183); 'Keeping His Love', *Manchester Guardian*, 29 November 1929 (VBA, G254); and 'A Man Must Be Considered', *Manchester Guardian*, 26 May 1931 (VBA, G344). The article entitled 'Keeping His Love' is included in Berry and Bishop (eds), *Testament of a Generation*, pp.127–9.

10. Vera Brittain, manuscript entitled 'A Man Must Be Considered. But As What?' (VBA, H99).

11. 'The New Woman', in Claire Buck (ed.), *Women's Literature A–Z*, London, Bloomsbury, 1994, n.p.

12. Sally Ledger, T*he New Woman: Fiction and Feminism at the* Fin de Siècle, Manchester, Manchester University Press, 1997, p.124.

13. Hugh Stutfield, 'Tommyrotics', in *Blackwood's Magazine*, vol.157, June 1895, p.837, cited in Ledger, *The New Woman*, p.17.

14. Ledger, *The New Woman*, p.11.

15. Ibid., p.23.

16. For detailed discussions of the New Woman and her attitudes to marriage see Ann Heilmann, *New Woman Fiction: Women Writing First-Wave Feminism*, London, Macmillan, 2000, pp.77–116, and Lyn Pykett, *The 'Improper' Feminine: The Women's Sensation Novel and the New Woman Writing*, London, Routledge, 1992, pp.143–53.

17. Heilmann, *New Woman Fiction*, p.77.

18. Ledger, *The New Woman*, p.1.

19. Anthea Trodd, *Women's Writing in English: Britain 1900–1945*, London, Longman, 1998, p.5.

20. Ibid., p.5.

21. Muriel Mellown, 'Vera Brittain: Feminist in a New Age', in Dale Spender (ed.), *Feminist Theorists: Three Centuries of Women's Intellectual Traditions*, London, Women's Press, 1983, p.316.

22. Bishop, 'Introduction to Vera Brittain's Journalism', in Berry and Bishop, *Testament of a Generation*, pp.37–8.

23. Brittain, *Testament of Youth*, p.41.

24. Ibid., p.73, emphasis in original.

25. Roland Leighton, letter dated 22.4.1914. See Alan Bishop and Mark Bostridge (eds), *Letters from a Lost Generation: First World War Letters of Vera Brittain and Four Friends*, London, Little, Brown and Company, 1998, p.14.

26. Olive Schreiner, unpublished letter, cited in Laurence Lerner, 'Olive Schreiner and the Feminists', in Malvern Van Wyk Smith and Don Maclennan (eds), *Olive Schreiner and After: Essays on South African Literature in Honour of Guy Butler*, Cape Town, David Philip, 1983, p.74.

27. Vera Brittain, letter dated 3.5.1914. See Bishop and Bostridge, *Letters from a Lost Generation*, p.16.

28. Roland Leighton, letter dated 7.9.1915. See Bishop and Bostridge, *Letters from a Lost Generation*, p.161.

29. Alan Bishop, '"With suffering and through time": Olive Schreiner, Vera Brittain and the Great War', in Smith and Maclennan, *Olive Schreiner and After*, p.88.

30. Alan Bishop (ed.), *Chronicle of Youth: Vera Brittain's War Diary 1913–1917*, London, Book

Club Associates, 1981, p.258.

31. Bishop, 'With suffering and through time', p.82.

32. Ibid., p.91.

33. Bishop, *Chronicle of Youth*, p.162 (my emphasis).

34. Olive Schreiner, *The Story of an African Farm* (1883), Oxford, Oxford University Press, 1992, p.150.

35. Olive Schreiner, unpublished letter, cited in Lerner, 'Olive Schreiner and the Feminists', p.73.

36. Schreiner, *African Farm*, p.156.

37. Lerner, 'Olive Schreiner and the Feminists', p.73.

38. Olive Schreiner, cited in Vera Brittain, manuscript dated July 1929, entitled 'The Crisis In Morals: Prudery versus Knowledge' (VBA, H106).

39. Schreiner, *African Farm*, p.246.

40. Olive Schreiner, *Woman and Labour*, London, Unwin, 1911, p.259, cited in Ridley Beeton, *Olive Schreiner*, Cape Town, Howard Timmins, 1974, p.75.

41. Schreiner, *Woman and Labour*, p.216, cited in Beeton, *Olive Schreiner*, p.74.

42. Schreiner, *Woman and Labour*, p.245, cited in Beeton, *Olive Schreiner*, pp.74–5.

43. Vera Brittain, 'Happiness and Sex. Do Women Enjoy Life Less Than Men?', *Yorkshire Post*, 19 December 1927 (VBA, G86).

44. Vera Brittain, *Women's Work in Modern England*, London, Nowell Douglas, 1928, p.37.

45. Vera Brittain, 'The Professional Woman: Careers Affected by Marriage', *Manchester Guardian*, 27 September 1928 (VBA, G145). A similar version of this article, entitled 'The Professional Woman: Careers And Marriage', is included in Berry and Bishop, *Testament of a Generation*, pp.123–6.

46. Beeton, *Olive Schreiner*, pp. 72–3.

47. Vera Brittain, 'Married Teachers and Social Hypocrisy', *The Nation and The Athenaeum*, 28 July 1928 (VBA, G131).

48. Vera Brittain, 'Superfluous Women are Really The Tennis Mad who Neglect their Homes', *Evening Standard*, 24 June 1929 (VBA, G223).

49. Ibid.

50. Linda Anderson, *Women and Autobiography in the Twentieth Century: Remembered Futures*, London, Prentice Hall/Harvester Wheatsheaf, 1997, p.82.

51. Ibid., p.82.

52. Brittain, 'Semi-Detachment. A Modern Solution of the Marriage Problem', *Evening News*, 4 May 1928 (VBA, G107). There are several versions of this article, one of which appears as '"Semi-Detached" Marriage' in Berry and Bishop, *Testament of a Generation*, pp.130–2.

53. Lucy Bland, 'Marriage Laid Bare: Middle-Class Women and Marital Sex 1880s–1914', in Jane Lewis (ed.), *Labour & Love: Women's Experience of Home and Family 1850–1940*, Oxford, Blackwell, 1986, p.142.

54. Brittain, manuscript dated July 1929, entitled 'The Crisis In Morals: Prudery versus Knowledge' (VBA, H106).

55. Ibid.

56. Heilmann, *New Woman Fiction*, p.79 and p.78.

57. Brittain, 'The Crisis In Morals: Prudery versus Knowledge' (VBA, H106).

58. Vera Brittain, 'The Modern "Old Maid"', *Daily Telegraph*, 8 December 1928 (VBA, G164).

59. Vera Brittain, 'Is It Foolish To Be An *Old Maid* From Choice?', *Modern Weekly*, 25 January 1930 (VBA, G271).

60. Brittain, 'Semi-Detachment. A Modern Solution of the Marriage Problem, *Evening News*, 4 May 1928 (VBA, G107).
61. Vera Brittain, 'Celibate Professions. Problem of the Married Woman Worker', *Daily Telegraph*, 27 March 1929 (VBA, G196).
62. Vera Brittain, 'The Husband in the Home', *Evening Standard*, 7 May 1928 (VBA, G110). See also Vera Brittain, 'Home-Making Husbands', *Yorkshire Post*, 3 January 1927 (VBA, G28), and Vera Brittain, 'Fathercraft. The Man in the Nursery', *Manchester Guardian*, 13 September 1928 (VBA, G141).
63. Schreiner, *Woman and Labour*, p.132, cited in Beeton, *Olive Schreiner*, p.74.
64. Vera Brittain, 'The Influence of Olive Schreiner. An Appreciation', *National Council of Women News*, February 1955. This article appears as 'The Influence of Olive Schreiner' in Berry and Bishop, *Testament of a Generation*, pp.313–5.
65. Heilmann, *New Woman Fiction*, p.112.
66. Ibid., p.85.
67. Vera Brittain, 'Wasted Women: The Tyranny of Houses', *Manchester Guardian*, 10 June 1927 (VBA, G55).
68. Vera Brittain, 'Reform the English Home! Household Drudgery That Kills Happiness', *Daily Dispatch*, 18 November 1929 (VBA, G250).
69. Brittain, 'Is It Foolish To Be An *Old Maid* From Choice?', *Modern Weekly*, 25 January 1930 (VBA, G271).
70. Brittain, 'The Husband in the Home', *Evening Standard*, 7 May 1928 (VBA, G110).
71. Brittain, 'The Influence of Olive Schreiner. An Appreciation' in the *National Council of Women News*, February 1955.
72. Vera Brittain, 'The Incomplete Woman: Wives and Spinsters', *Manchester Guardian*, 19 October 1927 (VBA, G74).

3. A Transatlantic Alliance
Patricia Pulham

1. Robert Browning, 'Inapprehensiveness', *Asolando: Fancies and Facts*, in *Poetical Works of Robert Browning*, vol. 17, London, Smith and Elder, 1894, pp.29–30, p.30.
2. Vernon Lee, *Studies of the Eighteenth Century in Italy*, London, W. Satchell, 1880.
3. Burdett Gardner, *The Lesbian Imagination (Victorian Style): a Psychological and Critical Study of 'Vernon Lee'*, New York and London, Garland Publishing Inc., 1987, p.44.
4. See Carlo Caballero, '"A Wicked Voice": On Vernon Lee, Wagner, and the Effects of Music', *Victorian Studies*, vol.35, no.4, Summer, 1992, pp.385–408; Jane Hotchkiss, '(P)revising Freud: Vernon Lee's Castration Phantasy', in Carola M. Kaplan and Anne B. Simpson (eds), *Seeing Double: Revisioning Edwardian and Modernist Literature*, London and Basingstoke, Macmillan, 1996, pp.21–38; Christa Zorn-Belde, 'Aesthetic Intertextuality as Cultural Critique: Vernon Lee Rewrites History through Walter Pater's "La Gioconda"', *Victorian Newsletter*, Spring 1997, pp.4–10; Catherine Maxwell, 'From Dionysus to "Dionea": Vernon Lee's Portraits', *Word & Image*, vol.13, no.3, July-September 1997, pp.253–69; Gillian Beer, 'The Dissidence of Vernon Lee: *Satan the Waster* and the Will to Believe', in Suzanne Raitt and Trudi Tate (eds), *Women's Fiction and the Great War*, Oxford, Clarendon Press, 1997, pp.107–31; Kathy Alexis Psomiades, *Beauty's Body: Femininity and Representation in British Aestheticism*, Stanford, Stanford University Press, 1997, especially Chapter 4, and '"Still Burning from This Strangling Embrace": Vernon Lee on Desire and Aesthetics', in Richard Dellamora (ed.), *Victorian Sexual Dissidence*, Chicago

and London, Chicago University Press, 1999, pp. 21–41; Angela Leighton, 'Ghosts, Aestheticism, and "Vernon Lee"', *Victorian Literature and Culture*, vol.28, no.1, 2000, pp.1–14.

5. Charlotte Perkins Gilman, *The Living of Charlotte Perkins Gilman: An Autobiography*, New York and London, D. Appleton-Century Co., 1935, pp.299–300.

6. Charlotte Perkins Gilman (Stetson), letter to Vernon Lee, 28.11.1900, 'Papers of Vernon Lee', Box 5, in the Lee Archive at Somerville College, Oxford.

7. Gilman, *The Living*, p.259.

8. These books also appear in the Vernon Lee Library collection at the British Institute in Florence.

9. Annotated edition of Charlotte Perkins Stetson, *Women and Economics: A Study of the Economic Relation between Men and Women as a Factor in Social Evolution.* 1899, in the Vernon Lee Library at the British Institute Florence, catalogue no.: VL/330.19396 STE., pp.132, 129.

10. Gilman (Stetson), letter of 28.11.1900, 'Papers'.

11. Vernon Lee, 'The Economic Parasitism of Women', *Gospels of Anarchy and Other Contemporary Studies*, London, T. Fisher Unwin, 1908, pp.263–97, p.263.

12. Lee, 'The Economic Parasitism of Women', pp.266–7.

13. Christa Zorn-Belde, 'Vernon Lee: Aesthetics, History and the Female Subject in the Nineteenth Century', Ph.D. thesis, University of Florida, 1994, p.63.

14. Zorn-Belde, 'Vernon Lee', p.63.

15. Zorn-Belde, 'Vernon Lee', p.54.

16. Zorn-Belde, 'Vernon Lee', pp.63–4.

17. This assertion is one that Gilman reiterates for, as Lisa Ganobcsik-Williams observes in her contribution to this collection, Gilman makes a similar statement in 'On Ellen Key and the Woman Movement'.

18. Charlotte Perkins Gilman, 'The Primal Power', *The Suffragette*, 6 June 1913, pp.562–3, p.562.

19. The dates of letters from Ethel Smyth to Vernon Lee quoted in this article are all accompanied by question marks, as they are in the collection of papers held at Somerville College, Oxford. Although we cannot be certain that these suggested dates are correct, they are consistent with Smyth's involvement with *The Suffragette*.

20. Ethel Smyth, letter to Vernon Lee, 15.11.1912 (?), 'Papers', Box 13.

21. Smyth, letter of 24.1.1913 (?), 'Papers'.

22. Smyth, letter of 24.1.1913 (?), 'Papers'.

23. Lee, 'The Economic Parasitism of Women', pp.293–4.

24. Vernon Lee, 'Why I want women to have the vote', 'Galleyproofs', Special Collections, Miller Library, Colby College, Waterville, Maine U.S.A.

25. Annotated edition of Charlotte Perkins Gilman, *The Home: Its Work and Its Influence*, New York, McClure, 1903, in the Vernon Lee Library, at the British Institute, Florence, catalogue no.: VL/301.4 GIL., pp.258–9.

26. Annotated edition of Gilman, *The Home*, p.259.

27. Zorn-Belde, 'Vernon Lee', p.65.

28. Gilman, letter of 15.12.1902, 'Papers'.

29. Gilman, letter dated 1904, 'Papers'.

30. Gilman, letter of 15.12.1902, 'Papers'.

31. Lee, 'The Economic Parasitism of Women', p.275.

32. Gilman, letter of 28.11.1900, 'Papers'.

33. Many thanks to the librarian at Somerville College, Oxford, to Mark Roberts at the

Vernon Lee Library, in the British Institute in Florence, and special thanks also to Nancy Reinhardt, Special Collections, Miller Library, Colby College, Waterville, Maine, for her cooperation and for allowing the publication of extracts from the Lee archive. This research was financed by the Central Research Fund and the Convocation Fund of the University of London.

4. Charlotte Perkins Gilman and *The Forerunner*
Lisa Ganobcsik-Williams

1. Charlotte Perkins Gilman, 'On Ellen Key and the Woman Movement', *The Forerunner*, vol.4, 1914, p.36.
2. Charlotte Perkins Gilman, *The Living of Charlotte Perkins Gilman*, Madison, University of Wisconsin Press (1935), 1990, p.304.
3. Gilman quoted in Larry Ceplair, *Charlotte Perkins Gilman: A Nonfiction Reader*, New York, Columbia University Press, 1991, p.93.
4. Charlotte Perkins Gilman, 'Announcement to All My Readers and Friends', *The Forerunner*, vol.7, 1916, p.56.
5. John Higham, *Strangers in the Land: Patterns of American Nativism 1860–1925*, Westport, Connecticut, Greenwood Press, 1981, p.159.
6. For a discussion of American immigration patterns, see Oscar Handlin, *Immigration as a Factor in American History*, Englewood Cliffs, New Jersey, Prentice-Hall, 1959, pp.1–15, and Higham, *Strangers*, 1981, p.88. For tables measuring the volume of immigration at ten-year intervals, see Maldwyn A. Jones, *The Limits of Liberty: American History 1607–1992*, Oxford, Oxford University Press, 1995, p.694.
7. Higham, *Strangers*, 1981, p.110, and Robert H. Weibe, *The Search for Order, 1877–1920*, London, MacMillan, 1967, p.288.
8. Ceplair, *Nonfiction Reader*, 1991, p.194, p.272.
9. Higham, *Strangers*, 1981, p.4.
10. On Gilman's family ancestry, see Ann J. Lane, *To 'Herland' and Beyond: The Life and Work of Charlotte Perkins Gilman*, Charlottesville, Virginia, University Press of Virginia, 1990, p.21, p.35.
11. Ceplair, *Nonfiction Reader*, 1991, p.194.
12. Dale M. Bauer, *Introduction* to Charlotte Perkins Gilman, 'The Yellow Wallpaper', Boston, Bedford Books, 1998, p.25.
13. David Leviatin, *Introduction* to Jacob Riis, *How the Other Half Lives: Studies Among the Tenements of New York*, New York, St. Martin's Press, 1996, pp.16–17.
14. Higham, *Strangers*, 1981, p.69, p.75, pp.101–6, p.234, p.238.
15. Susan S. Lanser, 'Feminist Criticism, "The Yellow Wallpaper," and the Politics of Color in America', *Feminist Studies*, vol.15, 1989, p.425.
16. Charlotte Perkins Gilman, 'The Making of Americans', *Women's Journal*, vol.8, 1904, p.258, and Charlotte Perkins Gilman, 'Malthusianism and Race Suicide,' *Women's Journal*, vol.9, 1904, p.282.
17. Gilman quoted in Ceplair, *Nonfiction Reader*, 1991, p.272.
18. These sentiments appear in *The Outlook*, vol. 79, 1905, and in the *World To-day*, vol.11, 1906. Both are cited in Higham, *Strangers*, 1981, p.110.
19. Higham, *Strangers*, 1981, p.110.
20. For a history of the American settlement movement, its founder Jane Addams, and an explanation of the movement's commitment to immigrants, see Allen F. Davis, *American*

Heroine: The Life and Legend of Jane Addams, New York, Oxford University Press, 1973. Also see Jane Addams, *Twenty Years at Hull House*, New York, MacMillan (1910), 1963.

21. On the growth of managerialism in social reform during the Progressive Era, see Weibe, *Search for Order*, 1967.

22. Charlotte Perkins Gilman, *Moving the Mountain*, *The Forerunner*, vol.2, nos.1–12, 1911, p.51, pp.79–81, p.109, p.135, p.140. Oscar Handlin, *The Uprooted*, Boston, Little, Brown, and Co. (1951), 1973, p.34–55, describes the hardships of the emigrant voyage and the development of government regulations between 1830–1900. On the transition from state to federal immigration controls and the 1892 establishment of the Ellis Island receiving station, see Higham, *Strangers*, 1981, pp.99–105. For primary documents on the immigrant passage and processing, see Virginia Yans-McLaughlin and Marjorie Lightman, *Ellis Island and the Peopling of America: The Official Guide*, New York, The New Press, 1997.

23. Gilman, *Moving the Mountain*, 1911, pp.80–1.

24. Higham, *Strangers*, 1981, pp.238, 242. Supported by churches, employers, and schools, Americanization was characterised by a campaign against bilingualism and 'an insistence on accentless speech, conformity in dress, and the performance of patriotic rites such as the daily pledge of allegiance to the flag in schools and the singing of the national anthem at sports events'. National Ethnic Coalition of Organizations, *Why Can't Those Immigrants Be More Like Us? A Century of Immigration in America, 1900–2000*, New York, Statue of Liberty National Monument/Ellis Island Immigration Museum, 2000.

25. Charlotte Perkins Gilman, 'Immigration, Importation, and Our Fathers', *The Forerunner*, vol.5, 1914, pp.117–19. This National Training School for immigrants bears striking similarities to a program Gilman suggested for socialising turn-of-the-century African-Americans into the 'American' work-ethic. See Charlotte Perkins Gilman, 'A Suggestion on the Negro Problem', 1908, reprinted in Ceplair, *Nonfiction Reader*, 1991, pp.176–83.

26. Gilman, 'Immigration', 1914, p.119.

27. Higham, *Strangers*, 1981, p.243.

28. Charlotte Perkins Gilman, 'Let Sleeping Forefathers Lie', *The Forerunner*, vol.6, 1915, pp.261–3. The view of immigrants as children needing to be taught was sufficiently popular as to appear in a 1921 letter from the United States Commissioner of Immigration to the Secretary of Labor: 'Ellis Island is not only the "gateway of the nation" but it is the nation's great kindergarten of Americanization, and what [immigrants] receive on the island they will live out in the nation'. Yans-McLaughlin and Lightman, *Ellis Island*, 1997, p.140.

29. Charlotte Perkins Gilman, *Herland*, London, Women's Press (1915), 1979. Van's emigration to Herland is chronicled in Charlotte Perkins Gilman, *With Her in Ourland*, *The Forerunner*, vol.7, nos 1–12, 1916.

30. Gilman, *Ourland*, 1916, pp.123, 154–7, 179–82, 213.

31. Gilman, 'Malthusianism,' 1904, p.282.

32. Gilman, *Ourland*, 1916, pp.152–5, 292. Gilman was not alone in these views. War-time anti-foreign sentiment led to the passage, in 1917, of a literacy test calculated to keep out Eastern and Southern European immigrants, and to the government-orchestrated 'Palmer Raid' arrests and deportations of foreign radicals in 1919. The Emergency Quota Act of 1921 and the National Origins Act of 1924, which set quotas disproportionately restricting the intake of immigrants from Eastern and Southern Europe, represented efforts 'to preserve the white, Anglo-Saxon culture of the United States'

by 'reinstating the ethnic profile…to what it was around 1890', and signified 'a repudiation of the asylum tradition'. These Acts continued to impose the virtual prohibition of Asians. Yans-McLaughlin and Lightman, *Ellis Island*, 1997, p.148. National Ethnic Coalition, *Why Can't Those Immigrants*, 2000. Jones, *Limits of Liberty*, 1995, p.439.
33. See Carmen Birkle's essay in this volume for a discussion of immigrant and 'ethnic' voices in the late nineteenth/early twentieth-century American popular press.
34. Charlotte Perkins Gilman, 'Among Our Foreign Residents', *The Forerunner*, vol.7, 1916, pp.145–6.
35. Charlotte Perkins Gilman, 'Is America Too Hospitable?', in Ceplair, *A Non-Fiction Reader*, New York, Columbia University Press, 1991, pp.288–95. In the early 1920s Gilman moved from New York City to rural New England and joined organisations promoting Americanization. Oral presentation and unpublished paper given at the Second International Charlotte Perkins Gilman Conference, Skidmore College. Judith A. Allen, 'The Late Gilman: Sexuality, Birth Control and Eugenics, 1911–1932', 1997, p.25, n.67.
36. Gilman, 'Is America Too Hospitable?', (1923), p.294.
37. Allen, 'The Late Gilman', 1997, p.1.
38. Ceplair, *Nonfiction Reader*, 1991, p.192.

5. Multiculturalism and the New Woman
Carmen Birkle

1. Since this volume in its entirety is dedicated to the New Woman, I will not go into a lengthy discussion of the term, but will assume the following definition—although originally applied to white middle-class women only—as an underlying concept emerging in all four writers and their short stories to be discussed here: 'The New Woman was never an objective historical reality. She was an ideal which, like most popular ideals, meant different things to different people…The keynote of the ideal was independence. The New Woman was self-reliant. She was determined to live her own life and to make her own decisions. She was eager for direct contact with the world outside her home. She held independent views. Often she managed to be financially independent as well, earning her own living and perhaps committing herself to a lifelong career. She was well educated. She was physically vigorous and energetic. Above all, she wanted to stand in a new relation to man, seeing herself as a companion—an equal—rather than as a subordinate or dependent.' Carolyn Forrey, 'The New Woman Revisited', *Women's Studies*, vol.2, 1974, p.39.
2. I should add to this list the African-American woman writer and journalist Pauline Hopkins, whose involvement in feminist and race matters is the focus of the essays by Sabina Matter-Seibel and Jill Bergman in this volume.
3. Patricia Okker, 'Native American Literatures and the Canon: The Case of Zitkala-ša', in Tom Quirk and Gary Scharnhorst (eds), *American Realism and the Canon*, Newark, University of Delaware Press, 1994, p.91.
4. Dexter Fisher, 'Foreward', in Zitkala-ša, *American Indian Stories* (1921), Lincoln, University of Nebraska Press, 1985, p.xv.
5. Carol Batker, '"Overcoming All Obstacles": The Assimilation Debate in Native American Women's Journalism of the Dawes Era', in Helen Jaskoski (ed.), *Early Native American Writing: New Critical Essays*, Cambridge, Cambridge University Press, 1996, pp.195–6.

6. 'It is significant that Bonnin used her Sioux name to sign the poem'. Laurie Lisa, 'The Life Story of Zitkala-ša / Gertrude Simmons Bonnin: Writing and Creating a Public Image', Ph.D. thesis, Arizona State University, 1996, p.92.

7. Daniel Littlefield, Jr, and James W. Parins, *American Indian and Alaska Native Newspapers and Periodicals, 1826–1924*, Westport, CT, Greenwood Press, 1984, pp.11–13.

8. Cf. Frederick J. Dockstader, 'Gertrude Simmons Bonnin (1875–1938)', in *Great North American Indians: Profiles in Life and Leadership*, New York, Van Nostrand Reinhold Company, 1977, p.41.

9. Cf. also Zitkala-ša, 'Editorial Comment: Hope in the Returned Indian Soldier', *American Indian Magazine*, vol.7, no.2, 1919, pp.61–2.

10. Zitkala-äa, 'The Red Man's America', *American Indian Magazine*, vol.5, 1917, p.64.

11. Lisa, 'The Life Story of Zitkala-ša', p.112.

12. Zitkala-äa, 'America, Home of the Red Man', *American Indian Magazine*, vol.6, 1918, p.166.

13. Zitkala-ša, 'America, Home of the Red Man', p.165.

14. Zitkala-ša, 'A Warrior's Daughter', in *American Indian Stories* (1921), Lincoln, University of Nebraska Press, 1985, p.141, p.140, p.142.

15. Ibid., p.143.

16. Ibid., p.145.

17. Ibid., p.150.

18. Ibid., p.151, p.152. Compare the fainted husband in Charlotte Perkins Gilman's 'The Yellow Wallpaper' (1892).

19. Ibid., pp.152–3.

20. Lisa, 'The Life Story of Zitkala-ša', p.56.

21. Jeanne Smith, '"A Second Tongue": The Trickster's Voice in the Works of Zitkala-ša', in Elizabeth Ammons and Annette White-Parks (eds), *Tricksterism in Turn-of-the-Century American Literature: A Multicultural Perspective*, Hanover, University Press of New England, 1994, pp.53–4; cf. also Zitkala-ša, 'Iktomi and the Ducks', in *Old Indian Legends* (1901), Lincoln, University of Nebraska Press, 1985, pp.1–15.

22. Sui Sin Far, 'Leaves from the Mental Portfolio of an Eurasian', *The Independent*, vol.66, no.3138, 21 January 1909, p.125.

23. Annette White-Parks, *Sui Sin Far / Edith Maude Eaton: A Literary Biography*, Urbana, University of Illinois Press, 1995, p.27.

24. Sui Sin Far, 'Leaves', p.127.

25. Ibid., p.128.

26. Ibid., p.129.

27. Martha Helen Patterson, '"Survival of the Best Fitted": The Trope of the New Woman in Margaret Murray Washington, Pauline Hopkins, Sui Sin Far, Edith Wharton and Mary Johnston, 1895–1913', Ph.D. thesis, University of Iowa, 1996, p.111.

28. Sui Sin Far, 'Leaves', p.128.

29. Amy Ling and Annette White-Parks (eds), *Mrs Spring Fragrance*, Urbana, University of Illinois Press, 1995, p.173.

30. Sui Sin Far, 'Leaves', p.132.

31. Sui Sin Far, 'Mrs Spring Fragrance', in Catherine Falvey (ed.), *Mrs Spring Fragrance*, Albany, NCUP, 1994, p.1.

32. Ibid.

33. Ibid., p.4.

34. Ibid., p.6.

35. White-Parks, *Sui Sin Far / Edith Maude Eaton*, p.165.

36. Ibid., p.168.

37. Gloria Velásquez Treviño, 'Cultural Ambivalence in Early Chicana Literature', in Geneviève Fabre (ed.), *European Perspectives on Hispanic Literature of the United States*, Houston, Arte Público Press, 1988, p.141.

38. Cf. Amy Doherty, 'Introduction', in Amy Doherty (ed.), *The Collected Stories of María Cristina Mena*, Houston, Arte Público Press, 1997, p.xii.

39. Matthew Hoehn, 'María Cristina Mena', in Matthew Hoehn (ed.), *Catholic Authors: Contemporary Biographical Sketches. 1930–1947*, Newark, St. Mary's Abbey, 1948, pp.118–19.

40. Hoehn, 'María Cristina Mena', p.119.

41. Elizabeth Ammons, *Conflicting Stories: American Women Writers at the Turn into the Twentieth Century*, New York, Oxford University Press, 1991, p.145.

42. Raymund A. Paredes, 'The Evolution of Chicano Literature', in Houston A. Baker, Jr. (ed.), *Three American Literatures: Essays in Chicano, Native American, and Asian-American Literature for Teachers of American Literature*, New York, The Modern Language Association of America, 1982, p.49.

43. Cf. also Américo Paredes and Raymund A. Paredes, 'Introduction', in Américo Paredes and Raymund A. Paredes (eds), *Mexican-American Authors*, Boston, Houghton Mifflin, 1972, p.1.

44. Doherty, 'Introduction', p.vii.

45. This story is republished in the same year in *The Monthly Criterion* and by Edward O'Brien in *The Best Short Stories of 1928 and the Yearbook of the American Short Story* in 1928.

46. Compare Lisa Ganobcsik-Williams's article in this volume. Ganobcsik-Williams discusses Gilman's growing nativism and ultimate rejection of immigration which, according to Gilman, threatened American democracy as well as her own status as a social reformer. While Gilman catered in this sense to the widespread attitude of nativism, the ethnic women writers discussed in my paper saw the need for a representation of the inter-relations of their ethnic and gender concerns in their fiction.

47. Doherty, 'Introduction', p.xxi.

48. Cf. ibid., p.xxiii.

49. Ibid., p.xxii.

50. Cited in ibid., p.xxii.

51. María Cristina Mena, 'The Gold Vanity Set' (1913), in Amy Doherty (ed.), *The Collected Stories of María Cristina Mena*, Houston, Arte Público Press, 1997, p.2.

52. Ibid.

53. Ibid.

54. The Virgin of Guadalupe is the 'patron of Mexico. Chicanos are familiar with the story of the miraculous appearance of the Virgin Mary to the Aztec peasant Juan Diego near the hill of Tepeyac in what is now Mexico City in the year 1531. She instructed him to go to the bishop with news that she wanted a church built on that site, which formerly had held a temple in honor of Tonanztín, the Aztec mother of all gods'. The bishop wanted proof of her existence. The Virgin instructed him to pluck roses in the middle of winter; 'he presented them to the bishop wrapped in his *tilma* (cloak), and as Juan opened it, revealing the roses, there also appeared on the *tilma* a full-length portrait of the Virgin of Guadalupe. The bishop took the cloak, complied with the request to build a chapel near Tepeyac, and placed the image in it'. Carl R. Shirley, 'Chicano History', in Francisco A. Lomelí and Carl R. Shirley (eds), *Chicano Writers:*

First Series, Dictionary of Literary Biography 82, Detroit, Bruccoli Clark Layman Book, 1989, p.297.

55. Mena, 'The Gold Vanity Set', p.5.
56. Ibid., p.6.
57. Ibid., p.11.
58. Ibid.
59. Beverly Seaton, 'Helen Reimensnyder Martin's "Caricatures" of the Pennsylvania Germans', *The Pennsylvania Magazine*, vol.104, no.1, January 1980, p.88.
60. This last name suggests an interesting coincidence of relation between the New England Penn family and the *Penn*sylvania German family Gladfelter.
61. Helen Reimensnyder Martin, 'Mrs Gladfelter's Revolt', in *Yoked with a Lamb and Other Stories* (1930), Freeport, NY, Books for Libraries Press, 1971, pp.60, 61, 63, 60.
62. Susanne Becker, *Gothic Forms of Feminine Fictions*, Manchester, Manchester University Press, 1999, p.18.
63. Ibid., p.58.
64. Ibid., p.61.
65. Martin, 'Mrs Gladfelter's Revolt', p.60.
66. Ibid.
67. Ibid., p.64.
68. Ibid., p.65, p.70.
69. Ibid., p.69.
70. Cf. Sandra Gilbert and Susan Gubar, *The Madwoman in the Attic: The Woman Writer and the Nineteenth-Century Literary Imagination*, New Haven, Yale University Press, 1984. Cf. Charlotte Perkins Gilman's 'The Yellow Wallpaper' in which her protagonist is considered to be sick only because she cannot come to terms with her new role as mother, and also Kate Chopin's *The Awakening* in which Edna Pontellier is supposed to see a physician because she rejects to fulfill the social expectations imposed on a mother, wife, and housewife.
71. Martin, 'Mrs Gladfelter's Revolt', p.70.
72. Ibid., p.72.
73. Ibid., p.73.
74. Mary Wilkins Freeman, 'The Revolt of "Mother"', in Nina Baym et al. (eds), *The Norton Anthology of American Literature*, 3rd edition, 2 vols, New York, Norton, 1989, vol.2, p.619.
75. Martin, 'Mrs Gladfelter's Revolt', p.73.
76. Ibid., p.72.

6. Pauline Hopkins's Portrayal of the African–American New Woman
Sabina Matter-Seibel

1. Frances E.W. Harper, 'Woman's Political Future', in Bert James Loewenberg and Ruth Bogin (eds), *Black Women in Nineteenth-Century American Life*, University Park: Pennsylvania State University Press, 1978, pp.244–7.
2. Rayford W. Logan, *The Negro in American Life and Thought: The Nadir, 1877–1901*, New York, Dial, 1954.
3. Hazel V. Carby, *Reconstructing Womanhood: The Emergence of the Afro-American Woman Novelist*, New York, Oxford University Press, 1987, p.95.
4. 'Editorial and Publisher's Anouncements', *Colored American*, September 1900, p.262.

5. Victoria Earle Matthews coined this term in her speech 'The Value of Race Literature' before the First Congress of Colored Women of the United States in 1895.

6. Pauline Hopkins, *Contending Forces: A Romance Illustrative of Negro Life North and South*, New York, Oxford University Press, 1988, p.15.

7. Ibid., p.202.

8. Ibid., p.241.

9. Ibid., p.241; 'Comment', *Colored American Magazine*, October 1901, p.479.

10. Hopkins, *Contending Forces*, pp.143–5.

11. M. Giulia Fabi, 'Taming the Amazon? The Price of Survival in Turn of the Century African-American Women's Fiction,' in Versluys Kristiaan (ed.), *The Insular Dream, Obsession and Resistance*, Amsterdam, 1995, p.236.

12. Hopkins, *Contending Forces*, p.107, p.349.

13. Elaine Showalter, *Sexual Anarchy: Gender and Culture at the* Fin de Siècle, New York, Viking, 1991, pp.38–42.

14. Hopkins, *Contending Forces*, p.115.

15. Kristina Brooks, 'New Woman, Fallen Woman: The Crisis of Reputation in Turn of the Century Novels by Pauline Hopkins and Edith Wharton,' *Legacy*, vol.13, no.2, 1996, p.91.

16. Hopkins, *Contending Forces*, p.154.

17. Ibid., pp.150–3.

18. Ibid., p.341.

19. In the 1850s and 1860s black women's articles appeared primarily in church organs like the *Repository of Religion and Literature and of Science and the Arts*, the *Christian Recorder* and the *Anglo-African* magazine or in abolitionist papers like the *Liberator* and *Frederick Douglass' Paper*.

20. Abby Arthur Johnson and Ronald Maberry Johnson, *Propaganda & Aesthetics: The Literary Politics of African-American Magazines in the Twentieth Century*, Amherst, University of Massachusetts Press, 1991, p.1.

21. August Meier, *Negro Thought in America, 1880–1915*, Ann Arbor, University of Michigan Press, 1988, p.154. Their readership was small, since in 1900, 45% of the total black population aged ten and over were illiterate. The geographical distribution of illiteracy was uneven, though, with only about 18.2% in the North and 47–49% in the South. Black magazines were therefore largely located in the big cities of the North. The readership included professionals like clergy, teachers and physicians, but also businessmen and artisans (Carby, *Reconstructing Womanhood*, pp.126–7).

22. On the cover of the first issue of the *Colored American Magazine*, 1900.

23. Hopkins, 'Higher Education of Colored Women in White Schools and Colleges', *Colored American Magazine*, October 1902, pp.446–7.

24. Hopkins, 'The Women's Department', *Colored American Magazine*, vol.1, 1900, p.121.

25. Hopkins, 'Echoes from the Annual Convention of the Northeastern Federation of Colored Women's Clubs', *Colored American Magazine*, October 1903, p.709.

26. Hopkins, *Contending Forces*, p.101.

27. Hopkins, 'Club Life among Colored Women', *Colored American Magazine*, August 1902, pp.273–7.

28. 'Hon. Frederick Douglass', *Colored American Magazine*, December 1900, pp.121–32; 'Booker T. Washington', *Colored American Magazine*, October 1901, pp.436–41; 'Toussaint L'Overture', *Colored American Magazine*, November 1900, pp.9–24.

29. 'Phenomenal Vocalists', *Colored American Magazine*, November 1901, pp.45–53.

30. Hopkins, 'Club Life among Colored Women', p.273.

31. 'Sojourner Truth: A Northern Slave', *Colored American Magazine*, December 1901, pp.124–32.
32. 'Harriet Tubman ("Moses")', *Colored American Magazine*, January/February 1902, p.212.
33. C.K. Doreski, 'Inherited Rhetoric and Authentic History: Pauline Hopkins at the *Colored American Magazine*,' in John Cullen Gruesser (ed.), *The Unruly Voice: Rediscovering Pauline Elizabeth Hopkins*, Chicago, University of Illinois Press, 1996, p.73.
34. Cited in Meier, *Negro Thought*, p.258.
35. The picture appeared in the issues of October and November 1900. It was offered for sale for a dollar in time for Christmas.
36. Booker T. Washington, N.B. Wood, and Fanny Barrier Williams, *A New Negro for a New Century*, New York, Arno, 1969.
37. Hopkins, *Contending Forces*, p.256.
38. Kevin Gaines, 'Black Americans' Racial Uplift Ideology as "Civilizing Mission": Pauline E. Hopkins on Race and Imperialism', in Amy E. Kaplan and Donald E. Pease (eds), *Cultures of United States Imperialism*, Durham, Duke University Press, 1993, p.441.
39. Johnson and Johnson, *Propaganda & Aesthetics*, p.3.
40. Ibid., 10–11.
41. 'Publishers' Announcements', *Colored American Magazine*, November 1904, p.700.
42. Later commentators said that her attitude was not conciliatory enough and that she lost financial support from white backers because she did not modify her writing; see Gruesser, Preface, *The Unruly Voice*, p.ix.
43. Fannie Barrier Williams, 'The Club Movement among Colored Women of America', in Washington, Wood, and Williams, *A New Negro for a New Century*, p. 424.
44. Fred Moore, 'In the Editor's Sanctum', *Colored American Magazine*, November 1904, p.693.
45. Even the covers of the magazine changed from a feminine to a more masculine layout as Bergman points out in her paper.
46. Johnson and Johnson, *Propaganda & Aesthetics*, pp.16–17.
47. *Voice of the Negro*, October 1904, pp.447–52.
48. Alain Locke described this development in *The New Negro* in 1925.
49. Gaines, 'Black Americans' Racial Uplift Ideology', p.434.
50. Hopkins, *A Primer of Facts Pertaining to the Early Greatness of the African Race*, Cambridge, 1905.
51. Hopkins, *Contending Forces*, p.389.

7. 'A New Race of Colored Women'
Jill Bergman

I would like to thank Sue Samson, Pam Marek and Patricia Collins at the University of Montana Mansfield Library for their generous assistance with this project.

1. Pauline Hopkins, 'Higher Education of Colored Women in White Schools and Colleges', *Colored American Magazine*, vol.5, no.6, October 1902, p.447.
2. Caroll Smith-Rosenberg, *Disorderly Conduct: Visions of Gender in Victorian America*. New York, Oxford University Press, 1985, p.245. Similarly, Martha Patterson refers to such a shift when she describes the New Woman as 'a liminal figure between the Victorian woman and the flapper.' 'Survival of the Best Fitted', *American Transcendental Quarterly*, vol.9, no.2, 1995, p.73.
3. Claudia Tate, *Domestic Allegories of Political Desire: The Black Heroine's Text at the Turn of*

the Century, New York, Oxford University Press, 1993.

4. This is a fairly common thesis among scholars. In particular, see Tate, *Domestic Allegories*; Hazel V. Carby, *Reconstructing Womanhood: The Emergence of the Afro-American Woman Novelist*, New York, Oxford University Press, 1987; Venetria Patton, *Women in Chains: The Legacy of Slavery in Black Women's Fiction*, Albany, State University of New York Press, 2000. For a discussion of prevalent stereotypes of African-American women in the 19th century, see Patricia Collins, *Black Feminist Thought: Knowledge, Consciousness, and the Politics of Empowerment*, New York, Routledge, 1991.

5. My argument here resembles a point made by Matter-Seibel, who asserts that one of Hopkins's characters must become a mother before becoming a new woman. Although Matter-Seibel describes a linear model, while I argue that Hopkins called for the simultaneous possession of True Woman and New Woman traits, we agree that Hopkins valued redemptive motherhood and claimed it as part of black New Womanhood.

6. The title of this article is 'Ethics of the New Woman in Social and Domestic Life', and is cited by Sandra Harmon in 'The Club Woman as New Woman: Late Nineteenth-Century Androgynous Images', *Turn-of-the-Century Women*, vol.1, no.2, 1984, pp.27-35.

7. Margaret Murray Washington, 'Club Work Among Negro Women', in Gerda Lerner (ed.), *Black Women in White America: A Documentary History*, New York, Vintage, 1973, pp.443-7.

8. Abby Arthur Johnson and Ronald Maberry Johnson, *Propaganda & Aesthetics: The Literary Politics of African-American Magazines in the Twentieth Century*, Amherst, University of Massachusetts Press, 1991, p.4.

9. This quotation appeared on the front cover of *Colored American Magazine* for most of the time the magazine was in print.

10. Hazel Carby, 'Introduction', *The Magazine Novels of Pauline Hopkins*, New York, Oxford University Press, 1988, p.xxxi.

11. William Stanley Braithwaite, 'Negro America's First Magazine', in Philip Butcher (ed.), *The William Stanley Braithwaite Reader*, Ann Arbor, University of Michigan Press, 1972, pp.114–21.

12. Smith-Rosenberg, *Disorderly Conduct*, p.245.

13. 'Pauline E. Hopkins', *Colored American Magazine*, vol.2, no.3, January 1901, p.218.

14. 'Here and There', *Colored American Magazine*, vol.1, no.1, May 1900, p.57 (emphasis mine).

15. 'Women's Department', *Colored American Magazine*, vol.1, no.2, June 1900, p.123; 'Here and There', *Colored American Magazine*, vol.2, no.2, December 1900, pp.134, 137; 'Here and There', *Colored American Magazine*, vol.2, no.4, February 1901, p.290; 'Here and There', *Colored American Magazine*, vol.2, no.3, January 1901, pp.204-7.

16. See Matter-Seibel's chapter for a fuller discussion of Sappho's status as a New Woman.

17. Pauline Hopkins, *Contending Forces: A Romance Illustrative of Negro Life North and South* (1900), New York, Oxford University Press, 1988. Although this novel was not published serially in the *Colored American Magazine*, as her subsequent novels would be, clear links exist between the novel and the journal. *Contending Forces* was published the same year that the *Colored American Magazine* began publication, and by the same publishing company. The novel was advertised extensively in the early issues of the journal, and was offered as a premium for subscription at one point.

18. 'Women's Department', *Colored American Magazine*, vol.1, no.2, June 1900, p.122.

19. 'Famous Women of the Negro Race XII: Higher Education of Colored Women in white Schools and Colleges', *Colored American Magazine*, vol.5, no.6, October 1902,

p.445–6. Hopkins reports the events of the General Federation of Women's Clubs meeting in 'Famous Women of the Negro Race IX: Club Life Among Colored Women', *Colored American Magazine*, vol.5, no.4, August 1902, pp.273–7. She describes it in less detail in the previous issue (vol.5, no.3, July 1902, p.210).

20. Jane Tompkins, *Sensational Designs: The Cultural Work of American Fiction, 1790-1860*, New York, Oxford University Press, 1985, pp.124, 125.

21. Ibid., p.145.

22. Fannie Barrier Williams, 'The Club Movement Among Negro Women', in J.W. Gibson and W.H. Crogman (eds), *Progress of a Race or The Remarkable Advancement of the Colored American*, Naperville, IL, JL Nichols & Co, 1902, 1912, p.199. See Bair's chapter on the continuing emphasis on the importance of motherhood to racial survival and progress.

23 'Echoes From the Annual Convention of Northeastern Federation of Colored Women's Clubs', *Colored American Magazine*, vol.6, no.10, October 1903, p.709.

24. Eric Sundquist, *To Wake the Nations: Race in the Making of American Literature*, Cambridge, Belknap Press of Harvard University Press, 1993, p.581.

25. 'Mrs Rosa D. Bowser', *Colored American Magazine*, vol.1, no.4, p.232.

26. Patricia Marks, *Bicycles, Bangs and Bloomers: The New Woman in the Popular Press*, Lexington, University Press of Kentucky, 1990, p.117.

27. Wilson Jeremiah Moses, *The Golden Age of Black Nationalism, 1850-1925*, New York, Oxford University Press, 1978, pp.105-8. Moses provides extensive information on the early antebellum period as background for his discussion of the years indicated in his book's title.

28. 'Famous Women: Club Life', pp.273-4.

29. The irony of this movement is that by subscribing to contemporary notions of racial hierarchies, Hopkins and others involved in the uplift movement participated in a similarly imperialistic effort on their African-American 'family' as whites had justified under slavery. Kevin Gaines, 'Black Americans' Racial Uplift Ideology as "Civilizing Mission": Pauline E. Hopkins on Race and Imperialism', in Amy Kaplan and Donald E. Pease (eds), *Cultures of United States Imperialism*, Durham, Duke University Press, 1993, pp.433–55.

30. 'Women's Department', p.121. Hopkins does not attribute the quoted portion of this statement to anyone.

31. C.K. Doreski makes a similar observation about Hopkins's work at the *Colored American Magazine* and the formation of a readership. 'Inherited Rhetoric and Authentic History: Pauline Hopkins at the *Colored American Magazine*', in John Cullen Gruesser (ed.), *The Unruly Voice: Rediscovering Pauline Elizabeth Hopkins*, Urbana, University of Illinois Press, 1996, pp.71–97.

32. 'Here and There', *Colored American Magazine*, vol.1, no.1, p.57. As Bair explains in the next chapter, Amy Jacques Garvey would create a similar forum twenty years later in the *Negro World*.

33. 'Here and There', *Colored American Magazine*, vol.1, no.2, p.126; 'Here and There', *Colored American Magazine*, vol.2, no.4, p.289; 'Here and There', *Colored American Magazine*, vol.2., no.5, p.379.

34. The source for this information is a 1912 article in *The Crisis*, but while this article does indicate that Hopkins had trouble at the magazine because 'her attitude was not conciliatory enough', it does not indicate that this was her reason for leaving the magazine.

35. See Bair's contribution for an insightful discussion of such beauty products.

8. 'Our Women and What They Think'
Barbara Bair

1. 'Mrs Garvey Delivers Ringing Message to White Women of London at Great Meeting', *Negro World*, 22 September 1928, p.3.
2. *Julius Caesar*, act 4, sc.3, line 217.
3. 'Speech by Marcus Garvey [at Century Theatre]', in Robert A. Hill, Barbara Bair, and Edith Johnson (eds), *The Marcus Garvey and Universal Negro Improvement Association Papers*, Berkeley, University of California Press, 1990, vol.7, pp.217–34.
4. *Negro World*, 22 September 1928, p.3.
5. Barbara Bair, 'True Women, Real Men: Gender, Ideology, and Social Roles in the Garvey Movement', in Dorothy O. Helly and Susan Reverby (eds), *Gendered Domains: Rethinking Public and Private in Women's History*, Ithaca, N.Y., Cornell University Press, 1992; Honor Ford-Smith, 'Women and the Garvey Movement in Jamaica', and Tony Martin, 'Women in the Garvey Movement', in Rupert Lewis and Patrick Bryan (eds), *Garvey: His Work and Impact*, Trenton, N.J., Africa World Press, 1991, pp.73–83, 67–72.
6. Amy Jacques Garvey (ed.), *Philosophy and Opinions of Marcus Garvey*, vols 1 & 2, (1923, 1925), reprint New York, Universal Publishing House, 1986. See also A.J. Garvey, *Garvey and Garveyism*, New York, Macmillan, 1963; Barbara Bair, 'Remapping the Black/White Body: Sexuality, Nationalism, and Biracial Antimiscegenation Activism in 1920s Virginia', in Martha Hodes (ed.), *Sex, Love, Race: Crossing Boundaries in North American History*, New York, New York University Press, 1999, pp.399–419; Mark Matthews, 'Our Women and What They Think: Amy Garvey and the Negro World', *Black Scholar*, May-June 1979, pp.2–13.
7. 'Women of Negro Race!' [ad], *Negro World*, 23 August 1924, p.16.
8. A.J. Garvey, 'Have a Heart', *Negro World*, 2 August 1924, p.12.
9. A.J.Garvey, 'Do Negro Women Want to Express Themselves?', *Negro World*, 15 November 1924, p.7.
10. A.J. Garvey, 'Send in Your Articles for This Page', *Negro World*, 6 February 1926, p.7.
11. 'Speech by Marcus Garvey [at Royal Albert Hall]', in Hill, Bair, and Johnson, *Garvey Papers*, 1990, vol.7, p.204.
12. Marie Trent, 'The Negro Woman's Call to Duty', *Negro World*, 15 November 1924, p.8.
13. Eunice Lewis, 'The Black Woman's Part in Race Leadership', *Negro World*, 19 April 1924, p.10.
14. *The Messenger*, July 1923, quoted from Ernest Allen, Jr., 'The New Negro', in Adele Heller and Lois Rudnick (eds), *1915: The Cultural Moment: The New Politics, the New Woman, the New Psychology, the New Art, and the New Theatre in America*, New Brunswick, N.J, Rutgers University Press, 1991, p.51.
15. Saydee E. Parham, 'The New Woman', *Negro World*, 2 February 1924, p.10.
16. 'Women's Party', *Negro World*, 2 February 1924, p.10.
17. Carrie Mero Leadett, 'Our Girls', *Negro World*, 2 February 1924, p.10.
18. 'The Very Latest Style' [dress ad], *Negro World*, 2 February 1924, p.10.
19. 'Weekly Text', *Negro World*, 2 February 1924, p.10.
20. 'England's Titled Socialist Visits America: Unemployment and Poverty Envelopes England', *Negro World*, 23 January 1926, p.7; 'Margaret Bondfield Is Return[ed] to Parliament', *Negro World*, 7 August 1926, p.7; 'Remove Sex from Politics Advises Mrs Pankhurst', *Negro World*, 6 March 1926, p.8; 'Suffrage in England', *Negro World*, 16 October 1926, p.6.
21. 'English House of Clergy Votes to Cut Out "Obey" from Bride's Ritual', *Negro World*,

6 December 1924, p.8; 'British Bridegroom Needn't Wear Ring', *Negro World*, 13 December 1924, p.8; 'A Woman's Right to Maiden Name', *Negro World*, 12 December 1927, p.7.

22. Matilda Ingleton, 'Four Essential Qualities in a Negro Woman', *Negro World*, 2 August 1924, p.12; see also A.J. Garvey, 'More Attention Given to Our Child Life' and 'The Hand that Rocks the Cradle', *Negro World*, 31 May 1924, p.10, 5 July 1924, p.12; Blanche Hall, 'Woman's Greatest Influence is Socially', *Negro World*, 4 October 1924, p.8; 'Women the Pivot of National Greatness', *Negro World*, 9 April 1927, p.7.

23. 'White Professional Women Discuss Matrimony at Meeting: Negro Women Should Encourage Motherhood and Let Their Race Live', *Negro World*, 16 October 1926, p.6.

24. Eunice Lewis, 'The Black Woman's Part in Race Leadership', *Negro World*, 19 April 1924, p.10.

25. Ibid.

26. Ibid.

27. Ibid.

28. A.J. Garvey, 'No Sex in Brains and Ability', *Negro World*, 27 December 1924, p.8.

29. Carrie Mero Leadett, 'Marriage Today and the Woman', *Negro World*, 21 June 1924, p.10.

30. Vera, 'The Kind of Girl Men Like', *Negro World*, 9 February 1924, p.10.

31. 'New "Mannish" Slenderstyle' [dress ad], *Negro World*, 25 October 1924, p.8; 'Fad for Boyish Form Called Health Menace', *Negro World*, 25 October 1924, p. 8; 'Physician Condemns Rubber Corsets', *Negro World*, 31 January 1925, p.8; 'Pope Pius Denounces Fashions for Women', *Negro World*, 25 December 1926, p.8; 'Scientist Fears Mannishness will Masculinize Girls', *Negro World*, 13 November 1926, p.7; 'Bobbed Hair Now Means Future Beards, Says Expert', *Negro World*, 20 September 1924, p.13; 'After the Bob Comes the Wig', and 'Use of Autos Injuring Women, Declares Doctor', *Negro World*, 18 October 1924, p.8; 'No "Bobs" for Russian Girls', *Negro World*, 6 February 1926, p.7. A.J. Garvey countered with 'Scanty Clothes Make Hardy Women', *Negro World*, 27 November 1927, p.5.

32. See A. J. Garvey, 'An Invitation to Our Teachers and Student Women' and 'Have a Heart', *Negro World*, 7 June 1924, p.10, 2 August 1924, p.12.

33. See Carrie Mero Leadett, 'The Obligations of Motherhood', *Negro World*, 29 March 1924, p.10.

34. Mabel Douglas, 'Emancipated Womanhood', *Negro World*, 15 November 1924, p.8.

35. 'Military Automatic' [gun ad], *Negro World*, 17 November 1926, p.5.

36. 'Negro Dolls' [ad], *Negro World*, 8 January 1927, p.10; 'Lovely Woman, be a Goddess', and 'Believe in Yourself', *Negro World*, 8 January 1927, p.6; A.J. Garvey, 'Are We Proud of Our Black Skins and Curly Hair?', 'Each Race Sees Beauty in Itself', and 'I Am A Negro—And Beautiful', *Negro World*, 1 August 1925, p.7, 8 May 1926, p.6, 10 July 1926, p.5.

37. 'Wanted: Agents, Hairdressers', and 'Have Your Feet Treated by Dr. Ethel May Brown' [ads], *Negro World*, 5 April 1924, p.10; 'Walker's System…Consult Miss Williams' and 'I Earned This Magnificent Fur Coat in Spare Time' [ads], *Negro World*, 30 January 1926, p.7; 'Ray Hoffman Scientific Beauty Parlor' [ad], *Negro World*, 31 May 1924, p.10; 'Dagley's Dressmaking School' [ad], *Negro World*, 16 October 1926, p.6.

38. 'Aunt Lydia's Wash Day Wonder' [ad], *Negro World*, 2 August 1924, p.12.

39. Henrietta Vinton Davis, 'The Exigencies of Leadership: Women Determined to Measure Up if Negro Men Fail', *Negro World*, 17 October 1925, p.7.

40. M.L.T. De Mena, 'Our Women', *Negro World*, 31 October 1925, p.7.
41. A.J. Garvey, 'Black Women's Resolve for 1926', *Negro World*, 9 January 1926, p.7.
42. A.J. Garvey, 'Away with Lip Service', *Negro World*, 6 February 1926, p.7.

9. Elizabeth Robins
Sue Thomas

In addition to the reviews of Robins's fiction cited directly in this essay, my broader comments on the reception of it are informed by a reading of all comment and reviews listed in my *Elizabeth Robins (1862–1952): A Bibliography*, St Lucia, Brisbane, Department of English, University of Queensland, 1994. See this bibliography for the grounds on which attributions of reviews are based. Robins collected reviews of her early fiction in scrapbooks which are now held among the Elizabeth Robins Papers, Fales Library, New York University. In citing reviews I have only read there I give the publishing information Robins notes. Sometimes she does not note dates of publication; rarely does she give page references.

1. See Elin Diamond, *Unmaking Mimesis: Essays on Feminism and Theatre*, London, Routledge, 1997; Linda Fitzsimmons and Viv Gardner (eds), *New Woman Plays*, London, Methuen, 1991; Joanne E. Gates, *Elizabeth Robins, 1862–1952: Actress, Novelist, Feminist*, Tuscaloosa and London, University of Alabama Press, 1994; Angela V. John, *Elizabeth Robins: Staging a Life, 1862–1952*, London and New York, Routledge, 1995; Jane Marcus, 'Elizabeth Robins', Ph.D. thesis, Northwestern University, 1973; Adrienne Scullion (ed.), *Female Playwrights of the Nineteenth Century*, London, Dent, 1996; Catherine Wiley, 'Staging Infanticide: The Refusal of Representation in Elizabeth Robins' *Alan's Wife*', *Theatre Journal*, vol.42, 1990, pp.432–46.
2. The quotation is from William Archer, review of *George Mandeville's Husband*, *Daily Chronicle*, 24 July 1894, Scrapbook 8, Elizabeth Robins Papers.
3. Lyn Pykett, *Engendering Fictions: The English Novel in the Early Twentieth Century*, London, Edward Arnold, 1995, p.57. Rita Felski observes: 'The most common metaphors in the history of modern thought for describing processes of social change are undoubtedly those of revolution and evolution. Revolution…gradually came to describe a decisive moment of rupture with the status quo and the inauguration of a new order' (*The Gender of Modernity*, Cambridge, MA, Harvard University Press, 1995, p.147). In feminist literary histories of change during the 1890s and of 'New Woman' fiction the modernity of the New Woman is conceptualized as a threat, revolutionary in potential. For Lyn Pykett, for example, she is 'a revolting daughter, in revolt against established literary conventions and modes of representation' (*Engendering*, p.57). Elaine Showalter's concept-metaphor is 'sexual anarchy'. 'History warns', she writes, 'that after the revolution comes the terror and decadence' (*Sexual Anarchy: Gender and Culture at the* Fin de Siècle, London, Bloomsbury, 1991, p.2). In her longer historical view in the Introduction to *Daughters of Decadence: Women Writers of the* Fin de Siècle, London, Virago, 1993, she places New Woman writers as part of the evolutionary 'genealogy of modernism', even calling them 'missing links' between the 'great Victorian women writers' and female modernists (p.viii).
4. In this collection, Christa Zorn in her essay on Lou Andreas-Salomé and Eveline Kilian in her essay on Dorothy Richardson work, as I do, through a close historical contextualization of writing by a woman often deemed anti-feminist to complicate and revise received opinion.

5. Michelle Elizabeth Tusan, 'Inventing the New Woman: Print Culture and Identity Politics During the Fin-de-Siecle' [*sic*], *Victorian Periodicals Review*, vol.31, no.2 (1998), p.177.

6. See Ellen Jordan, 'The Christening of the New Woman: May 1894', *Victorian Newsletter*, Spring 1983, pp.19–21. Tusan has traced the term to an 1893 headline in the *Woman's Herald*. Earlier dated instances were cited at the Feminist Forerunners Conference, Manchester Metropolitan University, 24–26 July 2000.

7. Sally Ledger, *The New Woman: Fiction and feminism at the* fin de siècle, Manchester and New York, Manchester University Press, 1997, pp.9–10.

8. Judith R. Walkowitz, *City of Dreadful Delight: Narratives of Sexual Danger in Late-Victorian London*, London, Virago, 1992, p.121. Walkowitz usefully elucidates the features of moral panics: 'the definition of a "threat"; the stereotyping of main characters in the mass media as particular species of monsters; a spiraling escalation of the perceived threat, the taking up of absolutist positions, including the mounting of "barricades"; and finally the emergence of an "imaginary" solution, in terms of tougher laws, moral isolation, and symbolic court action' (p.121). The role that the 1895 trials of Oscar Wilde ('symbolic court action') played in announcements of the demise of New Woman fiction, given the links made between the New Woman and sexual decadence, has been well elaborated by Ledger, *New Woman*, pp.94–7. Walkowitz cites Watney on p.121.

9. 'Miss Elizabeth Robins's First Story', letter, *Time and Tide*, vol.1, 1920, p.40.

10. Cited in 'The New Review, 1889–1897', in Walter E. Houghton (ed.), *The Wellesley Index to Victorian Periodicals 1824–1900*, vol.3, London, Routledge, 1979, p.304.

11. Elizabeth Robins, 'A Lucky Sixpence', in *Below the Salt*, London, Heinemann, 1896, p.8.

12. Anne McClintock, *Imperial Leather: Race, Gender and Sexuality in the Colonial Contest*, New York and London, Routledge, 1995, p.161.

13. Robins, 'Lucky Sixpence', p.10, p.22.

14. McClintock, *Imperial Leather*, p.161.

15. Robins, 'Lucky Sixpence', p.5, p.37.

16. Ann Ardis, *New Women, New Novels: Feminism and Early Modernism*, New Brunswick and London, Rutgers University Press, 1990, p.54, p.29.

17. Robins collected the press comment on 'A Lucky Sixpence' and ''Gustus Frederick' from which I quote (Scrapbook 8, Elizabeth Robins Papers).

18. Comment on 'A Lucky Sixpence', *Potts Guardian*; *Church Times*; *Public Opinion*; *Guardian*; *Westminster*, respectively, Scrapbook 8, Elizabeth Robins Papers.

19. Comment on 'A Lucky Sixpence', *Norfolk News*; *Hospital*; *Daily Free Press Aberdeen*; *Guardian*, respectively, Scrapbook 8, Elizabeth Robins Papers.

20. Comment on 'A Lucky Sixpence', *Church Times*, Scrapbook 8, Elizabeth Robins Papers.

21. Comment on 'A Lucky Sixpence', *Review of Reviews*, Scrapbook 8, Elizabeth Robins Papers.

22. Catherine Belsey, *Critical Practice*, London and New York, Methuen, 1980, pp.8–9.

23. Comment on 'A Lucky Sixpence', *European Mail*; *Guardian*; *Norfolk News*; *Hospital*; *Bristol Mercury*; *Northern Whig*, Belfast, respectively, Scrapbook 8, Elizabeth Robins Papers.

24. Comment on 'A Lucky Sixpence', *Leicester Chronicle*; *Potts Guardian*; *Morning Post*; *Lady's Pictorial*; *Public Opinion*; *St James's Gazette*; *Westminster*, respectively, Scrapbook 8, Elizabeth Robins Papers.

25. *Church Times*, Scrapbook 8, Elizabeth Robins Papers.

26. ''Gustus Frederick' is a sharp commentary on class discrimination in an upper-middle-

class woman's extolling of the joys of motherhood and on the artificiality of the middle-class view that those joys necessarily required legitimation by marriage, even a marriage of convenience. When first published in the *New Review* in March 1895 it had been criticized as 'coarse in conception and inconsistent in treatment' by A.W. in *Realm* and as 'a curious picture of the passion for maternity which is displayed by some women in defiance of law and public estimation' in the *Kendal Mercury*. The comment from which I quote is collected in Scrapbook 8, Elizabeth Robins Papers.

27. Arthur Waugh, 'Reticence in Literature', *Yellow Book*, vol.1, 1894, p.204.

28. [Arnold Bennett], 'Some Younger Reputations', *Academy*, 10 December 1898, pp.428–9.

29. Lyn Pykett, *The 'Improper' Feminine: The Women's Sensation Novel and the New Woman Writing*, London and New York, Routledge, 1992, p.42.

30. Reviews of *Below the Salt, British Weekly*, 22 October 1896; *Pall Mall Gazette*, 12 December 1896; *Vanity Fair*, 31 December 1896, p.458; *Woman*, 21 October 1896, p.6 (by 'Barbara', i.e. Arnold Bennett); *Manchester Guardian*, 13 October 1896; *Academy*, 28 November 1896, p.454, respectively. The reviews with no page references are cited from Scrapbook 8, Elizabeth Robins Papers.

31. Elaine Showalter, *A Literature of Their Own: British Women Novelists from Brontë to Lessing*, London, Virago, 1978, p.109.

32. Ardis, *New Women*, p.148.

33. Elizabeth Robins, *George Mandeville's Husband*, London, Heinemann, 1894, p.7, p.5.

34. R[alph] C. E[lliott], 'Satire', in Alex Preminger (ed.), *Princeton Encyclopedia of Poetry and Poetics*, enlarged edition, London, Macmillan, 1974, p.739.

35. William Heinemann, letter to Elizabeth Robins, 17.12.1900, Elizabeth Robins Papers.

36. Reviews of *George Mandeville's Husband, Daily Chronicle*, 24 July 1894 (by William Archer); *The Times*, 25 October 1894, p.14; *Publisher's Circular*, 18 August 1894; *Sketch*, 8 August 1894; *Great Thoughts*, 18 August 1894, p.316 (by Grant Richards), respectively. The reviews with no page references are cited from Scrapbook 8, Elizabeth Robins Papers.

37. The critic for the *Speaker*, 18 August 1894, declared of 'George Mandeville': 'No doubt she was capable of writing the kind of trash which nowadays finds favour with a considerable proportion of Mr. Mudie's subscribers, as well as with the modern school of reviewers, for the only quality which a woman needs to enable her to produce fiction of this kind is a taste for pruriency and an absence of shame' (p.195).

38. Reviews of *George Mandeville's Husband, Daily Chronicle*, 24 July 1894; *The Times*, 25 October 1894, p.14; *Publishers' Circular*, 18 August 1894; *Sketch*, 8 August 1894; *Great Thoughts*, 18 August 1894, p.316; *Daily News*, 15 August 1894; *Speaker*, 18 August 1894, p.195; *Bookman* (London), October 1894, p.56; *Woman*, 8 August 1894, p.9 (by Barbara, i.e. Arnold Bennett); *Christian Leader*, 16 August 1894, respectively. Bennett's 1898 commentary is in 'Some Younger Reputations'. The reviews with no page references are cited from Scrapbook 8, Elizabeth Robins Papers.

39. Waugh, 'Reticence', p.210.

40. Ardis, *New Women*, p.48

41. Ledger, *New Woman*, p.179.

42. On the significance of Waugh's essay see also Jane Eldridge Miller, *Rebel Women: Feminism, Modernism and the Edwardian Novel*, London, Virago, 1994, pp.16–17.

43. Graham Dawson, *Soldier Heroes: British Adventure, Empire and the Imagining of Masculinities*, London and New York, Routledge, 1994, p.65.

44. Kate Flint, *The Woman Reader 1837–1914*, Oxford, Clarendon Press, 1993, p.294, p.299.

45. Reviews of *George Mandeville's Husband*, *To-day* (by J.K. Jerome); *Daily Telegraph*, 27 July 1894. Cited from Scrapbook 8, Elizabeth Robins Papers.

46. Robins, *George*, pp.112–3.

47. Reviews of *George Mandeville's Husband*, *Illustrated London News*, 8 September 1894; *Daily Chronicle*, 24 July 1894; *Liverpool Mercury*, 15 August 1894; *Publisher's Circular*, 18 August 1894; *Academy*, 6 October 1894 (by John Barrow Allen), p.252; *Saturday Review*, 1 September 1894, p.241; *Speaker*, 18 August 1894, p.195, respectively. The reviews with no page references are cited from Scrapbook 8, Elizabeth Robins Papers.

48. 'What Her Body and Soul Permit', *Woman's Signal*, 4 October 1894, p.1.

49. Stead drew the comparison with *The Beth Book* in *Review of Reviews* (London), vol.19, 1899, p.81, the critic for the *New York World*, 15 January 1899, the comparison with *The Heavenly Twins*. George Bernard Shaw drew a comparison between Robins and George Eliot (letter to Elizabeth Robins, 13.2.1899, in Dan H. Laurence [ed.], *Collected Letters. Volume 2: 1898–1910*, London, Max Reinhardt, 1972, pp.76–8), and the critic for the *Argus* (Melbourne), 25 February 1899, p.4, compared Val with Maggie Tulliver in Eliot's *The Mill on the Floss*. The review in the *New York World* is cited from Scrapbook 12, Elizabeth Robins Papers.

50. This term is used in the *Guardian* [*Church Weekly*], 1 February 1899, Scrapbook 12, Elizabeth Robins Papers.

51. The reviewer for the *Aberdeen Free Press*, 28 November 1898, for instance, stated: 'The great strength of the book lies in the individualisation of characters'. Cited from Scrapbook 12, Elizabeth Robins Papers.

52. In his review Bennett wrote: 'it comes near to being an entire Rougon-Macquart in one volume' (*Academy*, 26 November 1898, p.333). The critic in the *Aberdeen Free Press* averred: 'The terrible fact of hereditary diseases is, after all, a fact and concerns most of us more than we are ready to confess; this fact the author does not hesitate to discuss boldly and his skilful use of it and deeply interesting manner of working it into the details of personal experience excite one's imagination as well as intellectual activity'. Her need to 'write the history of both branches of the family…discovers in her a remarkable talent for individual portraiture and a hardly less remarkable skill for following the intricacies of a many-pronged story with a firm hand and a cool head', wrote the critic for the *Westminster Gazette*, 12 December 1898. The reviews with no page references are cited from Scrapbook 12, Elizabeth Robins Papers.

53. The word 'genius' was used, for example, in the *St James's Gazette*, 16 November 1898, *Speaker*, 18 February 1899, p.215, and in the title of the review in *Country Life*, 24 December 1898. The reviews with no page references are cited from Scrapbook 12, Elizabeth Robins Papers.

54. Reviews of *The Open Question*, *New Age*, 29 December 1898, p.607; *Guardian*, 1 February 1899; *Review of Reviews*, vol.19, 1899, p.82; and *St James's Gazette*, 16 November 1898, respectively. The reviews with no page references are cited from Scrapbook 12, Elizabeth Robins Papers.

55. Ardis, *New Women*, p.55.

56. William Leonard Courtney, *The Feminine Note in Fiction*, London, Chapman and Hall, 1904, p.xii, p.vii.

57. The *Guardian* critic, for example, wrote: 'Up to the point when the problem-motive begins to trouble the art of the story the style is clear, precise, and cameo-like in its finish'. 1 February 1899, cited from Scrapbook 12, Elizabeth Robins Papers.

58. See, for instance, reviews in *Westminster Gazette*, 12 December 1898; *Daily News*, 12

December 1898; and *Review of Reviews*, vol.19, 1899, p.81. The reviews with no page references are cited from Scrapbook 12, Elizabeth Robins Papers.

59. Elizabeth Robins, *The Open Question: A Tale of Two Temperaments*, New York, Harper, 1899, p.202.

60. Instances of Ibsen cited sensationally as an influence may be found in reviews in the *Speaker*, 18 February 1899, p.215, *Westminster Gazette*, 12 December 1898, and *Daily News*, 12 December 1898. The *Daily News* reviewer stated that Ibsen 'has carried the proclamation of its [the ego's] sacredness into the domain of the drama; Schopenhauer is its high priest in philosophy; it is the gospel preached by Nietzsche'. The reviews with no page references are cited from Scrapbook 12, Elizabeth Robins Papers.

61. Flint, *Woman Reader*, pp.296–7.

62. Review of *The Open Question*, *Review of Reviews*, vol.19, 1899, p.85.

63. Belsey, *Critical*, p.13.

64. Robins, *Open*, p.328.

65. Review of *The Open Question*, *Review of Reviews*, vol.19, 1899, p.81.

66. *New Age*, 29 December 1898, p.607.

67. See the comment in the *Aberdeen Free Press* cited in n.52. The critic for the *Manchester Guardian*, 6 December 1898, praised Robins's handling of the issue: 'It is her honourable accomplishment to have presented such a theme with distinction, profound sympathy, and no parade of garish emotions'. Cited from Scrapbook 12, Elizabeth Robins Papers.

68. Review of *The Open Question*, *Westminster Gazette*, 12 December 1898, Scrapbook 12, Elizabeth Robins Papers.

69. Review of *The Open Question*, *Review of Reviews*, vol.19, 1899, p.85.

70. Elizabeth Robins, letter, *Daily Chronicle*, 16 December 1898, Scrapbook 12, Elizabeth Robins Papers.

71. Robins, *Open*, p.298.

72. Ibid., p.234.

73. Flint, *Woman Reader*, p.297.

74. William Archer, 'Pessimism and Tragedy', *Fortnightly Review*, vol.71, n.s. vol.65, March 1899, p.399.

75. Elizabeth Robins Papers, Series 11A, Scrapbook 12.

76. The term is used in the *Liverpool Courier* review, 2 January 1899, Scrapbook 12, Elizabeth Robins Papers.

77. Archer, 'Pessimism', p.390, p.399, p.397.

78. 'Pessimism in Fiction', *Literature*, 3 December 1898, p.510.

79. *Daily Telegraph*, 16 November 1898, Scrapbook 12, Elizabeth Robins Papers.

80. Courtney, *Feminine*, p.186, p.183.

81. *Daily Chronicle*, 16 December 1898, Scrapbook 12, Elizabeth Robins Papers.

82. 'Pessimism in Fiction', *Literature*, 3 December 1898, p.509.

83. Felski, *Gender*, p.211.

84. Ardis, *New Women*, p.56.

85. Courtney, *Feminine*, p.184.

86. Ledger, *New Woman*, p.179.

87. Waugh, 'Reticence', pp.201–19.

88. Courtney, *Feminine*. The quotation is from Ardis, *New Women*, p.55.

89. Ardis, *New Women*, p.29.

10. 'Der Mensch als Weib'
Christa Zorn

1. Translation: 'The Human Subject as Woman'. As of now, there is no English translation of Andreas-Salomé's essay collection *Die Erotik* in which 'Der Mensch als Weib' is included. The essay first appeared as 'Der Mensch als Weib: Ein Bild im Umriß' in *Neue Deutsche Rundschau*, vol.10, no.1, 1899, pp.225–43. All translations of quotations from the text are mine. Lou Andreas Salomé, *Die Erotik: Vier Aufsätze*. München, Ullstein, 1986, pp.7–44.

2. Vernon Lee, 'The Economic Parasitism of Women', *Gospels of Anarchy and Other Contemporary Studies*, London and Leipzig: T.Fisher Unwin, 1908, p.294.

3. Judith Ryan, in *The Vanishing Subject*, has described these new psychologies as two forms which Freud was to combine later: 'the originally Romantic theory of animal magnetism, whose philosophical basis was German idealism, and the introspective method, whose basis was critical empiricism'. Deriving the language of his psychology from literature, Freud created a paradigm that provided not only the material for stories but also a method for reading them. Judith Ryan, *The Vanishing Subject: Early Psychology and Literary Modernism*, Chicago and London, University of Chicago Press, 1991, pp.6–21.

4. When she arrived in Zurich in 1880, Salomé already belonged to the second wave of Russian women who had gained respect for their individual strength and intellectual achievement. See Renate Berger, *Malerinnen auf dem Weg ins 20. Jahrhundert: Kunstgeschichte als Sozialgeschichte*, Köln, DuMont, 1982, p.253. Because of rigid heredity laws, the desire for education and academic training was more readily granted to Russian daughters than, say, to Western European or American middle-class women, even though to become educated, Russian women had to travel abroad.

5. That such views are still alive in the 20th century is demonstrated in Stanley A. Leavy's *The Freud Journals of Lou Andreas-Salomé*, Trans. Stanley Leavy, New York, Basic Books, 1964, p.9. Leavy introduces Salomé as the embodiment of the 'femme fatale': 'Men longed for her, suffered for her, and it is possible that one or two even died for her'.

6. Ursula Welsch and Michaela Wiesner, *Lou Andreas-Salomé: Vom 'Lebensgrund' zur Psychoanalyse*, München, Internationale Psychoanalyse, 1988. Welsch and Wiesner— referring to Freud's elaborate and genteel praise of Salomé's 'Mein Dank an Freud'— raise the question whether he was just polite to her as a woman he admired or whether she did indeed contribute innovative and original ideas to psychoanalysis. In his letter, Freud admits that he has hardly ever praised others' psychoanalytical work and profusely compliments her 'genuine scientific synthesis' (p.19). Welsch and Wiesner convincingly argue that Salomé developed her own psychoanalytical theories without dismissing Freud's 'essentials'. She feminized his perspective and developed strikingly modern concepts of narcissism and femininity which anticipate recent developments in psychoanalytical thought.

7. Nietzsche in his letter to Paul Rée, 21.3.1882, cited in Cordula Koepcke, *Lou Andreas-Salomé: Leben, Persönlichkeit, Werk—eine Biographie*, Frankfurt/Main, Insel, 1986, p.72. In contradistinction to Salomé, who designed a working *ménage à trois* with Nietzsche and their mutual friend Paul Rée, Nietzsche was not envisioning collaboration but a heterosexual relationship so as to complement his philosophical project.

8. In her study of the Swedish poet Edith Södergran, Ebba Witt-Brattström argues that European female intellectuals from Ellen Key to Laura Marholm to Lou Andreas-Salomé modelled their new concepts of womanhood on Nietzsche to such an extent that they

were called 'Nietzsche-crazy women' ('Das Neue Weib im Norden', unpublished paper given at the conference on 'Wahlverwandtschaften, Grosstadt 1900' in Oslo, 1998, pp.2–3). Indeed, Nietzsche's vision of a new individual gave women a model according to which they could define themselves as autonomous erotic human beings. In Germany, Helene Stöcker (a friend of Salomé's) was one of the feminists who promoted Nietzschean individualism most radically. See Biddy Martin, *Woman and Modernity: The Lifestyles of Lou Andreas-Salomé*, Ithaca, Cornell University Press, 1991, pp.145–6.

9. Hedwig Dohm writes: 'Frau Lou Andreas-Salomé. Betrübt las ich ihre Schrift "Der Mensch als Weib" Frau Lou (ihr voller zu langer Name frißt zu viel Manuskript) Antifrauenrechtlerin!' [With dismay I read her treatise, 'The Human Subject as Woman.' Frau Lou (her full-size and overly long name takes too much space in the manuscript) anti-feminist!]. Hedwig Dohm, *Die Antifeministen*, Berlin, Dümmler, 1904, p.119.

10. Joan Burstyn, *Victorian Education and the Ideal of Womanhood*, Totowa, Barnes and Noble, 1980, pp. 36–9.

11. Ruth-Ellen Boettcher Joeres and Elizabeth Mittman, 'An Introductory Essay', in Joeres and Mittman (eds), *The Politics of the Essay: Feminist Perspectives*, Bloomington and Indianapolis, Indiana University Press, 1993, p.6.

12. In a letter to Ellen Key of 1898 she wrote, 'My own thoughts on this matter elude theoretical formulation—perhaps only till I have found it, perhaps also because I instinctively seek artistic expression for something I rather feel than think. But I may come to it presently ...'. Cited in Rudolf Binion, *Frau Lou: Nietzsche's Wayward Disciple*, Princeton, Princeton University Press, 1968, p.233.

13. Salomé's search was not singular but occurred under the influence of a religious messianic movement in Russia and the reception of Nietzsche in contemporary salon culture. Add the fascination with mysticism, eros and symbolism, and the result is the spiritual melding of divinity, body and creativity in the 'Lebensphilosophie' and neo-religious movements..

14. Biddy Martin's study *Woman and Modernity* discusses Salomé's ambivalence with great finesse by setting her in relation to the more rational discourses of the German women's movement at the time. Here and in a later essay, she evaluates this ambivalence as a challenge to feminist and other theoretical doctrine caught up in the constraints of realist discourses.—The German Studies journal *Seminar* (vol.36, no.1, February 2000) has recently dedicated a whole issue to Lou Andreas-Salomé. Several authors, while expressing their skepticism of her essentialist and biased idiom, argue convincingly that her innovative and daring assertions of womanhood present even to modern scholars interesting aspects for a re-assessment of the representation of female subjectivity.

15. On this point see Eveline Kilian's essay in this collection. Kilian positions Richardson's concept of 'impersonality' as an aesthetic and philosophical form of a female consciousness devoid of ideological constraints.

16. '[M]üßig aber ist es, darüber zu streiten, welche von beiden Arten wertvoller ist oder den mächtigeren Kraftaufwand bedingt.' 'Der Mensch', p.10.

17. 'Die verkehrte Auffassung des Weiblichen begeht im Grunde ein und denselben Fehler, gleichviel ob sie im passiv Abhängigen mehr das bloße Anhängsel des Mannes, oder ob sie vorwiegend das rein Mütterliche am Weibe betont, wenn es nur unter dem Bilde des passiven Empfangens, Austragens und Gebärens gefaßt wird, gestattet dieselben falschen Konsequenzen, und man kann sie auch bei den Vertreterinnen dieser Richtung innerhalb der Frauenfrage überall beobachten'. 'Der Mensch', pp.14–15.

18. 'Das Leben im Persönlichen wie im Allgemeinen...einigt sich eben bei den

Geschlechtern, kraft der Wesenstendenzen, die sich von vorn herein aus ihrer gegenseitigen Ergänzung herausdifferenziert haben, auf verschiedene Weise, kombiniert sich in ihnen verschieden und verleiht einem jeden von ihnen seine besondere Kraft im Leben.' 'Der Mensch', p.36.

19. This apparently reactionary statement, which was seen as a backlash to women's striving for professional recognition, assumes a much clearer psychological and philosophical meaning in her follow-up essay 'Zum Typus Weib,' *Imago*, vol.3, no.1 (1914), pp.1–14. In this essay she asserts that any cultural productions, male or female, converge in the common goal to achieve spiritual wholeness..

20. 'Für seine Erholung seine Sammlung, seine Lebensfreude muß er den ersehnten friedvollen Zusammenschluß da fertig vorfinden, wo das Weib waltet.' 'Der Mensch', p.31. Salomé's idea of female creativity here echoes the Romantic concept of *Bildung* (education) which is supposed to harmonize the alienated subject with the world. In Goethe's *Bildungsroman Wilhelm Meister*, for instance, *Bildung* is the (non-capitalist) good that returns to the protagonist in an ideal circle to produce a kind of pre-capitalist, ideal harmony between subjective and objective.

21. Martin, *Woman and Modernity*, p.147.

22. Ibid., p.13. Salomé's positive category of woman also resembles what Marilyn Frye defines in her essay 'The Necessity of Differences: Constructing a Positive Category of Woman', *Signs*, vol.21, no.4, 1996, p.1004: 'But if the category of women is constructed as a positive self-supporting category not constituted by universal exclusive relations to the-absence-of-it but by self-reliant structures of differentiation and relation, the identity or subjectivity associated with it has no built in exclusivity or closure against other identity categories, no analytically built in hostility to multiple category membership and subjectivities'.

23. 'Mit gleichem oder weitaus grösserem Schein von Recht hätte statt jener Phrase die Rede sein können von dem männlichen Bestandteil als dem anschlussbedürftigern, bedürftigern überhaupt.' 'Der Mensch als Weib', p.13.

24. Martin, *Woman and Modernity*, p.53.

25. Nietzsche allowed for only one explanatory model for the superman which could not accommodate female difference. Since he defined existence through deed and becoming, woman had to be defined by being. To avoid making female subjectivity merely an *Ersatz* human, Salomé changed the terms: if being was defined as active and doing as being driven (that is, rather passive) she could use the powerful Nietzschean shell without the implications of female inferiority. If woman wanted to be a subject in her own right, as Rudolf Binion puts it, 'her doing [could be] a mode of being'. (*Frau Lou*, p.235).

26. 'Der höchststehende Mann verzichtet auf eine ganz harmonische Auslebung seiner selbst in jenem Wechselspiel aller Kräfte, das schön, froh und gesund erhält, sobald er durch eine mächtige Spezialisierung seiner Kräfte ein ihm vorschwebendes Ziel errichen kann; die Sache, die er hochstellt, verstümmelt ihn unter Umständen, und gerade der Umstand, daß er dazu im Stande war, macht ihn männlich groß'. 'Der Mensch', p.25.

27. 'Die Repräsentanten der Reaktion verlangen diese Rechte aber nur—entweder zur privaten Daseinslust der Frau, oder insoweit sie ihrer Mütterlichkeit zu gute kommen. Und sie knüpfen daran die Bedingung, dass der Gebrauch der Freiheit ihre weibliche Eigentümlichkeiten nicht schädige...' Dohm, *Die Antifeministen*, 1904, p.118.

28. 'Bei Gott, wenn diese lieben und hochbegabten Dichterinnen so sehr gegen die Berufstätigkeit der Frau und ihre Konkurrenz mit dem Manne eifern: warum bleiben

sie denn nicht im Rahmen der Weiblichkeit, fern jeder Berufstätigkeit, warum produziren sie denn Fallobst und ähnliches Zeug?' Ibid., p.134.

29. Martin, *Woman and Modernity*, p.168.

30. 'Es giebt Amazonen und Opferlämmer, Hypatias und liebe, einfache Hausmütterchen—und alle wollen sich nach ihrer Wesensart bestätigen und alle haben Recht, tausendmal Recht'. *Die Zukunft*, vol. 29, 1899, p.282.

31. As an example, one only needs to read the 27-year old Freud's letters to his fiancée, in which he discredits Mill's views on gender equality which she had found intriguing: 'No, in this respect I adhere to the old ways, longing for my Martha as she is, and she herself will not want it different; legislation and custom have to grant to women many rights kept from them, but the position of woman cannot be other than what it is: to be an adored sweetheart in youth, and a beloved wife in maturity.' Ernst L. Freud (ed.), *Letters of Sigmund Freud*, translated by Tania and James Stern, New York, Dover, 1992, pp.75–6 (Letter 28).

32. 'Der Mensch', p.35.

33. Martin, *Woman and Modernity*, p.137.

34. 'Darum pflegt auch das traditionelle Mannes-Ideal fast lediglich in Frauenköpfen zu spuken…Hingegen ist es für das Weib weniger wichtig, daß es sich in etwas bedeutend betätigt, als vielmehr, daß es dies immer als Weib tut'. 'Der Mensch', p.35.

35. Georg Simmel, *On Women, Sexuality, and Love*, translated and introduced by Guy Oakes, New Haven and London, Yale, 1984, p.70.

36. Simmel, *On Women, Sexuality, and Love*, p.93.

37. 'Aber alles dies, was sie zu so vielem untauglicher macht als den Mann, beruht darin, daß sie nicht umhin kann, von jeglichem nur aufzunehmen, was sie nährt, was sie belebt, was sich assimilieren und zum Leben zurückverwandeln läßt.…Daher auch im Weibe das Verständnis für Dinge, die dem Verstand als solchem nicht plausibel zu machen sind; sie kann viel mehr Widersprüche in sich aufnehmen und organisch verarbeiten, wo der Mann dieselben erst theoretisch ausmerzen muß, um mit sich zur Klarheit zu kommen'. 'Der Mensch', p.25.

38. 'Why', Dohm asks in *Die Antifeministen*, 'do they (the anti-feminists) disguise their thoughts in picturesque drapery …?' (p.134).

39. Ursula Renner, 'Lou Andreas-Salomé: "Nicht nur Wissen, sondern ein Stück Leben"', in Barbara Hahn (ed.), *Frauen in den Kulturwissenschaften*, München, Beck, 1994, p.284.

40. Although in time, Salomé's language becomes more and more coloured by psychoanalytical terminology, she retained a highly individualized metaphoric diction, which makes her texts so hard to read, even for experts.

41. '[D]arum bedeuten die Worte "Reinheit" und "Keuschheit" und ähnliche, nicht nur etwas Negatives, sondern zugleich den ganzen klaren Glanz und die in sich vollendete Herrlichkeit einer Welt, die wir zugleich einseitig betrachten, wenn wir sie immer nur mit den Augen des geschlechtlich bewußten Menschen ansehen'. 'Der Mensch', p.19.

42. See Lorraine Markotic, 'Andreas-Salomé and the Contemporary Essentialism Debate', *Seminar*, vol.36, no.1, February 2000, p.67. In the same issue, in her article 'Renaming the Human. Andreas-Salomé's "Becoming Woman"', Gisela Brincker-Gabler argues that Salomé effectively revises ideas and notions of her time (especially those promoted by Simmel) in order to give woman 'a chance to be a human subject' (p.32).

43. Markotic, 'Andreas-Salomé and the Contemporary Essentialism Debate', p.70.

44. Martin, *Woman and Modernity*, p.175.

45. Michel Foucault, *The Use of Pleasure*, Harmondsworth, Penguin, 1987, p.5.

Feminist Forerunners

46. Welsch and Wiesner, *Lou Andreas-Salomé*, p.93. Salomé's subjectification process here comes close to Stuart Hall's recent influential reconceptionalization of identity as a 'suturing effect' which joins the subject to structures of meaning: 'Identities are thus points of temporary attachment to the subject positions which discursive practices construct for us'. Stuart Hall, 'Introduction: Who Needs "Identity"?', in Stuart Hall and Paul Du Gay (eds), *Questions of Cultural Identity*, London, Sage, 1996, p.6.
47. 'Der Mensch', p.30.
48. Stuart Hall, 'Introduction: Who Needs "Identity"?', pp.1–17.
49. Markotic, 'Andreas-Salomé and the Contemporary Essentialism Debate', p.68.
50. Ibid., p.68.
51. Renate Weber and Brigitte Rempp (eds), *Lou Andreas-Salomé: Das zweideutige Lächeln der Erotik: Texte zur Psychoanalyse*, Freiburg: Kore, 1990, pp.13–15.
52. Salomé's holistically conceived female subject here strikingly prefigures modernist notions of female consciousness, again, most notably, Dorothy Richardson's 'synthetic consciousness of woman' (see Eveline Kilian's essay). Independently from each other both women writers claim that women are able to move beyond the partial and compartmentalized view of men. In this sense, women are closer to the 'rich fabric of life' and they can guide their thoughts 'in all directions at once' because they can see 'life whole and harmonious'. Dorothy Richardson, 'The Reality of Feminism', *The Ploughshare*, n.s.2, 1917, pp. 245–6.
53. Rosemary Hennessy, *Materialist Feminism and the Politics of Discourse*, New York, Routledge, 1993, p.138.

11. 'Female Consciousness'
Eveline Kilian

1. Cf. e.g. Marylu Hill, *Mothering Modernity: Feminism, Modernism, and the Maternal Muse*, New York and London, Garland, 1999, pp. 84f.and 101; Ellen G. Friedman, '"Utterly Other Discourse": The Anticanon of Experimental Women Writers from Dorothy Richardson to Christine Brook-Rose', *Modern Fiction Studies*, vol.34, 1988, pp.357f.
2. Cf. e.g. Ann Rosalind Jones, 'Inscribing Femininity: French Theories of the Feminine', in Gayle Greene and Coppélia Kahn (eds), *Making a Difference: Feminist Literary Criticism*, London and New York, Methuen, 1985, p.92f.; Ann Rosalind Jones, 'Writing the Body: Toward an Understanding of *l'Écriture féminine*' (1981), in Elaine Showalter (ed.), *The New Feminist Criticism: Essays on Women, Literature and Theory*, London, Virago, 1986, pp.366–72; Toril Moi, *Sexual/Textual Politics: Feminist Literary Theory*, London and New York, Methuen, 1985, pp.110–13, 123 and 147–9.
3. Dorothy Richardson, *Pilgrimage* (1915–1967), 4 vols, London, Virago, 1979, vol.4, p.142.
4. Dorothy Richardson, 'The Reality of Feminism', *The Ploughshare*, n.s.2, 1917, p. 246.
5. Ibid., p.245.
6. Richardson, *Pilgrimage*, vol.1, p.443 and vol.2, p.27.
7. Richardson, 'The Reality of Feminism', p.246.
8. Richardson, *Pilgrimage*, vol.3, p.475.
9. Richardson, 'The Reality of Feminism', p.245.—Cf. Sydney Janet Kaplan, *Feminine Consciousness in the Modern British Novel*, Urbana, University of Illinois Press, 1975, pp.12–16.
10. Rachel Blau DuPlessis, 'For the Etruscans' (1981), in Showalter (ed.), *The New Feminist*

Criticism, p.276.

11. Richardson, *Pilgrimage*, vol.4, p.164; vol.3, p.324; vol.4, p.504.

12. Virginia Woolf, *A Room of One's Own* (1929), London, Granada, 1977, p.33.

13. Ibid., p.98.

14. Ibid., pp.55 and 94.

15. Richardson, *Pilgrimage*, vol.4, p.606.

16. Ibid., vol.1, p.443 and vol.4, p.490f.

17. Richardson, 'The Reality of Feminism', p.245.

18. This differs greatly from T.S. Eliot's definition of impersonality (cf. 'Tradition and the Individual Talent' [1919], in T.S. Eliot, *Selected Essays* [1932], London, Faber and Faber, third edition, 1951, pp.17f.), which implies that the poet must extinguish his personality in a 'process of depersonalization' (p.17) in order to assimilate the literary tradition. In stark contrast to Richardson's view, which emphasizes the subject's individuality, Eliot constructs a tension between tradition and individuality in which the latter finally disappears.

19. Besides Shakespeare and Jane Austen, Woolf specifically cites the Romantic poets as models for her theory (cf. *Room*, pp.55, 65, 94 and 98). And her statement that 'a great mind is androgynous' (ibid., p.94) explicitly takes up one of Coleridge's dicta (cf. Samuel Taylor Coleridge, *Table Talk*, recorded by Henry Nelson Coleridge and John Taylor Coleridge, ed. Carl Woodring, 2 vols, Princeton, NJ, Princeton University Press, 1990, vol.2, pp.190f.).

20. Richardson, 'The Reality of Feminism', pp.245 and 246.

21. Samuel Taylor Coleridge, *Biographia Literaria* (1817), in H.J. Jackson (ed.), *The Oxford Authors: Samuel Taylor Coleridge*, Oxford and New York, OUP, 1985, p.319.

22. 'The imagination...gives unity to variety; it sees all things in one' (Coleridge, *Table Talk*, vol.1, p.490; cf. also Coleridge, *Biographiy Literaria*, p.319)—Cf. Eveline Kilian, *Momente innerweltlicher Transzendenz: Die Augenblickserfahrung in Dorothy Richardsons Romanzyklus 'Pilgrimage' und ihr ideengeschichtlicher Kontext*, Tübingen, Niemeyer, 1997, pp.44–56.

23. Richardson, *Pilgrimage*, vol.4, p.419.

24. Ibid., vol.1, p.158; vol.2, p.28; vol.3, p.272; vol.4, p.491; vol.4, p.579; vol.4, p.607.

25. Ibid., vol.4, p.182.

26. Viktor Shklovsky, 'Die Kunst als Verfahren' (1917), trans. Rolf Fieguth, in Jurij Striedter (ed.), *Russischer Formalismus: Texte zur allgemeinen Literaturtheorie und zur Theorie der Prosa*, München, Fink, 1969, pp.3–35. A slightly modified version of this essay appeared as chapter 1 in Viktor Shklovsky, *Theory of Prose* (second edition, 1929), trans. Benjamin Sher, Elmwood Park, IL, Dalkey Archive Press, 1991, pp.1–14.—Once again we are reminded of the Romantic poets, who also defined the aim of poetry as stripping 'the veil of familiarity from the world' (Percy B. Shelley, 'A Defence of Poetry', in Donald H. Reiman and Sharon B. Powers [eds], *Shelley's Poetry and Prose*, New York and London, Norton, 1977, p.505) so that the reader's mind can be awakened 'from the lethargy of custom' (Coleridge, *Biographia Literaria*, p.314).

27. Dorothy Richardson, 'Narcissus', *Close Up*, vol.8, no.3, September 1931, p.183.

28. Cf. Richardson, 'Women and the Future', *Vanity Fair*, vol.22, April 1924, p.40.

29. *The New Adelphi*, n.s. 2, 1929, pp.347f.

30. Nat Arling, for example, lists the following among the New Woman's character traits: courage, self-respect, humility, modesty and independence ('What is the Rôle of the New Woman?', *Westminster Review*, vol.150, 1898, p.582; rpt. in Ann Heilmann [ed.], *The Late Victorian Marriage Question: A Collection of Key New Woman Texts*, 5 vols, London,

Routledge/Thoemmes, 1998, vol.2, n.p.).

31. Richardson, *Pilgrimage*, vol.4, p.167. In 'The Film Gone Male' Richardson highlights women's 'awareness of being, as distinct from man's awareness of becoming' (*Close Up*, vol.9, no.1, March 1932, p.36).—Cf. Shirley Rose, 'The Unmoving Center: Consciousness in Dorothy Richardson's *Pilgrimage*', *Wisconsin Studies in Contemporary Literature*, vol.10, 1969, pp.366–82; Carol Jane Bangs, 'The Open Circle: A Critical Study of Dorothy Richardson's *Pilgrimage*', Ph.D. thesis, University of Oregon, 1977, pp.174–8.

32. Dorothy Richardson, 'Spengler and Goethe: A Footnote', *Adelphi*, vol.4, 1926, pp.312 and 311.—Hypo Wilson in *Pilgrimage* is said to live in a 'world of ceaseless "becoming"' (vol.4, p.362).

33. Dorothy Richardson, 'The Queen of Spring', *Focus: A Periodical to the Point in Matters of Health, Wealth & Life*, vol.5, no.5, May 1928, p.262. The idea of stasis and immutability is also expressed in 'Women and the Future', where she claims that the womanly woman 'lives…in the deep current of eternity' and 'is relatively indifferent to the fashions of men, to the momentary arts, religions, philosophies, and sciences' (p.40).

34. Cf. Richardson, *Pilgrimage*, vol.4, p.362: 'Becoming versus being. Look after the being and the becoming will look after itself.'

35. Richardson, 'Women and the Future', p.40.

36. Ibid.

37. Dorothy Richardson, 'Women in the Arts: Some Notes on the Eternally Conflicting Demands of Humanity and Art', *Vanity Fair*, vol.24, May 1925, p.47.

38. Richardson, 'Women and the Future', p.40.

39. Ibid., p.39.

40. Ibid., p.40.

41. Ibid.

42. Richardson, *Pilgrimage*, vol.4, p.453.

43. Ibid., vol.4, p.565.

44. Richardson, 'Women and the Future', p.40.

45. Richardson, *Pilgrimage*, vol.1, p.9; vol.4, p.566.

46. Cf. John Keats, letter to George and Tom Keats, 27 (?) December 1817, in Robert Gittings (ed.), *Letters of John Keats*, Oxford, Oxford University Press, 1975, pp.43 and 157.

47. Coleridge, *Biographia Literaria*, p.320.

48. William Wordsworth, 'Preface to *Lyrical Ballads, with Pastoral and Other Poems* (1802)', in Stephen Gill (ed.), *The Oxford Authors: William Wordsworth*, Oxford and New York, OUP, 1984, p.604.—Cf. Kilian, *Momente*, pp.291 and 226–30.

49. Richardson, *Pilgrimage*, vol.1, p.385.

50. For Flaubert's definition of *impersonnalité* or *impassibilité* cf. Gustave Flaubert, *Correspondance* (1830–1868), 3 vols., ed. Jean Bruneau, Paris, Gallimard, 1973–1991, vol.2, p.204, vol.2, p.691, and vol.3, p.575.—We can also see a clear parallel between Flaubert's *impassibilité* and the concept of impersonality set forth by Stephen in James Joyce's *Portrait of the Artist as a Young Man* ([1916], St Albans, Panther, 1977) when he claims that the personality of the artist 'refines itself out of existence, impersonalizes itself' (p.194).

51. Dorothy Richardson, 'Talent and Genius' (1923), rpt. in Bonnie Kime Scott (ed.), *The Gender of Modernism: A Critical Anthology*, Bloomington and Indianapolis, Indiana University Press, 1990, p.409.

52. This corresponds to Miriam's description of 'men of letters': 'nothing but men sitting in studies doing something cleverly, being very important,…and looking out for appro-

bation' (Richardson, *Pilgrimage*, vol.2, p.130).

53. She says about *Madame Bovary*: 'an examination *de haut en bas* of a "small soul" is not great literature' ('Talent and Genius', p.410).

54. Richardson, *Pilgrimage*, 'Foreword', vol.1, p.9.

55. Ibid., vol.4, p.418.

56. Richardson, 'The Reality of Feminism', p.244.

57. Richardson, 'Women and the Future', p.40.

58. Ibid.

59. Ibid., p.39.

60. Ibid.

61. Cf. also Richardson, 'The Film Gone Male', p.36. Here we can see a clear parallel to Lou Andreas-Salomé's insistence on sexual difference and her repudiation of male culture based on fragmentation and specialization as a model for female expression. For an in-depth discussion of Salomé's position cf. Christa Zorn's essay in this book.

62. Richardson, 'The Reality of Feminism', p.246.

63. John Middleton Murry and Dr. James Carruthers Young, 'Modern Marriage', *The New Adelphi*, vol.2, no.3, March-May 1929, p.226.

64. Ibid.

65. Ibid. These views had a certain currency especially in male-authored comments about the New Woman. Grant Allen, for example, in *The Woman Who Did* ([1895], Oxford and New York, OUP, 1995), also points out 'that prime antithesis—the male, active and aggressive; the female, sedentary, passive, and receptive' (p.64).

66. Richardson, *Pilgrimage*, vol.4, p.240.

67. Cf. also Gillian Hanscombe and Virginia L. Smyers, *Writing for Their Lives: The Modernist Women 1910–1940*, London, Women's Press, 1987, pp.52–4.

68. Dorothy Richardson, 'Das Ewig-Weibliche', *The New Adelphi*, vol.1, June 1928, p.364.

69. Ibid., p.365.

70. Richardson, *Pilgrimage*, vol.2, p.220.

71. Woolf, *Room*, p.28.

72. Dorothy Richardson, rev. of *'In the Days of the Comet'*, by H.G. Wells, *The Crank*, vol.4, 1906, p.376.

73. Ibid.—A similar point about the 'terribly hampered and partial' knowledge of women in men's writing is made by Virginia Woolf in *Room*, p.79.

74. Richardson, 'In the Days of the Comet', p.376.

75. Dorothy Richardson, 'Novels', *Life and Letters To-Day*, vol.15, no.6, Winter 1936, p.188.

76. Richardson, *Pilgrimage*, vol.4, p.328..

77. Richardson, 'The Reality of Feminism', p.246.

78. 'For the woman…going into the world of art is immediately surrounded by masculine traditions' (Richardson, 'Women in the Arts', p.100)—Cf. also Woolf, *Room*, p.72.

79. Richardson, 'Women in the Arts', p.100.

80. Cf. Woolf, *Room*, p.51.

81. '[T]here exists for the woman no equivalent for the devoted wife or mistress' (Richardson, 'Women in the Arts', p.100). This recalls Aurora Leigh's reflections on the differences between herself and her male fellow writers, who have wives or mothers to love them and to appreciate their work (Elizabeth Barrett Browning, *Aurora Leigh* [fourth edition, 1859], ed. Margaret Reynolds, New York and London, Norton, 1996, V.516-539, pp.159f.).

82. Richardson, 'Women in the Arts', p.100.

83. Dorothy Richardson, 'Data for Spanish Publisher', ed. Joseph Prescott, *The London Magazine*, vol.6, no.6, June 1959, p.17.

84. Cf. Carol Watts, *Dorothy Richardson*, Plymouth, Northcote House in association with the British Council, 1995, pp.39–57. For a discussion of the New Woman and the modern city cf. also Sally Ledger, *The New Woman: Fiction and Feminism at the* fin de siècle, Manchester and New York, Manchester University Press, 1997, pp.150–76.

85. Dorothy Richardson, 'Leadership in Marriage', *The New Adelphi*, n.s.2, 1929, p.347.

12. 'Nature's Double Vitality Experiment'
Laurel Forster

1. May Sinclair, *Feminism*, London, Women Writers Suffrage League, 1912, pp.23–4, 27.

2. A few examples are Ethel in 'Lena Wrace' (1921); Katherine in *Audrey Craven* (1897); Barbara in *Mr Waddington of Wyck* (1921).

3. Suzanne Raitt, *May Sinclair: A Modern Victorian* (Oxford, Clarendon Press, 2000, pp.68–70) has suggested that in the figure of Audrey Craven, the eponymous heroine of Sinclair's first novel, 'Sinclair associated the "modern heroine" with decadence.' Leigh Wilson in the present volume considers the role of female chivalry in Sinclair's writings about the New Woman.

4. Sinclair was particularly influenced by the work of T.H. Green, whose major contribution to philosophy was the idea of the individual working towards a higher plane of consciousness which he called 'self-realisation', advocating a synergy between the private and the public good. See T.H. Green, *Prolegomena to Ethics*, Oxford, Oxford University Press, 1883, and *Lectures on the Principles of Political Obligation*, London, Longmans, Green and Co., 1907.

5. May Sinclair, *A Defence of Idealism*, London, Macmillan, 1917.

6. Sally Ledger, *The New Woman: Fiction and Feminism at the* Fin de Siècle, Manchester, Manchester University Press, 1997, pp.9–31.

7. Sinclair, *Feminism*; 'A Defence of Man', *Forum*, vol.48, July–December 1912, pp.409–20, also published as 'A Defence of Men', *English Review*, July 1912, pp.556–66. Almroth E. Wright, 'Sir Almroth Wright on Militant Hysteria', in 'Letters to the Editor', *Times*, 28 March 1912, pp.7–8. He later extended his letter to an essay: Almroth E. Wright, *The Unexpurgated Case Against Woman Suffrage*, London, Constable, 1913.

8. This was a precursor to the Tavistock Clinic; see Theophilus E.M. Boll, 'May Sinclair and the Medico-Psychological Clinic of London', *Proceedings of the American Philosophical Society*, vol.106, no.4, 1962, pp.310–26.

9. Sinclair was familiar with the holistic approaches in both William MacDougall, *Body and Mind*, London, Methuen, 1911, and Henry Maudsley, *Body and Mind: An inquiry into their connection and mutual influence, specially in reference to mental disorders* (1870), second edition, London, Macmillan, 1873.

10. 'Sir Almroth Wright on Militant Hysteria', all quotations this paragraph p.7.

11. Ibid., all quotations this paragraph pp.7–8.

12. For responses to Wright see 'Sir Almroth Wright's Letter' and 'Letters to the Editor', *Times*, 1 April 1912, p.6; 3 April 1912, p.6; 4 April 1912 p.7; 5 April 1912 p.8; and 8 April 1912 p.8, for various opinions from readers. In particular, Agnes Savill, female doctor and member of the Medico-Psychological Clinic, claims that Wright completely misunderstands the whole question of women. 'Reply by Dr. Agnes Savill', 'Letters', *Times*, 1 April 1912, p.6.

13. May Sinclair, 'Sir Almroth Wright on Woman Suffrage: Miss May Sinclair's Reply' (dated 31 March), *Times*, 4 April 1912, p.7.
14. Sinclair, *Feminism*, p.4.
15. Ibid., p.12.
16. Ibid., pp.22–7.
17. See for instance Henry Maudsley, 'Sex in Mind and in Education', *Fortnightly Review*, vol.21, 1874, pp.466–83.
18. Sinclair was not the first to discuss evolution and the New Woman; see M. Eastwood, 'The New Woman in Fiction and Fact', *Humanitarian*, vol.5, 1894, pp.375–9.
19. Sinclair, *Feminism*, p.27.
20. Ibid., pp.29–33.
21. Sinclair discusses Bergson in *Defence of Idealism*, chapter 2, 'Vitalism', pp.49–74.
22. Henri Bergson, *Time and Free Will: An Essay on the Immediate Data of Consciousness* (1910), translated by F.L. Pogson, London, George Allen Unwin, 1959.
23. Sinclair, *Feminism*, pp.28, 33.
24. Ibid., p.33.
25. Laura Otis, *Organic Memory: History and the Body in the Late Nineteenth and Early Twentieth Centuries*, London, University of Nebraska Press, 1994, pp.5–6. Also see L.J. Jordanova, *Lamarck*, Oxford, Oxford University Press, 1984.
26. For instance see Samuel Butler, *The Way of All Flesh* (1903). For an interesting discussion of the influence of Butler on Sinclair see Susanne Stark, 'Overcoming Butlerian Obstacles: May Sinclair and the Problem of Biological Determinism', *Women's Studies: An Interdisciplinary Journal*, vol.21, no.3, 1992, pp.265–83.
27. Herbert Spencer, *Essays on Education and Kindred Subjects* (1854–59), London, Dent, 1963; *The Principles of Psychology* (1855), third edition, 2 vols, London, D. Appleton, 1899.
28. Sinclair is joining in the response to Karl Pearson's 'Woman's Question' (see n.35), and in particular arguing against Cicely Hamilton's damning appraisal of the male sex in Cicely Hamilton, 'Man', *English Review*, vol.11, 1912, pp.115–25.
29. Sinclair, 'Defence of Man', p.412 (first two quotations), p.413 (last quotation).
30. A similar point is made by Ann Heilmann, *New Woman Fiction: Women Writing First-Wave Feminism*, Basingstoke, Macmillan, 2000, pp.1, 6.
31. See Sinclair, 'Defence of Man', pp.414–9.
32. Laura Chrisman, 'Empire, "race" and feminism at the *fin de siècle*: the work of George Egerton and Olive Schreiner', in Sally Ledger and Scott McCracken (eds), *Cultural Politics at the* Fin de Siècle, Cambridge: Cambridge University Press, 1995, pp.45–65. Chrisman argues that nineteenth-century white women writers articulated feminist identity through two registers: child-bearing and soul-making (p.45). Sinclair would seem to be also adopting this approach.
33. See May Sinclair, *The New Idealism*, London, Macmillan, 1922.
34. Sinclair argues that 'Whatever happens, the Immerweibliche will not be destroyed, for nature has too much need of it; too much need of woman's womanhood, of her eternal magic and eternal passion.' See 'Defence of Man', p.420.
35. See Lucy Bland, *Banishing the Beast: English Feminism and Sexual Morality 1885–1914* (London, Penguin, 1995, pp.10–14) for a full discussion of Karl Pearson's 1885 paper 'The Woman's Question' at the Men and Women's Club.
36. See for example Eliza Lynn Linton, 'The Wild Women as Social Insurgents', *Nineteenth Century*, vol.30, 1891, pp.596–605, and Mona Caird's rejoinder, 'A Defence of the "Wild Women"' in *The Morality of Marriage and Other Essays on the Status and Destiny of*

Woman, London, George Redway, 1897, pp.159–91; both repr. in Ann Heilmann (ed.), *The Late-Victorian Marriage Question: A Collection of Key New Woman Texts*, 5 vols, London, Routledge Thoemmes Press, 1998, vol.1.

37. Sinclair was friends with Evelyn Underhill who wrote *Mysticism* (1917) and took Sinclair sailing in her yacht.

38. For links between the two see Linda Dowling, 'The Decadent and the New Woman in the 1890's', in Lyn Pykett (ed.), *Reading Fin de Siècle Fictions*, London, Longman, 1996, pp.47–63. There is the sense in Sinclair's story of living beyond culture, beyond society's constraints; see Dowling p.60.

39. She is also superior to the over-stretched school-girls of the so-called 'forcing house' where she teaches. The irony of this is acknowledged towards the end of the text but is largely left unexplored by Sinclair.

40. Lloyd Fernando, *'New Women' in the Late Victorian Novel*, London, Pennsylvania State University Press, 1977, pp.2–4. Other theories are defined as the 'domestic theory' and the 'pedestal theory'.

41. Sinclair, 'Superseded' in *Two Sides of a Question*, London, Constable, 1901, p.275.

42. Spencer, *Essays on Education*, p.144.

43. May Sinclair, *The Creators: A Comedy*, London, Constable, 1910, p.334.

44. May Sinclair, *The Combined Maze*, London, Hutchinson, 1913. Underlying this novel are anti-degenerate, pro-exercise discourses such as those of Max Nordau. However, in other ways—such as her use of Mysticism—Sinclair opposes Nordau's ideas.

45. See for example her articles about the 'Two Women of Pervyse' (Baroness T'Serclaes and Mairie Chisholm) who had started out with Sinclair in Hector Munro's Field Ambulance for the Belgian Red Cross: 'In a Front-line Dug-out', *People*, 19 February 1918, page unknown. And more generally about female capability and athleticism: 'Women's War Work: II—At the Front', *Daily Chronicle*, date unknown (September 1915?), page unknown. These newspaper cuttings are in the 'Baroness T'serclass box file in the Imperial War Museum archive.

46. Sinclair, 'Women's War Work: II.-At the Front', see note above.

47. See for example Sarah Grand, *The Heavenly Twins*, 3 vols, London, Heinemann, 1893.

48. Olive Schreiner, *Woman and Labour*, London, T. Fisher Unwin, 1911.

49. See Ann Ardis, *New Women, New Novels: Feminism and Early Modernism* (London, Rutgers University Press, 1990, pp.165–76) for some helpful remarks about second-generation New Woman writers and modernism.

50. Sinclair, *Feminism*, p.42.

13. 'She in her "Armour" and He in his Coat of Nerves'
Leigh Wilson

1. For different perspectives on this, see Sheila Jeffreys, *The Spinster and Her Enemies: Feminism and Sexuality, 1880–1930*, London, Pandora, 1985 and Lucy Bland, *Banishing the Beast: Sexuality and the Early Feminists*, London, Penguin, 1995.

2. Catherine Belsey, *Desire: Love Stories in Western Culture*, Oxford, Blackwell, 1994, p.114.

3. For an account of how the violence of suffragette men also disturbed this balance, see Sandra Stanley Holton, 'Manliness and Militancy: The Political Protest of Male Suffragists and the Gendering of "Suffragette" Identity', in Angela V. John (ed.), *The Men's Share? Masculinities, Male Support and Women's Suffrage in Britain, 1890–1920*, London, Routledge, 1997, pp.110–34.

4. See Suzanne Raitt, *May Sinclair: A Modern Victorian*, Oxford, Oxford University Press, 2000.
5. See Sharon Ouditt, *Fighting Forces, Writing Women: Identity and Ideology in the First World War*, London, Routledge, 1994, pp.107–8; Laura Stempel Mumford, 'May Sinclair's *Tree of Heaven*: The Vortex of Feminism, the Community of War', in Helen M. Cooper, Adrienne Auslander Munich and Susan Merrill Squier (eds), *Arms and the Woman: War, Gender and Literary Representation*, Chapel Hill, University of North Carolina Press, 1989, p.179; Nicola Beauman, *A Very Great Profession: The Woman's Novel 1914–1939*, London, Virago, 1995, p.22.
6. Sir Almroth Wright, letter quoted in *The Freewoman*, 4 April 1912, p.393.
7. Ibid., p.392.
8. Ibid., p.393.
9. In this paper I am dealing with Sinclair's representation of heterosexual desire. Elsewhere, her work is incredibly suggestive about passion between women.
10. May Sinclair, *Feminism*, London, Women Writers Suffrage League, 1912, p.4.
11. Ibid., p.44.
12. James Burnet, 'Women War-workers and the Sexual Element', *The Medical Press*, 22 August 1917, p.140.
13. Ibid.
14. May Sinclair, 'Women War-workers and the Sexual Element', *The Medical Press*, 5 September 1917, p.179.
15. May Sinclair, 'Women's Sacrifices for the War', *Woman at Home*, February 1915, p.7.
16. See Rosemary Betterton, '"A Perfect Woman"': The Political Body of Suffrage', *An Intimate Distance: Women, Artists and the Body*, London, Routledge, 1996, pp.46–78; Lisa Tickner, *The Spectacle of Women: Imagery of the Suffrage Campaign, 1907–1914*, second edition, London, Chatto & Windus, 1989; Marina Warner, 'Introduction', *The Trial of Joan of Arc*, Evesham, Arthur James, 1996, pp.1–48.
17. May Sinclair, *Tasker Jevons: The Real Story*, London, Hutchinson, 1916, p.270; emphasis in original.
18. Ibid., p.129.
19. Ibid., p.317.
20. Ibid., pp.317–18; emphases in original.
21. From the *Suffragette*, 9 May 1913, quoted in Betterton, '"A Perfect Woman"': The Political Body of Suffrage', p.48.
22. Sinclair, *Tasker Jevons*, p.299.
23. For a discussion of the meaning of male wounding during the First World War, see Joanna Burke, *Dismembering the Male: Men's Bodies, Britain and the Great War*, London, Reaktion Books, 1996.
24. May Sinclair, *The Romantic*, London: W. Collins Sons & Co, 1920, pp.29–30.
25. For the further significance of this see Judith Marie Meyers, '"Comrade-Twin": Brothers and Doubles in the World War One Prose of May Sinclair, Katherine Anne Porter, Rebecca West and Virginia Woolf', Ph.D. thesis, University of Washington, 1985.
26. Sinclair, *The Romantic*, p.108.
27. Ibid., p.162.
28. Ibid., p.12.
29. Ibid., p.245.
30. See Jane Marcus, 'Corpus/Corps/Corpse: Writing the Body in/at War', in Helen M. Cooper, Adrienne Auslander Munich and Susan Merrill Squier (eds) *Arms and the*

Woman: War, Gender and Literary Representation, Chapel Hill, University of North Carolina Press, 1989, p.130.

14. Elizabeth Banks
Jane S. Gabin

1. Elizabeth Banks, 'Some Differences Between English and American Homes', *Cassell's Family Magazine*, vol.22, March 1895, p.259; 'Some American "Comparisons" and "Impressions"', *Nineteenth Century*, vol.37, April 1895, p.634; 'Paying Occupations for Gentlewomen', *Cassell's*, vol.23, April 1896, p.422 and September 1896, p.821.
2. 'I at first took up journalism in New York after my four years' stay in England'. Elizabeth Banks, *The Autobiography of a 'Newspaper Girl'*, New York, Dodd, Mead, 1902, p.196. Banks does not name the papers for which she freelanced or the 'yellow' journals to which she contributed when she was financially desperate.
3. Elizabeth Banks, 'American Country Parsons and Their Wives', *Quiver*, February 1899, p.327; 'The Story of Thanksgiving Day in the United States', *Quiver*, November 1899, p.40.
4. Elizabeth Banks, 'The American Negro and His Place', *Nineteenth Century*, vol. 46, July-December 1899, pp.459–74.
5. Elizabeth Banks, 'American "Yellow Journalism"', *Nineteenth Century*, August 1898, pp.328–40. Notice that Banks has adopted British spelling style. See also her article in *Living Age* (Boston), September 1898.
6. *Who's Who*, London, Adam Black, 1901. There is an entry for Elizabeth Banks in every annual edition from 1901 to 1938.
7. Elizabeth Banks, 'Maid-Servant in England and America', *World To-Day* (Chicago), vol.9, September 1905, pp.957–62; Mary Mortimer Maxwell, 'Window Boxes of London', *Good Housekeeping*, vol.48, April 1909, pp.401–9.
8. *London Illustrated Magazine*, June 1894, pp. 925–31. The series was published in 1894, so the title must have been inspired by Jacob Riis' famous work of the same name, published in 1888.
9. Elizabeth Banks, *The Remaking of an American* (1928), with an introduction by Jane S. Gabin, Gainesville, University Press of Florida, 2000, p.33.
10. Banks, *Remaking*, pp.279–80.
11 *On the Boat that Uncle Sam Built*, 10–page pamphlet copyrighted by Elizabeth Banks and printed by the Haycock-Cadle Co., 1917.
12. Banks, *Remaking*, p.10
13. Banks, *Remaking*, p.190.
14. Ibid., p.11.
15. Constitutional suffragists, held together in Millicent Garrett Fawcett's umbrella organization NUWSS (National Union of Women's Suffrage Societies), worked for voting rights through peaceful means and opposed the militant tactics of other groups.
16. Banks refers to her suffrage activities in *Remaking*, p.10. She is also listed as an active member of the Women Writers' Suffrage League in the *Suffrage Annual and Women's Who's Who*, London, Stanley Paul & Co., 1913, pp.134–7.
17. See 'Where the Vote is "The Thing"', *The Referee*, 3 November 1912, p.7, and 'VOTES FOR WOMEN. The "Referee" Competition', *The Referee*, 6 April 1913, p. 5. All of 'The Lady at the Round Table' columns were signed at the end: ENID.
18. Mary Mary Mortimer Maxwell, 'In Jail with the Suffragettes', *Harper's Weekly*, 3 August

1912, pp.9–10.

19. This is discussed in Viola Meynall (ed.), *Letters of J.M. Barrie*, London, Peter Davies, 1942, p.65.

20. Banks, *Remaking*, p.20.

21. When Banks referred to the 'antis', she meant political activists, progressives, pacifists.

22. Banks, *Remaking*, p.9.

23. F.R. Banks, *The New Penguin Guide to London*, Harmondsworth, Penguin, 1986, pp. 226–7.

24. This incident is related in Chapter 11 of *Remaking*, pp.125–36.

25. Banks, *Remaking*, p.77.

26. Banks describes this project in Chapter 9 of *Remaking*, pp.100–17, and this is substantiated by papers in the archives (Folio BEL 8) of the Imperial War Museum, London.

27. *Who's Who*, London, Adam Black. This information appears in every listing after 1914.

28. Letter of 3 March 1915 to W.E. Dowding, Esq. of the National Relief Fund. Original in the library of the Imperial War Museum, London.

29. Banks, *Remaking*, p.101.

30. Meynall, *Letters of J.M. Barrie*, p.65.

31. Banks mentions Henrietta several times in *Remaking*, and, as Mary Mortimer Maxwell, published an article in *Harper's Weekly* ('In Jail with the Suffragettes', see above) about the incarceration of Henrietta and others. However, the 'Roll of Honour' listing the names of hundreds imprisoned in Britain for suffrage activities between 1905 and 1914 does not mention anyone named Henrietta Marston (though there is a 'Miss Marson'). List courtesy of the Pankhurst Centre, Manchester.

32. *Who's Who*, London, Adam Black.

33. Banks, *Remaking*, p.202.

34. Ibid., p.218.

35. Ibid., p.219.

36. Elizabeth Banks, *School for John and Mary: A Story of Caste in England*, New York and London, Putnam, 1924. There was a second edition in 1926. The book was, understandably, more positively reviewed in the U.S. than in Britain.

37. *Who Was Who*, vol.3, 1929–1940, London, Adam and Charles Black, 1941, p.61. This is the final listing of Elizabeth Banks's biographical details.

38. Obituary, *New York Times*, 19 July 1938, p.22:5.

39. *Times*, 18 July 1938. For the article on the Jews under Nazi rule see p.10. Lengthy information on the Royal Visit to France can be found in a special French section added to the issue, pp.i–xxviii.

40. Will of Elizabeth Banks, dated 30.1.1933; copy obtained from the Principal Registry of the Family Division, London.

41. Banks, *Autobiography*, pp.211–12.

Select Bibliography

Ammons, Elizabeth, *Conflicting Stories: American Women Writers at the Turn into the Twentieth Century*, Oxford, Oxford University Press, 1991.

—and Annette White-Parks (eds), *Tricksterism in Turn-of-the-Century American Literature: A Multicultural Perspective*, Hanover, University Press of New England, 1994.

Ardis, Ann, *New Women, New Novels: Feminism and Early Modernism*, New Brunswick, Rutgers University Press, 1990.

Beauman, Nicola, *A Very Great Profession: The Woman's Novel 1914–1939*, London, Virago, 1995.

Beetham, Margaret, *A Magazine of Her Own? Domesticity and Desire in the Woman's Magazine, 1800–1914*, London, Routledge, 1996.

—(ed.), *The New Woman and the Periodical Press*. Special issue of *Media History*, vol.7, no.1 (2001).

Bjørhovde, Gerd, *Rebellious Structures: Women Writers and the Crisis of the Novel 1880–1900*, Oslo, Norwegian University Press, 1987.

Brandon, Ruth, *The New Women and the Old Men: Love, Sex and the Woman Question*, London, Secker & Warburg, 1990.

Carby, Hazel V., *Reconstructing Womanhood: The Emergence of the Afro-American Woman Novelist*, Oxford, Oxford University Press, 1987.

Collins, Patricia, *Black Feminist Thought: Knowledge, Consciousness, and the Politics of Empowerment*, London, Routledge, 1991.

Cooper, Helen M., Adrienne Auslander Munich and Susan Merrill Squier (eds), *Arms and the Woman: War, Gender and Literary Representation*, Chapel Hill, University of North Carolina Press, 1989.

Felski, Rita, *The Gender of Modernity*, Cambridge, MA, Harvard University Press, 1995.

Fitzsimmons, Linda and Viv Gardner (eds), *New Woman Plays*, London, Methuen, 1991.

Flint, Kate, *The Woman Reader 1837–1914*, Oxford, Clarendon Press, 1993, repr. 1999.

Gardiner, Juliet (ed.), *The New Woman*, London, Collins & Brown, 1993.

Gardner, Burdett, *The Lesbian Imagination (Victorian Style: A Psychological and Critical Study of 'Vernon Lee'*, New York, Garland, 1987.

Gardner, Vivien and Susan Rutherford (eds), *The New Woman and Her Sisters: Feminism and Theatre 1850–1914*, Ann Arbor: University of Michigan Press, 1992.

Gates, Joanne E., *Elizabeth Robins, 1862–1952: Actress, Novelist, Feminist*, Tuscaloosa and London, University of Alabama Press, 1994.

Gilbert, Sandra M. and Susan Gubar, *No Man's Land: The Place of the Woman Writer in the Twentieth Century*, 3 vols, New Haven, Yale University Press, 1988–1994.

Golden, Catherine J. and Joanna S. Zangrando (eds), *The Mixed Legacy of Charlotte Perkins Gilman*, Newark, University of Delaware Press, 2000.

Gough, Val and Jill Rudd (eds) *A Very Different Story: Studies on the Fiction of Charlotte Perkins Gilman*, Liverpool, Liverpool University Press, 1998.

Gruesser, John Cullen (ed.), *The Unruly Voice: Rediscovering Pauline Elizabeth Hopkins*, Chicago, University of Illinois Press, 1996.

Hanscombe, Gillian and Virginia L. Smyers, *Writing for Their Lives: The Modernist Women 1910–1940*, London, Women's Press, 1987.

Harman, Barbara Leah, *The Feminine Political Novel in Victorian England*, Charlottesville, University Press of Virginia, 1998.

Heilmann, Ann, *New Woman Fiction: Women Writing First-Wave Feminism*, Basingstoke, Macmillan, 2000.

—(ed.), *The Late-Victorian Marriage Question: A Collection of Key New Woman Texts*, London, Routledge Thoemmes Press, 1998.

—(ed.), *Masculinities, Maternities, Motherlands: Defying/Contesting New Woman Identities*. Special issue of *Nineteenth-Century Feminisms*, vol.4 (2001).

—and Stephanie Forward (eds), *Sex, Social Purity and Sarah Grand*, 4 vols, London, Routledge, 2000.

Heller, Adele and Lois Rudnick (eds), *1915: The Cultural Moment: The New Politics, the New Woman, the New Psychology, the New Art, and the New Theatre in America*, New Brunswick, Rutgers University Press, 1991.

Hill, Mary A, *Charlotte Perkins Gilman: The Making of a Radical Feminist 1860–1896*, Philadelphia, Temple University Press, 1980.

Hill, Marylu, *Mothering Modernity: Feminism, Modernism, and the Maternal Muse*, New York, Garland, 1999.

Hill, Robert A., Barbara Bair and Edith Johnson (eds), *The Markus Garvey and Universal Negro Improvement Association Papers*, Berkely, University of California Press, 1990.

Hodes, Martha (ed.), *Sex, Love, Race: Crossing Boundaries in North American History*, New York, New York University Press, 1999.

Hughes, Linda (ed.), *New Woman Poets: An Anthology*, London, The Eighteen Nineties Society, 2001.

Ingram, Angela and Daphne Patai (eds), *Rediscovering Forgotten Radicals: British Women Writers 1889–1939*, Chapel Hill, University of North Carolina Press, 1993.

Jaskoski, Helen (ed.), *Early Native American Writing: New Critical Essays*, Cambridge, Cambridge University Press, 1996.

Jeffreys, Sheila, *The Spinster and her Enemies: Feminism and Sexuality, 1880–1930*, London, Pandora, 1985.

Joannou, Maroula, *'Ladies, Please Don't Smash These Windows': Women's Writing, Feminist Consciousness and Social Change 1918–38*, Oxford, Providence, Berg, 1995.

John, Angela V., *Elizabeth Robins: Staging a Life, 1862–1952*, London, Routledge, 1955.

Johnson, Abby Arthur and Ronald Maberry Johnson (eds), *Propaganda & Aesthetics: The Literary Politics of African-American Magazines in the Twentieth Century*, Amherst, University of Massachusetts Press, 1991.

Kaplan, Carola M. and Anne B. Simpson (eds), *Seeing Double: Revisioning Edwardian and Modernist Literature*, Basingstoke, Macmillan, 1996.

Kersley, Gillian, *Darling Madame: Sarah Grand & Devoted Friend*, London, Virago, 1983.

Kilian, Eveline, *Momente innerweltlicher Transzendenz: Die Augenblickserfahrung in Dorothy Richardson's Romanzyklus 'Pilgrimage' und ihr ideengeschichtlicher Kontext*, Tübingen, Narr, 1997.

Kilcup, Karen L. (ed.), *Nineteenth-Century American Women Writers: A Critical Reader*, Oxford, Blackwell, 1998.

Kranidis, Rita S., *Subversive Discourse: The Cultural Production of Late Victorian*

Feminist Novels, Basingstoke, Macmillan, 1995.

Lane, Ann J., *To 'Herland' and Beyond: The Life and Work of Charlotte Perkins Gilman*, Charlottesville, University Press of Virginia, 1990.

Ledger, Sally, *The New Woman: Fiction and Feminism at the* Fin de Siècle, Manchester, Manchester University Press, 1997.

—(ed.), *Women's Writing at the* Fin de Siècle, special number of *Women's Writing*, vol.3, no.3, 1996.

—and Scott McCracken (eds), *Cultural Politics at the* Fin de Siècle, Cambridge, Cambridge University Press, 1995.

Lerner, Gerda (ed.), *Black Women in White America: A Documentary History*, New York, Vintage, 1973.

Livingstone, Angela, *Lou Andreas-Salomé*, London, Gordon Fraser, 1984.

Mangum, Teresa, *Married, Middlebrow, and Militant: Sarah Grand and the New Woman Novel*, Ann Arbor, University of Michigan Press, 1998.

Manos, Nikki Lee and Mari-Jane Rochelson (eds), *Transforming Genres: New Approaches to British Fiction of the 1890s*, New York, St Martin's Press, 1994.

Marks, Patricia, *Bicycles, Bangs, and Bloomers: The New Woman in the Popular Press*, Lexington, University Press of Kentucky, 1990.

Martin, Biddy, *Woman and Modernity: The Lifestyles of Lou Andreas-Salomé*, Ithaca, Cornell University Press, 1991.

Meier, August, *Negro Thought in America, 1880–1915*, Ann Arbor, University of Michigan Press, 1988.

Miller, Jane Eldridge, *Rebel Women: Feminism, Modernism and the Edwardian Novel*, London, Virago, 1994.

Mitchell, Sally, *The New Girl: Girls' Culture in England, 1880–1915*, New York, Columbia University Press, 1995.

Nelson, Carolyn Christensen, *British Women Fiction Writers of the 1890s*, New York, Twayne, 1996.

Newlin, Keith (ed.), *American Plays of the New Woman*, Chicago, Ivan R. Dee, 2000.

Ouditt, Sharon, *Fighting Forces, Writing Women: Identity and Ideology in the First World War*, London, Routledge, 1994.

Pykett, Lyn, *Engendering Fictions: The English Novel in the Early Twentieth Century*, London, Edward Arnold, 1995.

—*The 'Improper' Feminine: The Women's Sensation Novel and the New Woman*

Writing, London, Routledge, 1992.

—(ed.), *Reading Fin-de-Siècle Fictions*, London, Longman, 1996.

Raitt, Suzanne, *May Sinclair: A Modern Victorian*, Oxford, Clarendon Press, 2000.

—and Trudi Tate (eds), *Women's Fiction and the Great War*, Oxford, Clarendon Press, 1997.

Richardson, Angelique and Chris Willis (eds), *The New Woman in Fiction and in Fact:* Fin-de-Siècle *Feminisms*, Basingstoke, Palgrave, 2002.

Rudd, Jill and Val Gough (eds) *Charlotte Perkins Gilman: Optimist Reformer*, Iowa, University of Iowa Press, 1999.

Schaffer, Talia, *The Forgotten Female Aesthetes: Literary Culture in Late-Victorian England*, Charlottesville, University Press of Virginia, 2000.

Scott, Bonnie Kime (ed.), *The Gender of Modernism: A Critical Anthology*, Bloomington, Indiana University Press, 1990.

Showalter, Elaine, *A Literature of Their Own: British Women Novelists from Brontë to Lessing*, London, Virago, 1979.

—*Sexual Anarchy: Gender and Culture at the* Fin de Siècle, London, Bloomsbury, 1991.

—(ed.), *Daughters of Decadence: Women Writers of the* Fin de Siècle, London, Virago, 1993.

Smith-Rosenberg, Caroll, *Disorderly Conduct: Visions of Gender in Victorian America*, Oxford, Oxford University Press, 1985.

Tate, Claudia, *Domestic Allegories of Political Desire: The Black Heroine's Text at the Turn of the Century*, Oxford, Oxford University Press, 1993.

Thomas, Sue (comp.), *Elizabeth Robins (1862–1952): A Bibliography*, St Lucia, Brisbane, Department of English, University of Queensland, 1994.

Thompson, Nicola Diane (ed.), *Victorian Women Writers and the Woman Question*, Cambridge, Cambridge University Press, 1999.

Varty, Anne (ed.), *Eve's Century: A Sourcebook of Writings on Women and Journalism*, London, Routledge, 2000.

Watts, Carol, *Dorothy Richardson*, Plymouth, Northcote House in association with the British Council, 1995.

White-Parks, Annette, *Sui Sin Far / Edith Maude Eaton: A Literary Biography*, Urbana, University of Illinois Press, 1995.

Zangen, Britta, *A Life of Her Own: Feminism in Vera Brittain's Theory, Fiction, and Biography*. Frankfurt, Peter Lang, 1996.

Index